George Frederick Maclear

A Class-Book of the Catechism of the Church of England

George Frederick Maclear

A Class-Book of the Catechism of the Church of England

ISBN/EAN: 9783337180355

Printed in Europe, USA, Canada, Australia, Japan

Cover: Foto ©Lupo / pixelio.de

More available books at **www.hansebooks.com**

By the same Author.

A HISTORY OF CHRISTIAN MISSIONS DURING THE MIDDLE AGES. Crown 8vo. 10s. 6d.

THE WITNESS OF THE EUCHARIST; or, The Institution and Early Celebration of the Lord's Supper, considered as an Evidence of the Historical Truth of the Gospel Narrative and of the Atonement. Crown 8vo. 4s. 6d.

A CLASS-BOOK OF OLD TESTAMENT HISTORY. With Four Maps. *Third Edition.* 18mo. cloth. 4s. 6d.

A CLASS-BOOK OF NEW TESTAMENT HISTORY. Including the Connexion of the Old and New Testament. With Maps. *Second Edition.* 18mo. cloth, 5s. 6d.

A SHILLING BOOK OF OLD TESTAMENT HISTORY FOR NATIONAL AND ELEMENTARY SCHOOLS. With Map. 18mo.

A SHILLING BOOK OF NEW TESTAMENT HISTORY FOR NATIONAL AND ELEMENTARY SCHOOLS. 18mo.

MACMILLAN & CO. LONDON.

ELEMENTARY SCHOOL CLASS BOOKS.

The Volumes of this Series of ELEMENTARY SCHOOL CLASS BOOKS *are handsomely printed in a form that, it is hoped, will assist the young Student as much as clearness of type and distinctness of arrangement can effect. They are published at a moderate price to ensure an extensive sale in the Schools of the United Kingdom and the Colonies.*

PROFESSOR ROSCOE'S LESSONS IN ELEMENTARY CHEMISTRY. With numerous Illustrations, and chromo-litho. frontispiece of the Solar Spectra. *Seventh Thousand.* 18mo., 4s. 6d.

PROFESSOR OLIVER'S LESSONS IN ELEMENTARY BOTANY. With nearly 200 Illustrations. *Third Thousand.* 18mo., 4s. 6d.

MR. AIRY'S (ASTRONOMER ROYAL) POPULAR ASTRONOMY. With numerous Illustrations. *Fifth and Cheaper Edition.* 18mo., 4s. 6d.

PROFESSOR HUXLEY'S LESSONS IN ELEMENTARY PHYSIOLOGY. With numerous Illustrations. *Fourth Thousand.* 18mo., 4s. 6d.

MR. TODHUNTER'S EUCLID for COLLEGES and SCHOOLS. *New Edition.* 18mo., 3s. 6d.

MR. TODHUNTER'S ALGEBRA FOR BEGINNERS. 18mo., 2s. 6d. KEY. Crown 8vo., 6s. 6d.

MR. TODHUNTER'S TRIGONOMETRY FOR BEGINNERS. With numerous Examples. 18mo., 2s. 6d.

MR. TODHUNTER'S MECHANICS FOR BEGINNERS. With numerous Examples. 18mo., 4s. 6d.

MR. BARNARD SMITH'S SCHOOL CLASS-BOOK OF ARITHMETIC. Part I. and II. 18mo. limp cloth, each 10d.; Part III. 1s.; or 3 Parts in one Vol., 18mo. cloth, 3s. KEY. 3 Parts in 1 Vol., 18mo., price 6s. 6d.; or separately, 2s. 6d each.

MR. DALTON'S ARITHMETICAL EXAMPLES PROGRESSIVELY ARRANGED; with Exercises and Examination Papers. 18mo. 2s. 6d.

MR. JONES AND MR. CHEYNE'S ALGEBRAICAL EXERCISES. Progressively arranged. 18mo., 2s. 6d.

MR. MACLEAR'S CLASS-BOOK OF NEW TESTAMENT HISTORY. Including the Connexion of the Old and New Testament. *Second Edition.* With Maps. 18mo., 5s. 6d.

MR. MACLEAR'S CLASS-BOOK OF OLD TESTAMENT HISTORY. *Third Edition.* 18mo., with 4 Maps, 4s. 6d.

MR. ALDIS WRIGHT AND MR. EASTWOOD'S BIBLE WORD-BOOK: a Glossary of Old English Bible Words. 18mo., 5s. 6d.

MR. PROCTER'S ELEMENTARY HISTORY OF THE BOOK OF COMMON PRAYER. *Second Edition.* 18mo., 2s. 6d.

MR. WESTCOTT'S BIBLE IN THE CHURCH. *Second Edition,* 18mo., 4s. 6d.

MR. HODGSON'S MYTHOLOGY FOR LATIN VERSIFICATION: a Brief Sketch of the Fables of the Ancients, prepared to be rendered into Latin Verse for Schools. *New Edition,* revised. 18mo., 3s.

MR. THRING'S LATIN GRADUAL FOR BEGINNERS: a First Latin Construing Book. 18mo., 2s. 6d.

MR. THRING'S ELEMENTS OF GRAMMAR TAUGHT IN ENGLISH. *Third Edition.* 18mo., 2s.

MR. JEPHSON'S EDITION of SHAKESPEARE'S TEMPEST. 18mo., 1s. 6d.

MACMILLAN & CO. LONDON.

A CLASS-BOOK

OF

THE CATECHISM

OF

The Church of England.

Cambridge:
PRINTED BY C. J. CLAY, M.A.
AT THE UNIVERSITY PRESS.

A CLASS-BOOK

OF

THE CATECHISM

OF

The Church of England.

BY

THE REV. G. F. MACLEAR, B.D.

HEAD MASTER OF KING'S COLLEGE SCHOOL, LONDON,
AND PREACHER AT THE TEMPLE CHURCH.

London and Cambridge:
MACMILLAN AND CO.
1868.

"Ἵνα ἐπιγνῷς περὶ ὧν ΚΑΤΗΧΗΘΗΣ λόγων τὴν ἀσφάλειαν.—S. Lucas I. 4.

NOTICE.

The present Work forms a Sequel to the Author's *Class-Books of Old and New Testament History*.

Like them, it is furnished with notes, and references to larger Works, and it is hoped that it may be found, especially in the higher Forms of our Public Schools, to supply a suitable Manual of Instruction in the chief doctrines of our Church, and a useful Help in the preparation of Candidates for Confirmation.

CONTENTS.

		PAGES
INTRODUCTION	....	1—3

PART I.

THE CHRISTIAN COVENANT.

CHAPTER I.	*The Christian Name*..................	4—6
CHAPTER II.	*Christian Privileges*	7—9
CHAPTER III.	*The First Baptismal Vow*	9—12
CHAPTER IV.	*The Second Baptismal Vow*	12—14
CHAPTER V.	*The Third Baptismal Vow and the Obligation to keep our Vows*	15—17

PART II.

THE CREED.

CHAPTER I.	*Summary of the Creed*...............	18—20
CHAPTER II.	*The First Article*	20—23
CHAPTER III.	*The Second Article*	23—26
CHAPTER IV.	*The Third Article*	26—28
CHAPTER V.	*The Fourth Article*	29—34
CHAPTER VI.	*The Fifth Article*	34—38
CHAPTER VII.	*The Sixth Article*	39—43

		PAGES
CHAPTER VIII.	*The Seventh Article*	43—47
CHAPTER IX.	*The Eighth Article*	48—52
CHAPTER X.	*The Ninth Article*	53—61
CHAPTER XI.	*The Tenth Article*	61—65
CHAPTER XII.	*The Eleventh Article*	65—69
CHAPTER XIII.	*The Twelfth Article*	69—72

PART III.
THE TEN COMMANDMENTS.

INTRODUCTION	....	74—77

SECTION I.
OUR DUTY TOWARDS GOD.

CHAPTER I.	*The First Commandment*	77—79
CHAPTER II.	*The Second Commandment*	80—82
CHAPTER III.	*The Third Commandment*	82—84
CHAPTER IV.	*The Fourth Commandment*	84—86

SECTION II.
OUR DUTY TOWARDS OUR NEIGHBOUR.

CHAPTER I.	*The Fifth Commandment*	87—89
CHAPTER II.	*The Sixth Commandment*	90—92
CHAPTER III.	*The Seventh Commandment*	92—94
CHAPTER IV.	*The Eighth Commandment*	94—96
CHAPTER V.	*The Ninth Commandment*	96—98
CHAPTER VI.	*The Tenth Commandment*	98—100

PART IV.
THE LORD'S PRAYER.

INTRODUCTION	....	101—105
CHAPTER I.	*Structure of the Lord's Prayer*	105—107
CHAPTER II.	*The Invocation*	107—110

		PAGES
Chapter III.	The First Petition for God's Glory	111—113
Chapter IV.	The Second Petition for God's Glory	114—118
Chapter V.	The Third Petition for God's Glory	118—121
Chapter VI.	The First Petition for our own needs	121—124
Chapter VII.	The Second Petition for our own needs	124—127
Chapter VIII.	The Third Petition for our own needs	127—130
Chapter IX.	The Fourth Petition for our own needs	130—133
Chapter X.	The Doxology	133—137

PART V.

THE SACRAMENTS.

Section I.

NUMBER AND NATURE OF THE SACRAMENTS.

Chapter I.	Number of the Sacraments	138—140
Chapter II.	Nature of a Sacrament	140—143
Chapter III.	The Parts of a Sacrament	143—146

Section II.

THE SACRAMENT OF BAPTISM.

Chapter I.	The Outward Sign in Baptism.	146—151
Chapter II.	The Inward and Spiritual Grace of Baptism	151—156
Chapter III.	The Requirements for Baptism.	156—160
Chapter IV.	The Baptism of Infants	160—164

Section III.

THE SACRAMENT OF THE LORD'S SUPPER.

Chapter I.	The Object of the Institution of the Lord's Supper	164—168
Chapter II.	The Outward Part or Sign of the Lord's Supper	169—173
Chapter III.	The Inward Part of the Lord's Supper	173—177
Chapter IV.	The Benefits of the Lord's Supper	178—181
Chapter V.	Requisites for approach to the Lord's Supper	181—185

I. General Index	186—189
II. Index of Greek and Latin Words.........	190
III. Index of other Words	191

A Catechism,

THAT IS TO SAY,

AN INSTRUCTION TO BE LEARNED OF EVERY PERSON, BEFORE HE BE BROUGHT TO BE CONFIRMED BY THE BISHOP.

INTRODUCTION.

1. **A Catechism** is a course of instruction by question and answer in the first principles, or elements, of any subject.

2. **Derivation.** It is derived from a Greek word[1] which denotes, (i) *to sound down*, (ii) *to teach by word of mouth*. Thus St Luke states that he had composed his Gospel in order that Theophilus might *thoroughly know the certainty of the things wherein he had been orally instructed*[2], or, *catechised*, and Apollos is said to have been *mighty in the Scriptures*, and to have been *orally instructed*[3], or *catechised*, in the way of the Lord. He who thus teaches is called a *Catechist*[4], and he who is thus taught a *Catechumen*.

3. **The Catechism of the Church of England** is a course of instruction *in the first principles or elements*

---

[1] Κατηχέω, which comes from κατὰ = *down*, and ἦχος = *a sound*, whence the English word *echo*.

[2] Ἵνα ἐπιγνῷς περὶ ὧν κατηχήθης λόγων τὴν ἀσφάλειαν, Lk. i. 4.

[3] Οὗτος ἦν κατηχημένος τὴν ὁδὸν τοῦ Κυρίου, Acts xviii. 25; comp. also Rom. ii. 18, 1 Cor. xiv. 19, Gal. vi. 6.

[4] Which word is twice placed before questions in the Church Catechism.

of the Christian religion[1], and is "to be learned by every person, before he is brought to be confirmed by the Bishop."

4. **Division of the Catechism.** The first principles in which the Catechism gives instruction may be divided into Five Parts.

5. **The First Part** treats of *the Christian Covenant*, and instructs us concerning *the Christian Name*, and *the Privileges, and Obligations of our Baptism*.

6. **The Second Part** treats of *the Apostles' Creed* and its explanation, and instructs us in the *Faith*, to which our Covenant binds us.

7. **The Third Part** treats of the *Ten Commandments* and their summary, or the *Duty to God and Man*, to which our Covenant obliges us.

8. **The Fourth Part** treats of *Prayer*, and especially the Pattern Prayer, called *the Lord's Prayer*, given us by our Saviour.

9. **The Fifth Part** treats of the two Sacraments; (i) of *Baptism*, whereby we are admitted into the Christian Covenant, and (ii) of *the Lord's Supper*, whereby our Covenant-union with Christ is renewed, "our souls strengthened and refreshed," and "we be fed and sustained to spiritual and everlasting life[2]."

10. **History of the Catechism.** English Versions and Expositions of the Creed, the Lord's Prayer, and the Ten Commandments had existed in very early times[3]. Immediately before the Reformation, however,

---

[1] Compare the answer of the Bishops at the Savoy Conference: "The Catechism is not intended as a whole body of divinity, but as a comprehension of the Articles of Faith, and other doctrines most necessary to salvation."

[2] Noell's *Catechism;* Nicholson *On the Catechism*, p. 183.

[3] Thus, in Saxon times, the Council of Cealchythe, A.D. 785, directs, "that all shall know the Creed and the Lord's Prayer, and that all Sponsors shall promise to teach them their children." A Council held at Lambeth, A.D. 1281,

the knowledge of these elements of the Christian religion would seem to have been very scanty. The first Book of Service, therefore, put forth by the advisers of Edward VI. in the year A.D. 1549, contained the Catechism as far as the explanation of the Lord's Prayer, which, with certain alterations[1], still remains in our Prayer-Book. The Explanation of the Sacraments[2] was not added till after the Hampton Court Conference, A.D. 1604, in the reign of James I.

directs the clergy to explain, four times a year, the Ten Commandments and the Creed in the Vulgar or English tongue. The injunctions of Henry VIII., in 1536 and 1538, ordered the clergy to "teach the people the Lord's Prayer, the Creed, and the Ten Commandments, sentence by sentence, on Sundays and Holydays." See Procter *On the Book of Common Prayer*, pp. 389, 390.

[1] Till the year 1661 the Catechism was inserted in the *Order of Confirmation*, and the title in the Prayer-Books of Edward and Elizabeth was, *Confirmation, wherein is contained a Catechism for Children*.

[2] It is generally ascribed to Bishop Overall, the Prolocutor of the Convocation, and at that time Dean of St Paul's, but in all probability was translated by him from an old Latin formula.

PART I.
THE CHRISTIAN COVENANT.

What is your Name?—N. or M.

Who gave you this Name?— My Godfathers and Godmothers in my Baptism; wherein I was made a member of Christ, the child of God, and an inheritor of the kingdom of heaven.

What did your Godfathers and Godmothers then for you? —They did promise and vow three things in my name. First, that I should renounce the devil and all his works, the pomps and vanity of this wicked world, and all the sinful lusts of the flesh. Secondly, that I should believe all the Articles of the Christian Faith. And thirdly, that I should keep God's holy will and commandments, and walk in the same all the days of my life.

Dost thou not think that thou art bound to believe, and to do, as they have promised for thee?—Yes verily; and by God's help so I will. And I heartily thank our heavenly Father, that he hath called me to this state of salvation, through Jesus Christ our Saviour. And I pray unto God to give me His grace, that I may continue in the same unto my life's end.

CHAPTER I.
THE CHRISTIAN NAME.

1. **Names.** The first question in the Catechism is, *What is your name?* A man's Name signifies that he is a person, that he is a responsible being, and that he has in him an immortal soul, for which he, and he alone, must answer to God.

2. **Names in the Bible.** The Names which we find in the Bible were not given at random, but have definite meanings. Thus, to mention a few out of many,

Seth means *substituted*, because he was born to Adam *instead of* Abel (Gen. iv. 25); Abram means *high father*, but when God's covenant with him was renewed, he was called Abraham, or the *father of a great multitude* (Gen. xvii. 5); Isaac means *laughter*, because his mother Sarah *laughed* when she heard she should have a son in her old age (Gen. xxi. 5—7); Samuel means *the asked of God* (1 Sam. i. 20); Ichabod means *the glory is departed from Israel*, in memory of the capture of the ark by the Philistines (1 Sam. iv. 21).

3. **The Surname.** Persons now have two names, the Christian and the Surname. The Surname is so called because it is the name given *over and above*[1] the Christian name. At first it was given to a person either to mark something peculiar to him, or to preserve the name of his father. But at, or soon after, the landing of the Normans in this country, they introduced the use of surnames as fixed or family names, and this custom is now universal.

4. **The Christian Name.** The surname, which belongs to a person at the moment of his birth, is not the name asked for in the Catechism. This is the Christian Name, which does not belong to a person at his birth, but is *given to him*[2] at his Baptism, when he is admitted into the Christian Covenant, and as he carries it with him to the grave, always reminds him of that Covenant[3].

[1] From the French *sur*, Latin *super*, and nomen, = *the-over-and-above-Name*.

[2] Compare the Baptismal Service, *Then the Priest shall take the child into his hands, and shall say to the Godfathers and Godmothers,* "Name this child."

[3] This Name, thus imposed in infancy, is "each one's inalienable possession; and is afterwards used in the most solemn moments of life, in the marriage-vow, in all oaths and engagements, and on all occasions when the person is dealt with in his individual capacity." See *History of Christian Names*, I. 12. Even among the Greeks and Romans it

5. **When and by whom given.** In almost every civilized nation the giving of a name has been regarded as a solemn matter, and generally has been accompanied with some religious ceremony. Amongst the Jews it was given on the eighth day after birth when the child was circumcised (Gen. xxi. 3, 4; Lk. i. 59, 60)[1]. Amongst Christian nations the Christian name is given to the child at Baptism by his *Godfathers and Godmothers*, that is, by persons, who act as parents[2] to him in regard to God, and make for him[3] certain solemn promises, which "when he comes to age, he himself is bound to perform." Hence Godfathers and Godmothers are sometimes called sponsors[4] and sometimes sureties.

was usual for a slave, when emancipated, to assume a new name in token of his having entered on a *new, free* life.

[1] Among the Greeks the father gave the child its name at a solemn feast on the seventh, or tenth day after birth. The Romans inherited at least one name. But in early times the individual name (*prænomen*) was solemnly given to a boy at the age of fourteen. He then ceased to wear the *bulla* or golden ball which hung from the neck, and assumed the *toga virilis* or manly gown, of white with a purple hem. In later times the name was bestowed on boys on the 9th, on girls on the 8th day, and with a bathing of water. Hence the day was called *dies lustricus*, or *dies nominum*. See Smith's *Dict. Antiq.*, Art. *Nomen*; *History of Christian Names*, I. p. 12.

[2] Hence in ancient times they were called God-sibs (sib = kin), meaning *related in God*, whence the present word "gossip." See Trench, *English Past and Present*, p. 207.

[3] Hence in the Baptismal Service in the questions addressed to the Sponsors, and in their answers for the child, the *singular* number is used, because the child, not they, is considered as speaking.

[4] Called in Greek Ἀνάδοχοι, from ἀναδέχεσθαι = *to promise*, in Latin *Fide-jussores*, and *Sponsores*, from the Latin word spondere = *to vow, promise;* a surety means a *bondsman*, one who becomes bound for another; godfathers and godmothers become bound to see that a child shall be brought up in the faith of a Christian.

CHAPTER II.

CHRISTIAN PRIVILEGES.

1. **Baptism admits into Covenant.** The bestowal, however, of the Christian Name is but the least thing that was done for us at our Baptism. For whereas by nature we were *born in sin and were the children of wrath* (Eph. ii. 3), that is, strangers from the Church which is God's household, by Baptism we were admitted into the Christian covenant, and "the promises of forgiveness of sin, and of our adoption to be the sons of God by the Holy Ghost, were visibly signed and sealed to us[1]."

2. **The Old or Mosaic Covenant.** From the earliest times God has been pleased, of His free mercy and goodness, to enter into Covenant with man. Thus we read of His covenant with Noah[2]; of His covenant with Abraham[3]; of His covenant with the Israelites[4]. The last of these three covenants is called sometimes the Mosaic, sometimes the Old Covenant. It was concluded between God and the Israelites; it was solemnly ratified by the shedding of the blood of numerous victims (Exod. xxiv. 5—8); it was administered by *the hands of a Mediator*, Moses (Exod. xxiv. 2; Gal. iii. 19); and the ordained mode of entrance into it was by *circumcision* (Lev. xii. 3; Rom. iv. 11).

3. **The Christian Covenant.** This Covenant was not designed to last for ever, but to prepare for a new and better Covenant (Jer. xxxi. 31—33). This is the Christian Covenant or God's Covenant in Christ, which is not between Him and a single nation, like the Israelites, but between Him and *the whole world*

---

[1] See Article XXVII.; Noell's *Catechism.*
[2] Gen. ix. 8—16.   [3] Gen. xvii. 1—14.
[4] Exod. xix. 3—6.

(Heb. viii. 7—13). For the whole world the Mediator of this Covenant, JESUS CHRIST, shed His own blood upon the cross (Heb. ix. 12); to the whole world He bade His Apostles proclaim the glad tidings of remission of sins in His Name; and for all nations He ordained Baptism as the outward and visible sign of this Covenant, and the mode of entrance into it (Mtt. xxviii. 19, 20).

4. **Privileges of the Christian Covenant.** As, then, on the occasion of his circumcision, the Jew received his name (Lk. i. 59; ii. 21), and was admitted to all the privileges of the Old Covenant, so at his Baptism the Christian is admitted to all the privileges of the New Covenant, and to him individually they are then sealed (Col. ii. 11, 12). These privileges are set forth in the Catechism under three heads, and we are taught to say, each one for ourselves, "at my Baptism I was made (i) *a member of Christ*, (ii) *a child of God*, and (iii) *an inheritor of the kingdom of heaven.*"

5. **A member of Christ.** When our Lord Jesus Christ took upon Him our nature, He became to us a second Adam, and the beginning of a new nature and life. He also purchased for Himself a universal Church, and His relation to it is described in Scripture under the figures of (i) *a human body and its members*[1]; (ii) *a tree and its branches*[2]; (iii) *a building and the stones composing it*[3]. The first of these figures is alluded to in the Catechism. Of the Church, into which we are grafted by Baptism, Christ is the Head, and we are "very members incorporate in His mystical Body, which is the blessed company of all faithful people[4]."

---

[1] Rom. xii. 4, 5 ; 1 Cor. xii. 12—27.
[2] Jn. xv. 1—8; Rom. xi. 16—24.
[3] 1 Pet. ii. 4—8; Eph. ii. 19, 22 ; Rev. iii. 12.
[4] See the Thanksgiving in the post-Communion Service.

6. **The child of God.** The second Christian privilege flows from the first. For being in Baptism made members of Christ, who is the Son of God, in virtue of this union with Him we also become by adoption sons of God. Hence, after His Resurrection, our Lord bade Mary Magdalene go to His *brethren*, that is, to His Apostles, and say unto them, *I ascend unto My Father and your Father, and to My God and your God* (Jn. xx. 17); and St Paul says that *God sent forth His Son, that we might receive the adoption of sons* (Gal. iv. 4, 5), and that *having received the Spirit of adoption we might cry Abba, Father* (Rom. viii. 15; comp. Heb. ii. 11).

7. **An inheritor of the kingdom of heaven.** As the second Christian privilege flows from the first, so does the third from the second. For if, as members of Christ, we become sons of God, then also we become *heirs, heirs of God,* and *joint-heirs with Christ* of the Kingdom of Heaven (Rom. viii. 17; Gal. iii. 29; iv. 7). The expression "Kingdom of Heaven" is used in different senses in the Bible. Sometimes it means the Church of Christ "militant here in earth" (Mtt. iii. 2; xiii. 47, 48). Sometimes it means the Church of Christ in its future and glorified state, where we shall have "our perfect consummation and bliss, both in body and soul, in God's eternal and everlasting glory[1]." Of the kingdom of Heaven in the former of these senses we are members now; of the same kingdom in the latter sense we are "heirs through hope[2]" (Mtt. v. 20; Rev. xxi. 4, 27).

CHAPTER III.

THE FIRST BAPTISMAL VOW.

1. **Conditions of the Covenant.** Such, then, are

---

[1] See the Burial Service.
[2] See the Thanksgiving in the post-Communion Service.

the great privileges which, of His free mercy and grace, God has signed and sealed to us; such is His part of the Covenant, which He will "most surely keep and perform." But a Covenant supposes also certain conditions on our part, and these are contained in the "solemn vow, promise, and profession[1]," which our godfathers and godmothers made for us at our Baptism.

2. **The Baptismal Vow.** This Promise or Vow includes three things:

(i) *That we should renounce the Devil and all his works, the pomps and vanity of this wicked world, and all the sinful lusts of the flesh.*

(ii) *That we should believe all the Articles of the Christian Faith.*

(iii) *That we should keep God's holy will and commandments, and walk in the same all the days of our life.*

Our Baptismal Vow, then, may be summed up in three words; (1) Renunciation, (2) Faith, and (3) Obedience.

3. **Renunciation.** The Latin word[2], from which "renounce" comes, means *to break off, declare,* or *enlist oneself against.* A soldier enlists himself on the side of his sovereign, and engages to fight against all his enemies. So the Christian soldier is "signed with the sign of the Cross, in token that hereafter he shall not be ashamed to confess the faith of Christ crucified, and manfully to fight under His banner," and "to con-

---

[1] See the Exhortation in the Baptismal Service.

[2] Renuntiare. In the first Prayer-Book of King Edward VI. the word "forsake" was used instead of "renounce," which was substituted at the last review. The latter is clearly the better word. To *forsake* means to quit or give up. Now we do not actually forsake the Devil, the world, and the flesh, since they are with us go where we will. But we can renounce, or declare and show our antagonism to them, so as not "to follow nor be led by them."

tinue His faithful soldier and servant unto his life's end[1]."

4. **The Devil and all his works.** The first foe, against whom we promise to contend, is the Devil, the enemy of God and of all righteousness[2]. Created originally good, like all the works of God, *he abode not in the truth* (Jn. viii. 44), but rebelled against his Maker, and fell from his high estate (1 Tim. iii. 6), and henceforth, at the head of numerous other spirits, arrayed himself in open hostility to the Supreme, and *goeth about seeking whom he may devour* (1 Pet. v. 8). Every kind of sin may be called a "work of the Devil," but there are certain sins which may be peculiarly termed his works; such are *pride* (1 Tim. iii. 6), *lying* (Gen. iii. 4; Jn. viii. 44), *deceit and hypocrisy* Acts v. 1—4), *murder* (Jn. viii. 44), *hatred* (1 Jn. iii. 8, 10, 15), *envy* (Gen. iii. 1—5), *tempting others* (Mtt. xviii. 6, &c.).

5. **The pomps and vanity of this wicked world.** The second foe against which we undertake to fight manfully[3] is *the world*. By the "world" here is meant not the world we see around us, the heavens and the earth and the objects of glory and beauty which God has created therein, and which in the beginning He pronounced to be *very good* (Gen. i. 31). What is meant is *the world lying in wickedness* (1 Jn. v. 19), with its *seen and temporal* attractions, as opposed to the things that are *unseen and eternal* (2 Cor. iv. 18), with its vain, outward, show, its fleeting glory, and its low

---

[1] See the Baptismal Service.

[2] In Scripture he is called sometimes Satan, i. e. the Enemy (Matt. iv. 10); sometimes the Devil, i. e. the Slanderer (Matt. v. 1), because he slanders God to man (Gen. iii. 1—5), and man to God (Job i. 9—11; Rev. xii. 10); sometimes the Tempter (1 Thess. iii. 5); sometimes Apollyon or Abaddon, i.e. the Destroyer (Rev. ix. 11).

[3] See Baptismal Service.

maxims and principles of conduct. These things we promise to "renounce," and to seek the guidance of the Holy Spirit, remembering that the pomps of the world and the world itself are passing away (1 Jn. ii. 17; 1 Cor. vii. 31).

6. **The sinful lusts of the flesh.** The third Enemy we promise to contend against is *the flesh.* By the "flesh" here is meant the lower part of our nature, our natural appetites and passions, which we have in common with the animals. Though not in themselves necessarily sinful, they become so when indulged to excess instead of being kept in subjection (1 Cor. ix. 27). In renouncing, then, the sinful lusts of the flesh, we renounce all sloth, gluttony, drunkenness (Gal. v. 21), sensuality, and impurity (Eph. v. 3—5), *the end of which things is death* (Rom. vi. 21; viii. 13).

CHAPTER IV.
THE SECOND CHRISTIAN VOW.

1. **Faith.** Our second baptismal vow is *to believe all the Articles[1] of the Christian Faith,* is, in one word, a vow of *Faith.*

2. **Faith in man's natural life.** Faith is not a principle peculiar to religion. In a lower form we act upon it every day of our lives. In faith, in the firm persuasion that sleep will restore strength to our weary limbs, we betake ourselves to rest. In faith we commit the seed to the ground, fully believing that spring will be succeeded by summer, and summer by winter. In faith we entrust ourselves to the care of a physician, and, in the hope of a cure, submit to the medicines he prescribes. In short, "everything that we do from any

---

[1] Articles, from the Latin articulus—artus = *a joint,* denotes (1) a small joint, (2) a particular substance, (3) a single clause, term, or item.

motive whatsoever, beyond the impulses of the senses and the lusts of the moment, everything that we do in any way for the sake of others, or with a view to the future, though it be no further than the morrow, must needs be in some measure an act of faith[1]."

3. **Religious Faith.** Faith, in religion, is the same principle as faith in natural life, and differs only in its object. It is the firm persuasion of the being, existence, and character of God as made known to us in the Gospel of His Son, and an unfaltering trust and reliance on Him, His word, and His will (Heb. xi. 1, 6).

4. **Creeds.** From the earliest times all who sought to be baptized were required to make an open confession of their faith[2]. Such a confession is called in English a "Creed[3]," which is derived from the Latin word "Credo," *I believe*. At first these Creeds were very brief and simple (comp. Acts viii. 37), but, as the Church spread more widely, it became necessary, in consequence of false teaching, to make them more precise and definite, and so they were gradually enlarged, and assumed their present forms.

5. **The Apostles' Creed.** The Creed, which is

---

[1] Hare's *Victory of Faith*, p. 92.

[2] The first traces of Creeds may be found in such passages as 1 Cor. xv. 3—8; 1 Tim. iii. 16. See Heurtley's *Creeds of the Western Church;* Guericke's *Antiquities of the Christian Church*, p. 227.

[3] The earliest name, by which a Creed was designated, was Σύμβολον, Symbolum, *a symbol.* The meaning of the word is uncertain. It may denote (1) a summary of Christian doctrine; or (2), like the *Tessera militaris* among the Roman soldiers, a sign or watchword whereby Christians were distinguished from heathens and unbelievers. Comp. the *Catechism of Edward VI.* Q. "Why is this abridgement of the faith termed a symbol? *Answer.* A symbol is, as much as to say, a sign, mark, privy token, or watchword, whereby the soldiers of the same camp are known from their enemies." For other derivations see Bp. Browne *On the Articles*, Art. VIII.

treated of in the Catechism as containing the Articles of the Christian Faith, is commonly[1] called the *Apostles' Creed*. It is so called, not because it was drawn up by the Apostles, but because it contains the doctrines taught by them, and is in substance the same as has been used in the Church ever since their times[2].

6. **The Nicene Creed.** Besides the Apostles' Creed there are also the Nicene and Athanasian Creeds. The Nicene Creed was first drawn up at the Council of Nice in Bithynia, A.D. 325, and afterwards enlarged at the Council of Constantinople, A.D. 381. It was chiefly designed to meet the opinions of those[3] who taught that our Lord Jesus Christ was not the only-begotten Son of God, and therefore not God, and that the Holy Ghost was a creature. Hence it treats fully of the Godhead of the Son and of the Holy Ghost.

7. **The Athanasian Creed**, or the Creed of St Athanasius, a great bishop of Alexandria in the fourth century, is so called, not because it was drawn up by him (for it was not composed till 100 years after his death), but because it asserts those great truths which he spent his life in defending. These were the doctrines of the Holy Trinity and of the union of the Godhead and Manhood in our Lord Jesus Christ. It was drawn up in Latin, probably in Gaul, as some think, by Hilary of Arles, A.D. 429, or, as others, by Victricius, bishop of Rouen[4], A.D. 401.

---

[1] See Article VIII. of the Church of England.

[2] Another probable reason why it was so called is because the form most nearly like it is the Roman or Italian Creed found in the exposition of Rufinus of Aquileia. Now as the Church of Rome was the only Church in the West, which could certainly claim to have been founded by an Apostle, its See was called *the Apostolic See*, and its Creed the *Apostolic* or *Apostles' Creed*. Bp. Browne on Article VIII.; Heurtley's *Creeds of the Western Church*, p. 26; Bingham, *Antiq.* X. 3. 45.

[3] Especially Arius and Macedonius.

[4] See Waterland *On the Athanasian Creed*, ch. VIII.

CHAPTER V.

THE THIRD BAPTISMAL VOW,
AND THE OBLIGATION TO KEEP OUR VOWS.

1. **The Third Vow.** Our third Baptismal Vow is *to keep God's holy will and commandments, and to walk in the same all the days of our life*, or, in one word, it is a Vow of *Obedience*.

2. **The Ten Commandments.** The Commandments are Ten in number, whence their name "Decalogue," or *the Ten Words*. They are contained in the twentieth chapter of the Book of Exodus, and were uttered by God Himself in the hearing of the Israelites, when, after their delivery from Egypt, they were encamped before Mount Sinai (Ex. xix. xx.).

3. **The occasion of their delivery.** Their delivery marks a most momentous epoch in the history of the world. At a time when men were falling more and more away from God, were *worshipping and serving the creature rather than the Creator* (Rom. i. 25), and forgetting the dictates of the Law *written in their hearts* (Rom. ii. 15), it pleased Him solemnly to republish the Law of Nature. Out of the midst of fire and cloud and thick darkness, with thunderings and lightnings and voices (Deut. v. 22), He uttered the Ten Commandments, and afterwards caused them to be inscribed in visible characters on two Tables of Stone, and delivered them to Moses to be kept from age to age (Exod. xxxii. 15, 16; 2 Cor. iii. 7, 13).

4. **The Moral Law not done away.** By these Commandments God has borne a fixed and unalterable testimony against sin, and shown us the path of duty towards Himself and one another, in which He would have us walk. Hence Christ Himself came not *to destroy the Law, but to fulfil it* (Mtt. v. 17), and He has taught

us how its precepts reach not only to the outward acts, but to the thoughts and intents of the heart[1]. From obedience, therefore, to the Moral Law "no Christian man whatsoever is free[2]." Even as the Son of God came down from heaven *not to do His own will, but the will of Him that sent Him* (Jn. vi. 38), so must we learn to walk in the narrow way that leadeth unto life, marked out for us by God's commandments.

5. **Duty of keeping our Vows.** Such, then, are our Baptismal Vows of Renunciation, Faith, and Obedience, and we must remember that as the privileges then signed and sealed to us are real gifts to us through God's free grace, and that He will "surely keep and perform" His part of the Covenant, so the Vows we make on our part are binding upon us in the most solemn manner. Promises made to our fellow-creatures are meant to be kept, much more those made to Him in whom *we live and move and have our being* (Deut. xxiii. 21).

6. **Need of Divine Grace.** Hence in the Catechism we say, "we verily think we are bound to believe and to do" as was promised for us at our Baptism, and declare that by God's help we will so believe and do. We say *by God's help*, for in the lifelong battle we promise to wage "we have no power of ourselves to help ourselves[3]." Through "the weakness of our mortal nature" we can do no good thing without God's merciful aid, but He is "the strength of all them that put their trust in Him[4]," and by the help of His grace He can enable us to keep His commandments, and walk in the laws

---

[1] See His Comments in the Sermon on the Mount on the Sixth and Seventh Commandments (Mtt. v. 21, 22; 27, 28).
[2] See Article VII. of the Church of England.
[3] Collect for the Second Sunday in Lent.
[4] Collect for the First Sunday after Trinity.

which He hath set before us (Jn. xv. 5; Phil. ii. 13; iv. 13).

7. Thankfulness for privileges. Momentous, therefore, are the Vows we have undertaken, and we should ever remember that it is an inestimable privilege to have been brought into covenant with God through Jesus Christ. Thus to have been placed in a state of salvation[1] calls for hearty thanksgiving to our heavenly Father, and for earnest prayer that He will give us His grace that we may not fall away from, but continue in the same, and "daily increase in His Holy Spirit until we come unto His everlasting kingdom[2]" (Eph. iii. 14—19; Phil. i. 9—11; iv. 8).

---

[1] That is, "on the road to and in process of salvation." A state of salvation does not imply a state, in which we are certain to be saved, but a state in which we *are being saved*. Compare the expression τοὺς σωζομένους in Acts ii. 47.

[2] See the Prayer of Confirmation, and compare the Collect for Christmas Day; "Almighty God, who hast given us thy only-begotten Son to take our nature upon him, and as at this time to be born of a pure Virgin; Grant that we being regenerate, and made thy children by adoption and grace, may daily be renewed by thy Holy Spirit; through the same our Lord Jesus Christ, who liveth and reigneth with thee and the same Spirit, ever one God, world without end. *Amen.*"

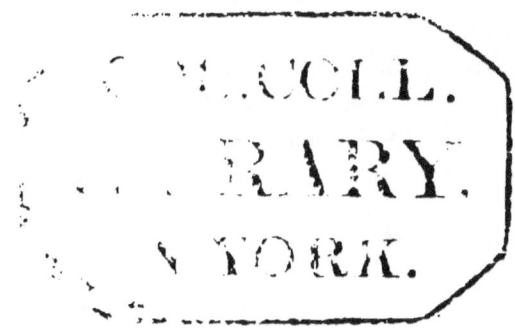

PART II.

THE CREED.

Rehearse the Articles of thy Belief.—*I believe in God the Father Almighty, Maker of heaven and earth: And in Jesus Christ his only Son our Lord, Who was conceived by the Holy Ghost, Born of the Virgin Mary, Suffered under Pontius Pilate, Was crucified, dead, and buried, He descended into hell; The third day he rose again from the dead, He ascended into heaven, And sitteth at the right hand of God the Father Almighty; From thence he shall come to judge the quick and the dead. I believe in the Holy Ghost; The holy Catholic Church; The Communion of Saints; The Forgiveness of sins; The Resurrection of the Body; And the Life everlasting. Amen.*

What dost thou chiefly learn in these Articles of thy Belief?—First, *I learn to believe in God the Father, who hath made me, and all the world.* Secondly, *In God the Son, who hath redeemed me, and all mankind.* Thirdly, *In God the Holy Ghost, who sanctifieth me, and all the elect people of God.*

CHAPTER I.

SUMMARY OF THE CREED.

1. **The Creed**, which we are taught in the Catechism to rehearse[1], is the Apostles' Creed, as being the most simple and elementary, and in most frequent[2] use amongst us.

2. **The Articles** it contains are Twelve in number, and though the first word *I believe* occurs but twice in the Creed, it really belongs to each of these Articles, and to every part or single truth contained in them[3].

---

[1] From the French *rehercer* (*re* again, and *herce* a harrow) = lit. *to harrow again,* thence *to repeat, recite.* Comp. Judg. v. 11; 1 Sam. xvii. 31.

[2] As (1) in the Baptismal Services, (2) the Visitation of the Sick, (3) at Morning and Evening Prayer.

[3] See Pearson *On the Creed*, Art. I.

3. **Summary of the Creed.** From these Articles we chiefly learn to believe in the All-Holy Trinity, into whose Name we were baptized. For, though there is but One living and true God (Exod. xx. 3, Isai. xliv. 6), yet in the Unity of the Godhead there are three Persons, *the Father, the Son, and the Holy Ghost* (Matt. xxviii. 19).

4. **God the Father.** Of the Twelve Articles one relates to the First Person in the Trinity, God the Father, "Who hath made us and all the world[1]."

5. **God the Son.** Six Articles relate to the Second Person in the Trinity, God the Son, "who hath redeemed us and all mankind."

6. **God the Holy Ghost.** One Article relates to the Third Person in the Trinity, God the Holy Ghost, "who sanctifieth us and all the elect people of God."

7. **The Holy Catholic Church.** The remaining four Articles relate to the Holy Catholic Church, and the privileges conferred on us[2] as its members.

8. **The Twelve Articles,** then, of the Creed are

Art. I.—*I believe in God the Father, Almighty, Maker of heaven and earth.*

Art. II.—*And in Jesus Christ, His only Son, our Lord;*

Art. III.—*Who was conceived by the Holy Ghost, born of the Virgin Mary;*

Art. IV.—*Suffered under Pontius Pilate, was crucified, dead, and buried;*

Art. V.—*He descended into Hell, the third day He rose again from the dead;*

Art. VI.—*He ascended into heaven, and sitteth at the right hand of God, the Father Almighty;*

---

[1] See Becon's *Catechism*, Parker Society's Works.
[2] See Nicholson *On the Catechism*, p. 30.

Art. VII.—*From thence He shall come to judge the quick and the dead.*
Art. VIII.—*I believe in The Holy Ghost;*
Art. IX.—*The Holy Catholic Church, the Communion of Saints;*
Art. X.—*The Forgiveness of sins;*
Art. XI.—*The Resurrection of the Body;*
Art. XII.—*And the Life everlasting.*

CHAPTER II.

THE FIRST ARTICLE.

I believe in God the Father, Almighty, Maker of heaven and earth.

1. **I.** With this little word the Creed commences, and by the use of the singular instead of the plural number brings the faith home to each one of us, as our own faith, and not that of any other person[1].

2. **I believe.** The belief here intended is far more than a bare confession, opinion, or assent of the mind. It implies not merely a belief that God is, but that we put our whole trust[2], hope, and confidence in Him, that we rely upon Him, and adhere to Him.

3. **I believe in God.** The first Article in the Creed declares the existence of God, a truth, which is

---

[1] Nicholson *On the Catechism*, p. 31.

[2] The first words of the Creed in Latin are not Credo Deum, = *I believe that God is*, which, as St James says (Jas. ii. 19), the devils do and tremble; nor are they Credo Deo = *I believe that the word of God is true;* but Credo in Deum = *I believe in God, I put my whole trust and confidence in Him*. See the Appendix to Noell's *Catechism*.

the foundation of all religion, and to which there is no age so distant[1], no country so remote, no people so barbarous, but they have testified in some form or other.

4. **The Father.** Though, as has been already said, there is but one living and true God, yet in the unity of the Godhead there are Three Persons, of whom the first is God the Father. It is true that the Fatherhood of God was not unknown to the Jews, for Isaiah says, *Thou, O Lord, art our Father, our Redeemer, Thy Name is from everlasting* (Isai. lxiii. 16); and Malachi asks, *Have we not all one Father, hath not one God created us?* (Mal. ii. 10). It is true also that the Greeks and Romans and other heathen nations had dim conceptions of a great All-Father, "the Father of Gods and men," as St Paul acknowledged when he quoted to the Athenians the words of one of their own poets, for *we are the offspring of God* (Acts xvii. 28). But when our Lord Jesus Christ took upon Him our nature and shed His blood for us, then we really knew that God is our Father not only because He created us, and *in Him we live and move and have our being* (Acts xvii. 28), but also because by virtue of our union with His Son he has adopted us into His family, has given us *power to become the Sons of God* (Jn. i. 12), and has bestowed upon us *the Spirit of adoption, whereby we cry, Abba, Father* (Rom. viii. 15).[2]

5. **Almighty.** And not only is He the Father, but He is also Almighty, or Omnipotent. He can do all things, and *none can stay His hand, or say unto Him What doest Thou?* (Dan. iv. 35; Job xlii. 2); He is the source of all power, *the blessed and only Potentate, King of kings and Lord of lords* (1 Tim.

---

[1] See Pearson *On the Creed*, Art. I.
[2] See Barrow's *Sermons on the Creed*.

vi. 15); He ruleth and disposeth all things, and directeth them according to His will[1]; *He hath prepared His throne in heaven, and His kingdom ruleth over all* (Ps. ciii. 19).

6. **Maker of heaven and earth.** This Article of the Creed once ended with the word Almighty[2], but now we go on to declare our belief in a great proof of God's Almighty power, which distinguishes Him from all false gods; for, as the Psalmist says, *all the gods of the nations are but idols, but the Lord made the heavens* (Ps. xcvi. 5)[3]. The goodly frame of things around us, the heaven above, the earth beneath, and the waters under the earth did not come into existence of themselves, nor do they subsist of themselves. Of His infinite power He made them all by His Son (Heb. i. 2)[4], and with His Spirit (Gen. i. 2), and having made them He ever sustains and upholds them by His Providence. He rules the motions of the sun and moon and stars; He orders the ministrations of angels and archangels, of cherubim and seraphim (Ps. ciii. 20, 21); He numbers *the very hairs of our head*, and without Him

---

[1] The words *Creator of heaven and earth* were not in the earliest Creeds, but were probably "introduced in the East, at a very early period, to arrest the truth against the blasphemy of those who denied that the Father of our Lord Jesus Christ and the Creator of the world were one and the same God;" Heurtley's *Creeds of the Western Church*, p. 129.

[2] The word rendered by us Almighty is in the Latin Creed *Omnipotens*, and in the Greek Παντοκράτωρ. This last word is the same as the Hebrew *Sabaoth* (comp. Isai. xlviii. 2; Jer. l. 34), *the Lord of Hosts*, importing "God's universal conduct and managery of all creatures; for all things in the world, as being ranged in a goodly and convenient order (like an army marching in array, or marshalled to battle), are called armies, or *sabaoth*." Barrow's *Sermons*.

[3] Comp. 2 Kings xix. 15, 19; Jer. x. 11; Acts xiv. 15, xvii. 24.

[4] Compare the Nicene Creed.

not a sparrow falleth to the ground (Mtt. x. 29, 30; Lk. xxi. 18).

CHAPTER III.

THE SECOND ARTICLE.

And in Jesus Christ, His only Son, our Lord.

1. **The Second Part of the Creed.** Next after our belief in "God the Father, who made us and all the world," comes our belief "in Jesus Christ, His only Son, our Lord." Hence the six following Articles of the Creed set forth His Person, His Office, and His Work of Redemption.

2. **Jesus.** And the first point to consider is the ever-blessed Name by which the second Person in the Trinity was known as a man among men. This was JESUS, for so was He called before His birth by the angel Gabriel (Lk. i. 31; Mtt. i. 21), and so was He named by His earthly parents at His circumcision (Lk. ii. 21). It is a Hebrew word, and is the same as Joshua, the name of the valiant companion of Moses and the conqueror of Palestine[1]. He was first called Hoshea, *a Saviour* or *Deliverer*, but afterwards Jehoshua, or Joshua, *Jehovah the Saviour*, or *Jehovah's Salvation* (Num. xiii. 16; xiv. 6, 30). In the Greek translation of the Bible the name Joshua is always rendered by the word ʼΙΗΣΟΥΣ, JESUS, whence its use in the New Testament.

3. **Meaning of the Name.** *Thou shalt call His Name* JESUS, or THE LORD WHO SAVES, said the Angel

---

[1] Comp. Acts vii. 45, *Which also our fathers that came after brought in with* JESUS, *i. e.* JOSHUA, *into the possession of the Gentiles;* and Heb. iv. 8, *For if* JESUS, *i. e.* JOSHUA, *had given them rest, then would he not have spoken of another day.*

Gabriel to Joseph, *for He shall save His people from their sins* (Lk. i. 31). Such is the import of the Name *which is above every name* (Phil. ii. 9). The first Joshua was but a man, and by the power of Jehovah[1] enabled the Israelites to vanquish the Canaanites, and divided the Land of Promise among their tribes. But JESUS was at once God and a Saviour (Mtt. i. 21—23); He Himself came down from the highest heaven, and as our Saviour delivered us from the guilt and power of sin, *destroyed him that hath the power of death, that is, the devil* (Heb. ii. 14), and will hereafter bring His people into the presence of God, and assign to them *the mansions* He is *preparing* for them (Jn. xiv. 2).

4. **Christ.** But the second Person in the Godhead is not only called Jesus, but also Christ. This is a Greek word and means *Anointed*, and is the same as the Hebrew Messiah, a title which the Jews for many generations gave to their expected Deliverer (Dan. ix. 25; Jn. i. 41). Amongst the Jews men were solemnly anointed to three offices, those of the *priest*, the *prophet*, and the *king*. Thus Aaron was an anointed priest[2]; Elisha an anointed prophet[3]; Saul an anointed king[4]. But in the person of our Redeemer the three offices met which were never conjoined in any other[5]. Melchizedek, indeed, was king and priest, David was king and prophet, but none, save Jesus, was all three, the anointed Priest, the anointed Prophet, the anointed King. With the unction of the Holy Spirit (Lk. iv. 18) He was anointed as Priest[6], *to put away sin by the sacrifice of Himself* (Heb. ix. 26); as Prophet, to reveal

---

[1] Comp. Josh. i. 6 (margin) with Josh. i. 9.
[2] Exod. xxx. 30.   [3] 1 Kings xix. 16.
[4] 1 Sam. xvi. 1, 13.
[5] Nicholson *On the Catechism*, p. 40.
[6] On this threefold office of Christ, see Butler's *Analogy*, Pt. II. chap. 5.

the Divine will to man (Lk. iv. 18); as King, *to reign over the house of Jacob for ever*, and exercise dominion for all ages (Lk. i. 32, 33).

5. **His Only Son.** But the second Person in the ever-blessed Trinity is not only Jesus Christ, He is also the only, or only-begotten[1], Son of God, begotten of His Father before all worlds[2], and of the same substance, majesty, might, and power with His Father. This is a great mystery, but it is expressly declared in Scripture. *In the beginning, says St John, was the* WORD, *and the* WORD *was with God, and the* WORD *was God* (Jn. i. 1); *and the* WORD, he continues, *became flesh, and dwelt among us, and we beheld His glory, the glory as of the only-begotten of the Father, full of grace and truth* (Jn. i. 14[3]). *God, who at sundry times and in divers manners spake in time past unto the fathers by the prophets, hath in these last days spoken unto us by His Son, whom He hath appointed heir of all things, by whom also He made the worlds; who is the brightness of His glory and the express image of His Person* (Heb. i. 1—3).

---

[1] Compare the Creed in the Baptismal Service.

[2] The simple confession in the Apostles' Creed, *And in Jesus Christ, His only Son, our Lord*, is expanded in the Nicene Creed into *And in one Lord Jesus Christ, the only-begotten Son of God, begotten of His Father before all worlds, God of God, Light of Light, very God of very God, begotten, not made, being of one substance with the Father, by whom all things were made.* Here it is to be observed, that (i) " Very God of very God" means *true God of* (from) *true God: very* being an adjective signifying "true," "real," from the Latin *verus*, Fr. *vrai*. Compare Gen. xxvii. 21, *Art thou my very son Esau?* and Jn. vii. 26, *Do the rulers know indeed that this is the very Christ?* (See *Bible Word-Book*, p. 510.) (ii) The Article, *by whom all things were made*, refers to the Son, not to the Father (of whom it has been already said), and contain in fact the words of St John i. 3.

[3] Comp. 1 Jn. iv. 9; and Heb. i. 2, 3.

6. **Our Lord.** Moreover the eternal Son of God is *our Lord*. The word Lord is that name of God, which in the Hebrew is expressed by Jehovah[1], and this was distinctly applied to Christ by the Angels at His birth. *Unto you*, said they to the shepherds, *is born this day in the city of David*, a Saviour, which is Christ *the Lord* (Lk. ii. 11). But it is also the title of a King or Ruler, and in this sense is specially applicable to Christ. For to Him the Father hath delegated authority over man, angels, and all things, so that He is King of kings and Lord of lords, and He, by taking upon Him our nature, has *bought us with a price* (Comp. Heb. ii. 14; Acts xx. 28), so that He is for ever our Lord and Master and we are His servants[2] (1 Cor. vi. 20).

CHAPTER IV.

THE THIRD ARTICLE.

Who was conceived by the Holy Ghost, born of the Virgin Mary.

1. **The Incarnation.** Having set forth generally the Name and Offices of our blessed Lord, the Creed passes on to treat of what He has done and suffered,

---

[1] In Greek Κύριος, in Latin *Dominus;* both in Ps. lxxxiii. 18, where we read, *Thou, whose name alone is Jehovah, art the most high in all the earth*, and in Exod. vi. 3, where God saith, *I appeared unto Abraham, unto Isaac, and unto Jacob, by the name of God Almighty; but by my Name Jehovah was I not known unto them,* "for the name *Jehovah*, the Greek translation, which the Apostles followed, hath no other name but *Lord;* and therefore, undoubtedly, by that word which we translate *the Lord* did they understand the proper name of God, Jehovah." Pearson *On the Creed*, Art. II.

[2] Moreover, in our Baptismal Vow we bind ourselves unto His service. See Pearson *On the Creed*, Art. II.

what He continues to do still, and will do finally[1] "for us men and for our salvation." And first it deals with His Incarnation, or His taking upon Him our nature.

2. **The Promise of Redemption.** When through the transgression of our first parents, mankind fell into captivity to sin and death (Rom. v. 12), it was promised that *the Seed of the woman should bruise the serpent's head* (Gen. iii. 15), and win back for man his lost inheritance. At length, *when the fulness of time was come* (Gal. iv. 4), in His infinite love[2] for man and the world which He had made, God sent forth His Son to take our nature upon Him, and the Son out of the same infinite love condescended to *make Himself of no reputation*, to *be made in the likeness of men*, and to become Emmanuel, *God with us* (Mtt. i. 23; Phil. ii. 7; Heb. ii. 14).

3. **He was conceived by the Holy Ghost.** But since the taint and corruption of our nature descends to all men, who are born in the natural way of the offspring of Adam[3], it was not possible that the Most Holy One could be conceived after the ordinary manner of men. The secret power, therefore, and operation of the Holy Ghost (Mtt. i. 20; Lk. i. 35), who in the beginning brooded over the waters and brought order out of chaos and life out of death (Gen. i. 2), caused that the Eternal Son of God should, in accordance with the word of prophecy[4], be conceived of a pure Virgin[5].

4. **Born of the Virgin Mary.** The humble maiden, thus divinely and pre-eminently favoured (Lk. i. 28), was

---

[1] Abp. Secker's Lectures on the Catechism.
[2] See Barrow's Sermons on *the Incarnation of our Lord*, and compare the Collect for *the Sunday before Easter*, and Jn. iii. 16, 1 Jn. iv. 9.
[3] See the VIIIth Article of the Church of England.
[4] See Isaiah vii. 14.
[5] Compare the Collect for *Christmas Day*.

named MARY, or Miriam, of the royal tribe of Judah and of the lineage of David[1] (Lk. i. 32; Rom. i. 3). While living in the retired village of Nazareth, in northern Palestine, the Angel Gabriel announced to her that the *Holy Ghost should come upon her, and the power of the Highest overshadow her, and that the Holy Thing which should be born of her should be called the Son of God* (Lk. i. 35).

5. **At Bethlehem.** The miraculous birth thus announced from heaven took place, as had been predicted[2], at Bethlehem, a village of Judæa. Thither the holy Virgin had gone up with her husband Joseph, a carpenter of Nazareth, in consequence of a decree of the Emperor Augustus, that the whole Roman world should be taxed[3] (Lk. ii. 1). While they were there, the hour long ago foreseen in the counsels of eternity arrived; *the days were accomplished that she should be delivered; and she brought forth her firstborn Son, and wrapped Him in swaddling clothes, and laid Him in a manger* (Lk. ii. 7).

6. **Perfect God and Perfect Man.** Thus "in great humility[4]" was He, who was with the Father before all worlds, pleased to be conceived and born, and "to commence His residence on earth for our salvation[5]." Remaining perfect God He became perfect Man, "of a reasonable soul and human flesh subsisting[6]." Remaining the Son of God Most High, He became JESUS, the Son of Mary, and *increased in wisdom and stature, and in favour with God and man* (Lk. ii. 52).

[1] See *Class-Book of New Testament History*, p. 130.
[2] See Micah v. 2, and compare Mtt. ii. 5, 6.
[3] See *Class-Book of New Testament History*, pp. 134, 135.
[4] See Collect for *the First Sunday in Advent*.
[5] Mill's *Lectures on the Catechism*, p. 81, and Archer Butler's Sermon *on the Mystery of the Incarnation*, Vol. I. p. 72.
[6] See the Athanasian Creed, and Hooker, *Eccl. Pol.*, Bk. IV. 53, 3.

CHAPTER V.

THE FOURTH ARTICLE.

He suffered under Pontius Pilate, was crucified, dead, and buried.

1. **He suffered.** Having confessed that for us men and for our salvation, the Eternal Son of God came down from heaven and was made Man, the Creed passes on to the equally marvellous truth, that "He suffered under Pontius Pilate, was crucified, dead, and buried."

2. **His Sufferings predicted.** For as the first Adam brought sin into the world and death by sin (Rom. v. 12, 14), so from the beginning it was predicted, with more or less clearness, that the Second Adam, who knew no sin but came to *put away sin*, should *suffer* and *die* (Mk. ix. 12; 1 Pet. i. 11). Thus the earliest prophecy had declared that the Seed of the woman should *bruise the Serpent's head*, but at the same time had whispered that the Serpent should *bruise His heel*[1] (Gen. iii. 15). The Prophets, moreover, who were raised up one after the other to foreshadow the Person, Office, and Work[2] of the Messiah, intimated that His triumph would not be that of an earthly conqueror. Isaiah spoke of the coming of *a Man of sorrows and acquainted with grief;* of His being *wounded for our transgressions* and *bruised for our iniquities;* of His being *oppressed and afflicted,* of His being *brought as a Lamb to the slaughter,* and of His *being stricken for the transgression of His people* (Isai. liii. 1—10); Zechariah, again, had predicted that the Messiah should be

---

[1] That is, *His human nature.*
[2] See Micah v. 2; Isai. vii. 14; Zech. vi. 13; Isai. lxi. 1, and read Pearson *On the Creed*, Art. IV.

smitten (Zech. xiii. 7); and Daniel had declared that *He should be cut off, but not for Himself*[1] (Dan. ix. 26).

3. **And fulfilled.** And even so was it fulfilled. For our blessed Lord having grown up to man's estate in the despised town of Nazareth (Jn. i. 46), at length came forth on His errand of wondrous Love. Having been baptized in the Jordan by his forerunner John the Baptist (Mtt. iii. 15, 16; Lk. iii. 21, 22), for three years He went about the towns and villages of Palestine, declaring in discourses and parables such as *never man spake* the will of His Father, and proving Himself victorious over nature and the spirit-world, over disease and death. But though *He came to His own, His own received Him not* (Jn. i. 11). Though he went about doing good, His lowly birth caused Him to be despised and rejected (Mtt. xiii. 55—57); the rulers of the nation hated Him, and sought to kill Him; one of His own disciples betrayed Him; and at length He was brought as a prisoner before Pontius Pilate[2], the Roman[3] governor of Judæa, as One who deserved to die, because *He made Himself the Son of God* (Jn. xix. 7).

[1] Moreover, while "the Prophets *said* in express terms that the Messiah, whom they foretold, should suffer, Moses *said* so in those ceremonies which were instituted by his ministry," (1) in the sacrifice of the Pascal lamb, (2) in the uplifting of the brazen serpent in the wilderness, (3) in the Sacrificial ritual generally, which all pointed to a greater and a perfect Sacrifice. And what the prophets predicted, and the Law of Moses foreshadowed, our Lord Himself declared to His Apostles would be fulfilled (Lk. xviii. 31).

[2] By the mention of the name of this governor the Creed determines the time when the Saviour suffered. For from the monuments of history (Tacitus, *Annals*, xv. 44), we know that Pontius Pilate was sent forth by Tiberius Cæsar to be procurator of Judæa in A.D. 26, and that he held this office till the year A.D. 36. See *Class-Book of New Testament History*, pp. 150—152.

[3] For "the power of life and death was not in any court

4. **He suffered under Pontius Pilate.** When the Holy One was brought before his tribunal, Pilate examined Him and the charges brought against Him, and three times declared that he *found no fault in Him* (Jn. xviii. 38). But though he pronounced Him to be innocent, though he washed his hands in token of it, and knew well that it *was for envy* that the chief priests and rulers had *delivered Him up* (Mtt. xxvii. 18), he did not release Him. Carried away by the furious clamour of His accusers he first gave orders that He should be scourged. This painful and horrible[1] punishment the Holy One *suffered.* The soldiers of Pilate executed his command with their wonted severity, and not content with inflicting upon Him cruel stripes, they placed a reed in His right hand, they saluted Him in mockery *Hail, King of the Jews*, they struck Him with the reed, they spat in His face, and heaped upon Him indignities unspeakable[2].

5. **Was Crucified.** But this spectacle of terrible suffering borne without a single murmur drew forth no pity from the Jews. *Crucify*[3] *Him, Crucify Him*, was their cry (Jn. xix. 6). For awhile Pilate hesitated, but at length, *willing to content the people* (Mk. xv. 15), he delivered the Holy One to a band of soldiers, who led

---

of the Jews, but in the Roman governor alone as supreme." See Pearson *On the Creed*, Art. IV., and Lightfoot on Mtt. xxvi. 3.

[1] See *Class-Book of New Testament History*, p. 305, n.

[2] Compare Mtt. xxvii. 28—30; Mk. xv. 18, 19; John xix. 2.

[3] Crucifixion was not a Jewish but a Roman punishment, and only inflicted by them on slaves and the lowest criminals. Had the Jews been at liberty to inflict the punishment due by their law for the crime of blasphemy, that punishment would have been by *stoning* (Levit. xxiv. 16). See Pearson *On the Creed*, Art. IV; *Class-Book of New Testament History*, p. 309 and notes.

Him forth without the city to a place called Golgotha, *the place of a skull*[1] (Mtt. xxvii. 33). There the soldiers stripped Him of His garments, nailed His hands and feet to a Cross, placed a title over His head, *This is Jesus, the King of the Jews,* and thus crucified Him between two malefactors, one on His right hand, the other on His left (Mtt. xxvii. 37, 38).

6. **Dead.** In the Nicene, as also in some of the earlier Creeds, we say that our Lord was "crucified under Pontius Pilate and suffered." But the Apostles' Creed adds that He "died," that is, that His crucifixion ended in a real death[2]. And this is added in opposition to the opinions of those who taught that His death was not real, but only apparent[3]. The truth however of His death is clearly set forth in the Gospels. For they tell us that after He had hung upon the Cross about six hours, *i.e.* from nine in the morning till three in the afternoon, He cried with a loud voice, *Father, into Thy hands I commend My Spirit* (Lk. xxiii. 46), and gave up the ghost, which means that His spirit was separated from His body, and, as death consists in this separation, so far as He was Man, He died. Moreover, when the soldiers deputed for this purpose by Pilate, at the request of the Jewish rulers[4], came to Golgotha, they broke the

---

[1] In Greek called *Kranion*, probably from the shape of its rounded summit. The Vulgate has rendered it *in locum Calvariæ*, whence comes the English *Calvary* (Lk. xxiii. 33).

[2] Compare the third Article of the Church of England, "who truly suffered, was crucified, dead, and buried."

[3] The error of the Docetæ. See Bp. Browne *On the Articles*, Art. II.

[4] Death by crucifixion did not generally supervene till after three days, and was at last the result of gradual numbing and starvation. During this time the Romans permitted the sufferers to linger on, instead of shortening their agonies. The Mosaic law did not permit such barbarities, see Deut. xxi. 22, 23.

legs of the two malefactors, but when they came to the body of Jesus, they found that He was dead already (Jn. xix. 33). They broke, therefore, not a bone of His body[1], but one of the soldiers thrust his spear into His side, thus inflicting a wound of itself sufficient to cause death[2], and immediately there flowed forth blood and water (Jn. xix. 34), showing by this separation of the blood from the water, that he was truly dead.

7. **And buried.** And as He truly died, so also was He truly "buried[3]." For the Gospel narratives relate, that before the tidings of the Saviour's death could reach the ears of Pilate, Joseph of Arimathaea, a man of wealth, a member of the Sanhedrin, and a secret disciple of Jesus, boldly went to the procurator and requested that the Body of the Redeemer might be given up to him (Mk. xv. 43). Assured by the centurion who had been present at the crucifixion, that death had really taken place, Pilate assented, and Joseph having purchased fine linen proceeded to Golgotha with Nicodemus, who had bought *a mixture of myrrh and aloes, about an hundred pound weight* (Jn. xix. 39). Arrived there, they took down the Holy Body, wrapped it in the linen clothes with the myrrh and aloes, and conveyed it to a new tomb that Joseph

---

[1] Thus unconsciously fulfilling the type of the Paschal lamb (Ex. xii. 46; Ps. xxxiv. 20), just as the piercing of the side fulfilled the words of Zechariah, that men should *look upon Him whom they had pierced* (Zech. xii. 10).

[2] The spear used is called λόγχη (Jn. xix. 34), i.e. the Roman *hasta*, the iron head of which was *the width of a handbreadth*, and pointed at the end.

[3] The burial of our Lord formed a distinct subject of St Paul's preaching, as appears from 1 Cor. xv. 4. And since in *Baptism* the Christian is said to *be buried with Christ* (Col. ii. 12) *into death* (Rom. vi. 4), the afternoon of Easter Eve was in the Early Church one of the most favourite times for baptizing. See Guericke's *Antiq. of the Christian Church*, p. 149, and compare the Collect for Easter Even.

had hewed out of a rock in a garden which he possessed near the place of crucifixion. There, in the presence of Mary Magdalene and other women, they laid the Body, rolled a great stone to the entrance, and departed[1].

CHAPTER VI.

ARTICLE V.

He descended into Hell, the third day He rose again from the dead.

1. **He descended into Hell.** Thus in accordance with His own prediction (Mtt. xii. 40), in respect to His body was the Holy One truly buried, and thus did He make *His grave with the rich* (Isai. liii. 9). The Creed now proceeds to declare what became of His soul, or spirit, which in death He commended into His Father's hands (Lk. xxiii. 46), and says that in it "He descended into Hell[2]."

2. **The word Hell** here used is the English equivalent of the Greek word Hades, which literally means *the unseen or hidden place*[3]. It does not denote the

---

[1] Mtt. xxvii. 60; Mk. xv. 46; Lk. xxiii. 53, 54.

[2] This Article is not found in the oldest Creeds. It first occurs in the Creed of the Church of Aquileia, about A. D. 400, whence in all probability it was taken into the Apostles' Creed. All the earlier fathers, however, of the Church laid great stress on the belief in Christ's descent to Hades, as establishing the true doctrine of His humanity, viz. that He was "perfect Man, of a reasonable soul and human flesh subsisting;" "for whereas His Body was laid in the grave, and His soul went down to Hades, He must have had both Body and Soul." Bp. Browne *On the Articles*, p. 81; Heurtley *On the Creeds*, pp. 134—137.

[3] The word Hell is derived from the A. S. hælen=*to cover* or *conceal*, and denotes, like the Hebrew Sheol, "the covered place," the invisible underworld. Γέεννα is the Greek word for "the place of torment," and ἡ ἄβυσσος for

place of torment, for which a different Greek word is always used, but *the place of departed spirits*[1].

3. **Scripture Proof.** That our Lord did descend into Hades is plain from His own words to the penitent thief, *Verily I say unto thee, To-day shalt thou be with Me in Paradise*[2] (Lk. xxiii. 43). Now "Paradise" or the "Garden of Eden" was a term applied by the Jews to that part of Hades containing the souls of the blessed in their intermediate state[3]. Moreover, St Peter, in his address to the Jews on the day of Pentecost, quoting the sixteenth Psalm, *Thou wilt not leave My soul in Hades, neither wilt Thou suffer Thine Holy*

"the bottomless pit." See Lk. viii. 31, and comp. Trench *On the Miracles*, p. 471 n.

[1] The phrase used in the earlier Creeds in which this word occurs is in Greek εἰς τὰ καταχθόνια, (comp. Eph. iv. 9), in Latin *ad inferna* or *in inferna*, in later times *ad inferos*, "to the inhabitants of the Inferna," as one Anglo-Saxon version exactly renders it, *He nither astah to helwarum*.

[2] From the Greek word παράδεισος = *a walled garden*, or park of a king, rich in fruits and flowers. The Jews disposed of the souls of the righteous till the resurrection under a threefold phrase; (1) "The Garden of Eden" or "Paradise;" (2) "under the throne of glory" (= "under the altar" Rev. vi. 9); (3) "in Abraham's bosom" (Lk. xvi. 22). See Lightfoot's *Hor. Heb.* on Lk. xvi. 22; and Bp. Browne on the third Article.

[3] The Creed does not state *the purpose* of Christ's descent into Hades, but from 1 Peter iii. 19, according to the most probable interpretation of the verse, we gather that *He went and preached*, or rather *made proclamation* (ἐκήρυξεν) *to the spirits in prison*, i. e. in *ward* or *guardianship* (ἐν φυλακῇ) in Hades; and as to the subject of His proclamation, what can "be more probable than that He should have proclaimed to them that their Redemption had been fully effected, that Satan had been conquered, that the great Sacrifice had been offered up? If *angels joy over one sinner that repenteth* (Lk. xv. 10), may we not suppose Paradise filled with rapture, when the Soul of Jesus came among the souls of His redeemed, Himself the Herald (κῆρυξ) of His own victory?" See Bp. Browne on the third Article; Horsley's *Sermons*, Vol. I. xx.; and Noell's *Catechism*.

One to see corruption, distinctly states that the Psalmist spake of *the resurrection of Christ, that His soul was not left in Hades, neither His flesh did see corruption* (Acts ii. 25—31). From these passages, then, we infer that, as when human beings die, their bodies are laid in the grave, while their souls pass to the realm of spirits, even so our Lord descended thither also, "that He might fulfil the conditions also of death proper to human nature[1]."

4. **The third day.** The Body of our Lord, as we have seen, was laid in the tomb on the day preceding the Jewish Sabbath, that is, on Friday evening, and there, during Friday night, Saturday, and Saturday night[2], it remained. But early in the morning of the first day of the week, *our Lord's Day* (Rev. i. 10), Mary Magdalene and the other women set out thither to complete the embalming of the Body (Lk. xxiv. 1). While they were musing who should roll away the great stone from the entrance, the earth quaked beneath their feet, and an Angel descended and rolled away the stone and sat upon it.

5. **He rose again from the dead.** Though be-

---

[1] Bp. Browne on the third Article.

[2] It was the custom of the Jews to call the same time *three days and three nights* (1 Sam. xxx. 12, 13), or *after three days*, or *on the third day* (2 Chron. x. 5, 12), putting the whole for a part. Hence the Saviour in one place says that *as Jonas was three days and three nights in the whale's belly, so shall the Son of Man be three days and three nights in the heart of the earth* (Matt. xii. 40); in another place He says, *Destroy this temple, and in three days I will raise it up* (Jn. ii. 19); in another place He says, *After three days I will rise again* (Matt. xxvii. 63). We must understand, therefore, by the expression, *He rose from the dead the third day*, not that He continued the space of three whole days dead, but that during Friday night, Saturday, and Saturday night, He lay in the grave, and on the third day, our Lord's day, He rose again. See Pearson, *On the Creed*, Art. v. and the notes.

wildered by these strange events, the women advanced nearer, and perceived not only that the stone was rolled away, but that the sepulchre was empty (Lk. xxiv. 3); and as they were standing full of awe and wonder, an Angel announced to them that their *Lord was risen* (Lk. xxiv. 5, 6), and bade them go tell the joyful news to His Apostles. Filled at once with mingled fear and joy they hurried with all speed to the Apostles, who at first regarded their words as no better than *an idle tale* (Lk. xxiv. 11). But soon they found that the announcement of the Angel was true. *Their Lord was risen indeed*, and from time to time[1] during a period of forty days they were privileged to see Him, and that not only separately but together[2], not by night only but by day, and they were permitted not merely to see Him but to touch Him, to converse with Him, to eat with Him, to examine His person, and to assure themselves that "He had truly risen again from death[3]," and came forth the Conqueror of the Grave.

6. **According to the Scriptures.** Thus, then, on the third day, as prophets had foreshewn, and He

---

[1] Comp. Acts i. 3, ὁπτανόμενος, *appearing from time to time*, in opposition to His continued sojourn before. See Westcott's *Gospel of the Resurrection*, p. 111.

[2] For the risen Saviour manifested Himself (1) to Mary Magdalene (Jn. xx. 11—18); (2) to the other ministering women (Mtt. xxviii. 9); to the two disciples journeying towards Emmaus (Lk. xxiv. 13—33); (4) to St Peter (Lu. xxiv. 34; 1 Cor. xv. 5); (5) to the ten Apostles (Lu. xxiv. 33—46); (6) to the eleven Apostles (when Thomas was present, Jn. xx. 24—31); (7) to seven Apostles by the Lake of Tiberias (Jn. xxi. 1—14); (8) to the eleven Apostles, and probably the 500 brethren, on the appointed mountain (Mtt. xxviii. 16—18, 1 Cor. xv. 6); (9) to James (1 Cor. xv. 7); (10) to the Apostles in or near Jerusalem just before the Ascension (1 Cor. xv. 7, Lk. xxiv. 50). See Wieseler's *Chronol. Synopsis;* Tischendorf's *Synopsis Evangelica;* Ellicott's *Lectures*, p. 414 n.

[3] See Article IV.

Himself had predicted (Mtt. xvi. 21; xvii. 22, 23), did the Lord rise again, and the fact was attested by His Apostles (Acts i. 3), by His Enemies (Mtt. xxviii. 11—15), and by Angels from heaven (Lk. xxiv. 4—7[1]). From the earliest times His Resurrection has formed one of the Articles of the Creed, for it is the keystone of the Christian Faith. It is one of the plainest proofs of His Divinity (Rom. i. 4; Jn. x. 18); it is the sign and seal of the acceptance of the Sacrifice He offered upon the Cross[2] (Rom. iv. 25; 1 Cor. xv. 56, 57); it is the earnest and pledge[3] of our Resurrection (1 Cor. xv. 20—22); it is the fount and source of all our means of grace in this life, of all our hopes and assurances as regards the next.

[1] The commemoration, moreover, of Christ's Resurrection *from the very earliest times* (Jn. xx. 19, xx. 26, Acts xx. 7, 1 Cor. xvi. 2), on the first day of the week, or *the Lord's Day* (Rev. i. 10), is a strong testimony to its truth, and that it was not added to our religion in any later age, after the history of the time was forgotten, and the truth of the account could not be examined. See Westcott's *Gospel of the Resurrection*, p. 106, 2nd Edit.

[2] On the day our Lord rose from the dead, the 16th of the Jewish month Nisan, the first ripe sheaf of barley was brought into the temple sanctuary, and there waved by the priest before the Lord, till which was done, no produce of the now ripening harvest might be eaten (Lev. xxiii. 9—11). As that ripe sheaf was the pledge and earnest of the whole harvest, so is the Resurrection of Christ the Firstfruit, the pledge of the harvest and ingathering of all men.

[3] "By His death we know that He suffered for sin, by His resurrection we are assured that the sins for which He suffered were not His own; had no man been a sinner, He had not died; had He been a sinner, He had not risen again; but dying for those sins which we committed, He rose from the dead to shew that He had made full satisfaction for them, that we believing in Him might obtain remission of our sin, and justification of our persons." Pearson, *On the Creed*, Art. v.

CHAPTER VII.

ARTICLE VI.

He ascended into heaven, and sitteth at the right hand of God the Father Almighty.

1. **The Great Forty Days.** After His glorious Resurrection the Saviour remained upon this earth for a space of *forty days* (Acts i. 3). During this period He satisfied His Apostles from time to time respecting His death and the prophecies which had foreshadowed it, instructed them in *the things concerning His kingdom* (Acts i. 3), and gave them His last commission *to go and make disciples of all nations, baptizing them into the Name of the Father, and of the Son, and of the Holy Ghost* (Mtt. xxviii. 19, 20).

2. **The Walk to Olivet.** At length this solemn period drew to a close. Warned it may be by the Saviour Himself, or attracted by the near approach of the festival of Pentecost, the Apostles left Galilee, and returned to Jerusalem. There they once more saw their risen Lord, and received His command to remain in Jerusalem, till they should be *baptized with the Holy Ghost, and endued with power from on high* (Acts i. 5). At last He bade them accompany Him along the road towards Bethany and the Mount of Olives (Lk. xxiv. 50). Convinced that something mysterious was about to happen, and thinking that He intended to commence His long-expected reign, they began to enquire, *Lord, wilt Thou at this time restore the kingdom to Israel?* But their enquiries were solemnly silenced. It was not for them *to know the times or the seasons, which the Father had put in His own power:* it was their duty and privilege to be witnesses to the Lord *in Jerusalem, and in all Judæa, and in Samaria, and unto the uttermost part of the earth* (Acts i. 8).

3. **He ascended into heaven.** Thus conversing they followed Him even to the borders of the district[1] of Bethany, to one of the secluded hills which overhang the village on the eastern slope of Olivet. There they received his last solemn and abiding blessing (Lu. xxiv. 50), and while his hands were yet uplifted in benediction (Lu. xxiv. 51), a marvellous change took place. By the power of His inherent Deity he began *to be parted from them,* and there came a cloud in which He rose from Olivet, and *was carried up into heaven out of their sight* (Lk. xxiv. 51; Acts i. 9). Long time stood the Eleven looking upwards and watching Him as He receded more and more from view (Acts i. 10). At length two angelic beings clad in white apparel addressed them, *Ye men of Galilee, why stand ye gazing up into heaven? This same Jesus, who hath been taken from you into heaven, shall so come in like manner as ye have seen him go into heaven* (Acts i. 11).

4. **The difference** between the Resurrection and the Ascension[2] is very noticeable. When exactly the Lord rose again, how He looked when He arose, no man knoweth, for no man saw. But when He ascended, when it was of the utmost importance that men should be assured that He had gone up to the same blest abode, where He was with the Father *before the world was* (Jn. xvii. 5), then, in the presence of many witnesses, did He withdraw, and that not swiftly and imperceptibly, like Enoch, who *was not, for God took him*

---

[1] "Not altogether into Bethany, but so far as the point where Bethany came into sight." Stier. "A more-secluded spot could scarcely have been found so near the stir of a mighty city; the long ridge of Olivet screens the hills, and the hills themselves screen the village beneath from all sound or sight of the city behind." Stanley's *Sinai and Palestine,* p. 454.

[2] The Ascension had been foretold by our Lord Himself; see Jn. vi. 62, vii. 33, xiv. 28, xvi. 5, xx. 17.

(Gen. v. 24), nor *with a chariot of fire, and horses of fire* (2 Kings ii. 11), as in the case of Elijah, but gradually and quietly, without pomp or circumstance, as though it was but the natural close of His Divine life on earth.

5. **He sitteth at the right hand of God.** Thus, then, as David had predicted, did the Holy One *ascend up on high, and lead captivity captive, and receive gifts for men* (Ps. lxviii. 18)[1]; thus did He enter into His glory, and bear our redeemed humanity *far above all heavens* (Eph. iv. 10), into the very presence of God, into "that place of all places in the universe of things in situation most eminent, in quality most holy, in dignity most excellent, in glory most illustrious, the inmost sanctuary of God's temple above[2]." Having stated this, the Creed passes on to speak of what He does in the highest heavens. *He sitteth*, it says, *at the right hand of God, the Father Almighty* (Ps. cx. 1). Now God is a Spirit, and hath not hands like a man. Therefore we must understand, by this session[3] at God's right hand, that in the heavens our Lord now occupies the

---

[1] Compare also the Proper Psalms appointed for Ascension-Day, the eighth, fifteenth, twenty-first, twenty-fourth, forty-seventh, and one hundred and eighth.

[2] Barrow's sermon on the Ascension. Compare the words of Pearson, *On the Creed*, Art. vi.: "whatsoever heaven is higher than all the rest which are called heavens; whatsoever sanctuary is holier than all which are called holies; whatsoever place is of greatest dignity in all those courts above, into that place did He ascend, where in the splendour of His Deity He was before He took upon Him our humanity."

[3] We must not understand His session as determining any posture of His body in the heavens, for in one place St Paul merely says, that He *is at the right hand of God* (Rom. viii. 34, 1 Pet. iii. 22), and St Stephen affirmed that He saw Him *standing on the right hand of God* (Acts vii. 56). The word signifies (i.) habitation, possession, and continuance; (ii.) rest and quietness; (iii.) dominion, sovereignty, and

place of greatest honour, of most exalted majesty[1], and of most perfect bliss, and that God hath conferred upon Him all pre-eminence of dignity, power, favour, and felicity.

6. **As our Priest.** But we are not to conceive of the session of our Lord as though it implied a state of inactive rest. In the highest heavens He exerciseth the twofold functions, typified by Melchizedek, of Priest and King (Heb. vii. 21). As the Jewish high-priest entered once every year, on the great day of Atonement, into the Holy of Holies, with the blood of various victims, which he sprinkled before the mercy-seat (Lev. xvi. 15), even so as our high-priest Christ has entered into the true Holy of Holies with His own Blood (Heb. ix. 12), and pleads face to face with God the merits of His sacrifice (Rom. viii. 34). For even in that glorious world He still retains a perfect sense of our infirmities, and of all the mystery of human pain which He learnt on earth, and out of His perfect love, knowledge, and sympathy, He, as our Advocate, intercedes for us, and through His intercession our prayers ascend to and are accepted at the Throne of Grace (Heb. iv. 14, vii. 25; 1 Jn. ii. 1, 2; Rev. viii. 3).

7. **As our King.** And not only as our *Great High Priest* (Heb. iv. 14), but as King of kings and Lord of lords does He sit at the right hand of God. There with infinite power, wisdom, and providence He is guiding the destinies of the Universe, and especially of the

majesty. Ipsum verbum *sedere* regni significat potestatem. Pearson, *On the Creed*, Art. VI.

[1] "Because the most honourable place amongst men is the right hand, as when Bathsheba went unto King Solomon, he *sat down on his throne, and caused a seat to be set for the king's mother, and she sat on the right hand* (1 Kings ii. 19, compare also Matt. xx. 21), therefore the *right hand* of God signifies the glorious majesty of God." Pearson, *On the Creed*, Art. VI.

redeemed family of man. Slowly indeed, as we count slowness[1], but yet surely He is directing all things towards their destined end, and employing the agency of heaven and earth for the government and defence of His people. As yet, indeed, we do not *see all things put under Him* (Heb. ii. 8), but as He *is able*, so will He *subdue all things unto Himself* (Phil. iii. 21), and in due time *the last enemy, even death* (1 Cor. xv. 26), shall be destroyed, and the Victory, for which all creation waiteth, shall be finally and completely won.

CHAPTER VIII.

ARTICLE VII.

From thence He shall come to judge the quick and the dead.

1. **From thence He shall come.** When He was upon earth our Lord declared not only that he should ascend into heaven (Jn. vi. 62), but also that from thence He should come again. Sometimes He stated this under various images, as that of a "master returning to his household" (Mtt. xxiv. 45—51), or "a nobleman returning from a far country" (Lk. xix. 12—27), or "a bridegroom coming for his bride" (Mtt. xxv. 1—12). Sometimes He spoke of it expressly, as when He told His disciples that He was going away *to prepare a place* for them, and would *come again and receive them unto Himself* (Jn. xiv. 2, 3); or when He

---

[1] "Men are impatient, and for precipitating things: but the Author of Nature appears deliberate throughout His operations, accomplishing His natural ends by slow successive steps. And there is a plan of things beforehand laid out, which, from the nature of it, requires various systems of means, as well as length of time, in order to the carrying on of its several parts into execution." Butler's *Analogy*, Part II. Chap. IV, and note in Fitzgerald's edition.

declared to the Jewish rulers that hereafter they should see the Son of Man sitting on the right hand of power, and *coming in the clouds of heaven* (Mtt. xxvi. 64). Thus also the angels, who appeared to the Apostles at the Ascension, distinctly stated that the same Jesus, who had been taken from them into heaven, should *so come in like manner as they had seen Him go into heaven* (Acts i. 11).

2. **To judge.** The second coming, however, of the Saviour will not be, like His first, "in great humility[1]," but in "glorious majesty," and with all His holy angels to execute judgment in the earth. This is His own express declaration. *The Father*, He saith, *judgeth no man, but hath committed all judgment unto the Son, and hath given Him authority to execute judgment because He is the Son of Man*[2] (Jn. v. 22, 27). Thus also St Paul said to the Athenians on Mars' hill, *God hath appointed a day, in the which He will judge*

---

[1] See the Collect for the First Sunday in Advent.

[2] *Because He is the Son of Man.* This remarkable title is never applied by the writers of the Gospels to the Eternal Son of God. Wherever it is applied, it is by our Lord Himself. There are only three exceptions to this rule, Acts vii. 56, Rev. i. 13, and Rev. xiv. 14. During, however, the period of His sojourn in this world, there was no title our Lord was pleased so often and so constantly to apply to Himself; for a few out of many instances compare Jn. i. 51, iii. 13; Lk. v. 24, vi. 22; Mk. ix. 31, x. 33; Mk. xiv. 62. Observe, it is not Son of a Man, but "Son of Man." The word in the original used for man implies human being, and the expression denotes that He who was the "Son of God" from all eternity became the "Son of Man" in time, the second Adam; "It pleased not the Word or Wisdom of God to take to itself some one person amongst men, for then should one have been advanced, which was assumed, and no more; but wisdom, to the end she might save many, built her house of that nature which is *common unto all,* she made not this or that man her habitation, but dwelt *in us.*" Hooker, *Eccl. Pol.* Book v. lii. 3.

the world in righteousness by that Man whom He hath ordained (Acts xvii. 31; comp. Rom. ii. 16).

3. **The quick and the dead.** Concerning the nature of this Judgment it has been revealed to us that it will extend alike to the quick[1] and to the dead, that is, to those who shall be alive at that Day, and to those who shall have died before it arrives. *I charge thee,* writes St Paul to Timothy, *before God and the Lord Jesus Christ, who shall judge the quick and dead at His appearing and His kingdom* (2 Tim. iv. 1). *Who,* writes St Peter of profane men, *shall render an account to Him that is ready to judge both the quick and dead* (1 Pet. iv. 5). For *we shall not all sleep,* i.e. the sleep of death, *but we shall all be changed, in a moment,* in *the twinkling of an eye, at the last trump* (1 Cor. xv. 51)...and *the dead, both small and great,* shall stand before the Judgment-seat of Christ (Rev. xx. 12).

4. **According to their works.** Moreover, it will extend to the thoughts (1 Cor. iv. 5), words (Mtt. xii. 36), and actions[2] (Rev. xx. 13) of men. For He, before whom nations (Mtt. xxv. 32) will be then assembled, knoweth *what is in man* (Jn. ii. 25). He will *bring to light the hidden things of darkness, and will make manifest the counsels of the hearts* (1 Cor. iv. 5). He will exact

---

[1] Quick means *living, moving,* from the A.-S. *cwic, cwuc,* Germ. *queck.* Comp. Lev. xiii. 10; Num. xvi. 30; Ps. lv. 15; cxxiv. 3; also Chaucer's *Knight's Tale,* 1017:
    Nat fully quyk, na fully deed they were.
Shakespere, *Hamlet,* Act v. Sc. 1:
    'Tis for the dead, not for the quick.
See *The Bible Word-Book,* p. 393.

[2] Beside the direct testimony of the Word of God we are convinced of a future judgment (1) by our conscience, (2) by reflection on God as a just God, (3) by the consent of almost all mankind. See Pearson, *On the Creed,* Art. VII.; Butler's *Analogy,* Bk. I. Ch. III.

a strict account of the *deeds done in the body, whether they be good or whether they be evil* (2 Cor. v. 10), and on His sentence will depend issues of inconceivable moment; for they that have done evil shall *go away into everlasting punishment, but the righteous into life eternal* (Mtt. xxv. 46).

5. **The Judge**, then, on this great and terrible Day will be no other than the *Son of Man*, whom Daniel foresaw *coming with the clouds of heaven* (Dan. vii. 13, 14). For though the right and power of judging inseparably pertains to God Almighty, whose creatures and servants we are[1], yet He hath delegated this authority to His Son (Jn. vi. 27). All the revelations of Scripture imply that the future Judgment will be transacted in a regular, public, and most solemn manner, in the face and audience of all the world, before angels and men. But the glorious presence of God we could not endure. He dwelleth in the light which no man can approach unto, so that *no man hath seen nor can see Him* (1 Tim. vi. 16). *Thou canst not see My face*, said He to Moses, *for there shall no man see Me and live* (Exod. xxxiii. 20). As, then, the *only-begotten Son, who is in the bosom of the Father* (Jn. i. 18), alone ever declared, or manifested Him to His creatures, so to Him God hath delegated the universal and ultimate judgment of mankind, so that "as in our nature He performed all that was requisite to save us, as in our nature He was exalted to God's right hand to rule and bless us, so He shall in our nature appear to judge us[2]."

---

[1] See Barrow's sermon *On the Circumstances of the Future Judgment*.

[2] Barrow's *Sermons*. Compare also Pearson *On the Creed*, Art. VII. "The Father, who is only God, and never took upon Him either the nature of man or angels, *judgeth no man* (and the same reason reacheth also to the Holy Ghost); *but hath committed all judgment to the Son*, and the reason

6. **Because He is the Son of Man,** therefore is He decreed and determined by God to be our Judge (Jn. vi. 27). For this high office he unites proprieties which could not be found in any other even the highest archangel. For not only, as the Gospel records assure us, is He our Redeemer and endued with perfect equity of mind, and immutable love of right; not only has He the divine faculty of searching men's hearts, so that He knows all matters of fact that ever were, and can discern the right in every case; but He alone from experience of human life can possess that "exact temperament of affection toward man, which is requisite to the distribution of equal justice towards them, according to due measures of mercy and severity[1]."

7. **Summary.** This, then, is the sum of the second part of the Christian Faith, "wherein is contained the whole story of our redemption by Jesus Christ[2]," His Incarnation, His sufferings under Pontius Pilate, His Death, His Burial, His descent into Hades, His Resurrection on the third day, His ascent into heaven, His session at the right hand of God, His future coming to judge the quick and the dead[3].

---

why He hath committed it to Him is, *because He is*, not only *the Son of God*, and so truly God, but also *the Son of Man*, and so truly Man; *because He is* that *Son of Man* who suffered so much for the sons of men."

[1] Barrow.   [2] Noell's *Catechism*.

[3] After the words *to judge both the quick and the dead*, the Nicene Creed adds the clause *Of whose kingdom there shall be no end*, which is said to have been directed against the opinion of those "who taught that, at the Day of Judgment, the Word would return into the bosom of the Father, whence He came forth, and cease to have a distinct personal subsistence, and by consequence a distinct personal reign." Heurtley, pp. 139, 140.

CHAPTER IX.

ARTICLE VIII.

I believe in the Holy Ghost.

1. **I believe.** Having confessed our faith in God the Father, "who hath made us and all the world," and in God the Son, "who hath redeemed us and all mankind," we now proceed to confess our faith in God the Holy Ghost, "who sanctifieth us and all the elect people of God." Before this Article repeat again the first word of the Creed, *I believe*, because of the many particulars concerning the Son and His work of Redemption which have intervened.

2. **I believe in the Holy Ghost**[1], then, or Holy Spirit, is the Eighth Article of the Creed, or, as it is more fully expressed in the Nicene Creed, *I believe in the Holy Ghost, the Lord*[2] *and Giver of Life, who proceedeth from the Father and the Son, who with the Father and the Son together is worshipped and glorified, who spake by the Prophets*[3].

3. **The Holy Ghost a Person.** By these words we profess our belief that the Holy Ghost is "not a virtue, nor a gift, but a Person[4]." And this may be proved from Scripture. For He is called by our blessed

---

[1] From A.-S. *gást*, G. *geist*, *i.e.* spirit, breath, opposed to body. Hence the expression in the Catechism "our ghostly enemy" = our "spiritual enemy."

[2] That is, *the Lord God and the Giver of Life*, τὸ Κύριον καὶ τὸ ζωοποιόν. These words were added to the Nicene Creed at the second General Council of Constantinople; see Pearson *On the Creed*, Art. VIII., and the notes.

[3] Compare the statements in the Athanasian Creed, and the words of the Fifth Article, *The Holy Ghost, proceeding from the Father and the Son, is of one substance, majesty, and glory, with the Father, and the Son, very and eternal God.*

[4] Pearson *On the Creed*, Art. VIII.; Nicholson *On the Catechism.*

Lord the Comforter[1] (Jn. xiv. 26); He is said to *come* to men (Jn. xvi. 7), to *speak* to men (Acts x. 19, 20; xiii. 2), to *bid* men do things for Him (Acts xiii. 2, 4), to *give gifts* unto men (1 Cor. xii. 8—11), to *intercede* for men (Rom. viii. 26), to *love* men (Rom. xv. 30), to *be grieved* by the actions of men (Eph. iv. 30); and these expressions imply that He is a Person.

4. **And proceedeth from the Father and the Son.** Moreover, while the Scriptures ever speak of the Son of God as *begotten* of the Father, so they speak of the Holy Ghost as *coming forth* or *proceeding* from the Father and the Son. He proceeds from the Father, for He is called *the Spirit of the Father* (Mtt. x. 20), He is described as *sent by the Father* (Jn. xiv. 26), as *given by the Father* (Jn. xiv. 16), and in express words as *proceeding from the Father* (Jn. xv. 26). Again, He proceeds from the Son[2], for He is called the *Spirit of*

---

[1] Παράκλητον, *the Paraclete*. This word strictly denotes an Advocate, and in this sense it is used in 1 Jn. ii. 1, *We have an* Advocate (παράκλητον) *with the Father, Jesus Christ the righteous*. But as an advocate is one, who being summoned to the side of the accused or imperilled man, stands by to aid and encourage, so the word also means the Comforter, that is, the *Strengthener*, and *Supporter*, from the late Latin *comfortare* (Fr. *conforter* from *con* and *fortis*= strong) = to strengthen. The idea of *strengthening* and *supporting* has been lost sight of in the modern usage of the word, which now signifies to *console*. But when Wiclif first used the word, he intended it in the sense of strengthening or supporting. Thus he renders Phil. iv. 13, "I may alle thingis in him that *comfortith* me" = strengtheneth me. Again, he renders Isai. xli. 7, "and he *comfortide* hym with nailes, that it shoulde not be moved," where our present version translates "and he fastened it with nails." See Hare's *Mission of the Comforter*, pp. 521—527; *The Bible Word-Book*, p. 116.

[2] The words Filioque, "and from the Son," are not in the Nicene Creed, but were gradually adopted in the West. They first appear in the acts of an assembly of bishops at Braga, A.D. 412. Their use gave rise to the great schism between

Christ (Rom. viii. 9; Gal. iv. 6), He is described as *sent by the Son* (Jn. xv. 26), and as *given by the Son*[1] (Jn. xx. 22).

5. **Is God.** But while proceeding from the Father and the Son, He is "of one substance, majesty, and glory with them, being very and Eternal God[2]." For the Scriptures ascribe to Him the attributes of Deity. He is eternal (Heb. ix. 14); He is omniscient (1 Cor. ii. 10); He is omnipotent (Lk. i. 35); He was associated with the Son in the act of creation (Gen. i. 2); He *knoweth the deep things of God* (1 Cor. ii. 10); to sin against Him is to sin against God (Acts v. 3, 4); and into His Name we are baptized (Mtt. xxviii. 19). Hence in the Nicene Creed is He truly termed "the Lord," that is, "the Lord God."

6. **The Giver of Life.** But in the same Creed He is called not only "the Lord," but also the "Giver of Life." For we read that at the creation of the world the Spirit of God brooded over *the face of the waters* (Gen. i. 2), and awoke order out of chaos, and life out of death, and again at the new creation of the world, when the Saviour rose triumphant from the tomb, He is said to have been *quickened by the Spirit* (1 Pet. iii. 18). Moreover, He is the Author and Giver of intellectual life. To Him is ascribed all supernatural wisdom and knowledge (Ex. xxxi. 3; 1 Cor. xii. 8); He in old times "spake by the prophets," and as they were moved and inspired by Him, so they wrote (2 Pet. i. 21). He, on the day of Pentecost, came from heaven upon the Apostles, *like a mighty rushing wind* (Acts ii. 2), to teach

---

the East and the West, A.D. 1053; the Eastern Church refusing to use an expression which had not been sanctioned by a General Council. Bp. Browne *On the Articles;* Hardwick's *Middle Ages,* pp. 195, 298, and the notes.

[1] See Pearson *On the Creed.*
[2] Comp. Article v.

them and to lead them into all truth, "giving them both the gift of divers languages, and also boldness with fervent zeal constantly to preach the Gospel unto all nations[1]," and He afterwards strengthened them and the Churches they founded with manifold gifts of grace, as *the word of wisdom, the word of knowledge, healings, the working of miracles, prophecy, discerning of spirits, divers kind of tongues*, and *the interpretation of tongues, dividing unto every man severally as he would* (1 Cor. xii. 6—11).

7. **The Spirit of Holiness.** And not only is He called the Giver of Life, but also the "Holy Spirit," or the "Spirit of Holiness" (Rom. i. 4). And since we are in ourselves unholy and impure, and without holiness it is impossible to please God (Heb. xii. 14), He inspires us with holy desires, and prompts us to good counsels (Eph. v. 9); He creates in us the first dispositions towards truth and holiness (Gal. v. 22, 23); He prevents, i. e. goes before us, "that we may have a good will, and works with us when we have that good will[2]" (Rom. viii. 14); He renews us unto repentance (Heb. vi. 6); and if we thwart not His gracious influences by wilful sin, He sanctifieth us and all the elect[3] people of God, i. e. all members of the Church of Christ.

---

[1] See the proper Preface in the Communion Service for Whitsunday, i.e. Pentecost-day (compare the Teutonic forms *Pfingsten-tag* and *Whingsten*). Others derive it from *Wytson-day*, i.e. *wit* or *Wisdom*-Day, in memory of the gift of wisdom bestowed on the Apostles. See Procter, *On the Book of Common Prayer*, pp. 290, 291 and notes.

[2] Art. X. Cranmer's *Catechism*, Oxford Edition, p. 122.

[3] As under the Old Covenant the *whole* Jewish nation were *elected*, or *chosen*, to be God's peculiar people, to have the covenant and the promises (Deut. vii. 6; xxvi. 18, 19; Amos iii. 1, 2), so the Apostles teach that the *whole* Church, composed of both converted Jews and Gentiles, is His *elect*, or *chosen*, people, under the New Covenant (Comp. Rom. i. 6, 7; 1 Cor. i. 24; Phil. i. 1; 1 Pet. ii. 9, 10,

8. **The Comforter.** But, lastly, as the Comforter or "Strengthener," it is His office to strengthen and sustain us in our doubts and difficulties, distresses and afflictions, to beget in us joy and peace in believing, to *help our infirmities*, and whereas *we know not what to pray for as we ought*, to make, as our Advocate, *intercession for us* (Rom. viii. 26). And as He is ever ready to shed forth His gracious influences within us, it is our duty to yield them a ready entrance and a kind welcome into our hearts; to hearken attentively to His voice speaking to us through our consciences[1]; to beware of *quenching* the divine light He kindles within us (1 Thess. v. 19), of *resisting* Him when He prompts us to pure thoughts and holy acts, of *grieving* Him when He would take up His abode in the temples of our souls (Eph. iv. 30; 1 Cor. vi. 19); and by the steady use of every means of grace we ought to seek to foster His gracious work within us, that so He "may in all things direct and rule our hearts[2]."

compared with Ex. xix. 5, 6). Hence in the Liturgy, Catechism, and Homilies, we find the elect regarded "as identical with the baptized, or, what is the same thing, with the Church of Christ throughout the world." Bp. Browne on the xviith Article.

[1] Barrow's Sermon *On the Divinity of the Holy Ghost;* "It is through the whisperings of conscience that the Spirit speaks. If, then, men are willingly deaf to their consciences, they cannot hear the Spirit. If hearing, if being compelled to hear, the remonstrances of conscience, they nevertheless decide, and resolve, and determine to go against them; then they grieve, then they defy, then they do despite to the Spirit of God." Paley's Sermon *On Spiritual Influence*, Part III.

[2] Collect for the Nineteenth Sunday after Trinity.

CHAPTER X.

ARTICLE IX.

The Holy Catholic Church; the Communion of Saints.

PART I.

THE HOLY CATHOLIC CHURCH.

1. **The Church.** In the last Article we confessed our belief in the Holy Ghost, whose special office it is "to sanctify us and all the elect people of God." The "elect people of God," as we have seen above[1], includes all members of the Church of Christ throughout the world. In the present Article, therefore, we naturally pass on to speak of the Church, the great sphere of the Spirit's operations, and which is here defined[2] to be "Holy" and "Catholic."

2. **Meaning of the Word.** The word which we have rendered "Church," i.e. *the Lord's House*[3], is in

---

[1] See above, p. 51 note.
[2] And in the Nicene Creed, Εἰς μίαν καθολικὴν καὶ ἀποστολικὴν Ἐκκλησίαν = *And in One Catholic and Apostolic Church.*
[3] From the Greek κυριακή, a feminine adjective, from Κύριος, *the Lord*, and οἰκία, *a house*. The word Κυριακὸς occurs in 1 Cor. xi. 20, Rev. i. 10. From κυριακή comes the German *kirche*, and the Scotch *kirk*. The presence of a Greek word in the vocabulary of our Anglo-Saxon forefathers has been thus explained. "While the Anglo-Saxons and other tribes of the Teutonic stock were almost universally converted through contact with the Latin Church in the Western provinces of the Roman empire, or by its missionaries, some Goths on the Lower Danube had been brought at an earlier date to the knowledge of Christ by Greek missionaries from Constantinople; in this κυριακή, or 'church,' did, with certain other words, pass over from the Greek to the Gothic tongue; and these Goths, the first converted, and the first therefore with a Christian vocabulary, lent the word in their turn to the other German tribes, among these to our Anglo-Saxon

the Greek language *Ecclesia*[1]. This originally denoted an *assembly* of persons called out from among others by the voice of a herald, as e.g. at Athens, for the purpose of legislation. In the sense of *an assembly* or *congregation* it is often applied in the Old Testament to the Israelitish nation[2], which was "called out" by God from the rest of the world, to bear witness to His Unity, to preserve His laws, to keep alive the hope of Redemption, and to exhibit the pattern of a people living in righteousness and true godliness.

3. **Foundation of the Church.** Now, when our Lord declared His intention of building His Church (Mtt. xvi. 18; xviii. 17), He used this word *Ecclesia*[3],

forefathers; and by this circuit it has come round from Constantinople to us." See Hooker, *Eccl. Pol.* v. xiii. 1. Wordsworth's *Theophilus Anglicanus*, p. 1 and note.

[1] From ἐκ = *out* and καλέω = *I call*. Hence the French *église*.

[2] Hence the expressions so often occurring, *the congregation of Israel* (Ex. xii. 6; Num. xvi. 9), *the elders of the congregation* (Lev. iv. 15; Num. xvi. 2), *the Tabernacle of the congregation* (Lev. iv. 4; Ex. xxxv. 21), *the day of the assembly* or *congregation* (Deut. ix. 10; xviii. 16). Hence St Stephen says of Moses that *he was in the church* (or *congregation*, ἐκκλησία) *in the wilderness with the angel that spake to him in the Mount Sina* (Act vii. 38). Again, David says in Ps. xxii. 22 (quoted in Heb. ii. 12), *I will declare Thy name unto my brethren, in the midst of the church* or *congregation* (ἐν μέσῳ ἐκκλησίας) *will I sing praise unto Thee*. Again he says in Ps. xxvi. 12, *My foot standeth in an even place: in the congregation* (ἐκκλησίαις) *will I bless the Lord*. Comp. also Ps. lxviii. 26. The Hebrew קָהָל is rendered in the Septuagint sometimes by the word ἐκκλησία, sometimes by συναγωγὴ, both being = *congregation*. In the XIXth Article the Church is called a "Congregation of faithful men," Cœtus fidelium.

[3] "As συναγωγὴ, synagogue, was the more frequent word for the congregation of the Jews; so perhaps our Lord and His Apostles, adopted, by way of preference and for distinction's sake, the word ἐκκλησία, *church*, for the congregation of Christians." Bp. Browne on the XIXth Article.

or *Congregation*, and in His last command to His Apostles bade them call members into it, not from one nation only like the Jews, but from the whole world (Mtt. xxviii. 19, 20). Accordingly, His Church was founded on the day of Pentecost through the preaching of the Apostle Peter after the descent of the Holy Ghost, and *numbered about three thousand souls* (Acts ii. 41).

4. **Spread of the Church.** Though small at first, like *the grain of mustard seed*, to which Christ had compared it (Mtt. xiii. 31), the Church spread gradually from Jerusalem to Samaria and Galilee, and thence to the uttermost parts of the earth. As it spread, the word "Church" was naturally applied sometimes to the whole collective body of Christians, partakers of *one hope, one faith, and one baptism* (Eph. iv. 4); sometimes to the community of Christians in a particular town or country, as at Jerusalem (Acts viii. 1), at Antioch (Acts xiii. 1), at Ephesus (Acts xx. 17), at Corinth (1 Cor. i. 2, comp. Rev. ii. iii.); sometimes to a single body of Christians meeting or living in a private house, as that of Aquila and Priscilla (Rom. xvi. 5), that of Nymphas (Col. iv. 15), or that of Philemon (Philem. 2).

5. **The Church,** then, spoken of in the Apostles' Creed is the collective Society[1], or Congregation of believers, which Christ first called out from the rest of the world by the preaching of His Apostles, of which He is the Head, having purchased it for Himself with His own Blood (Acts xx. 28); to which He is ever adding *such as shall be saved* (Acts ii. 47); against which, by virtue of His all-sufficient promise, *the gates of hell shall not prevail* (Mtt. xvi. 18): and which "has been,

[1] "The Church is always a visible *Society* of men." Hooker, *Ecc. Pol.* III. i. 14.

now is, and hereafter shall be, so long as the sun and moon endure[1]."

6. **Holy.** Now the Church of Christ is called in the Creed Holy[2], not because every member of it is holy, for in this mortal life *the tares* will be ever mingled with *the wheat*[3] (Mtt. xiii. 24), but for two chief reasons, first, in respect to its Author, and secondly, in respect to the object for which it was founded. It is Holy in respect to its Author, because it was founded by, is united to (Eph. v. 29—32), receives life from (Jn. xv. 5), is ruled by (Heb. iii. 6), and is the mystical Body of Christ, who is *the Holy one* (Mk. i. 24; Acts iii. 14). Again, it is Holy, in respect to the object for which it was founded, viz. to put down evil, to exhibit a pattern of, to beget and to increase in the world, *holiness* (1 Cor. i. 2; 2 Tim. i. 9), and to form a community of persons showing forth the praises of Him, who *hath called them out of darkness into His marvellous light* (1 Pet. ii. 9).

7. **Catholic.** But in the Creed the Church is called

---

[1] Pearson *On the Creed*, Art. IX.; Cranmer's *Catechism*, p. 124.

[2] In the Nicene Creed the Church is also called *one*, or united, for all its members have *one* God and Father (Eph. iv. 6), are sheep of *one* Fold under *one* Shepherd (Jn. x. 16), are all baptized into *one* Spirit (1 Cor. xii. 13), and have all *one* Faith and *one* Hope of their calling (Eph. iv. 2—5). See Barrow *On the Unity of the Church*. In the same Creed it is called Apostolic, as being built on the foundation of the Apostles and Prophets, Jesus Christ Himself being the Head Corner Stone, and as continuing steadfastly in the doctrine of the Apostles. See Acts ii. 42; Eph. ii. 20; and the Collect for SS. Simon and Jude's Day.

[3] Our Lord also compares it to a Threshing Floor containing Grain and Chaff (Mtt. iii. 12); to a Fold with Sheep and Goats in it (Mtt. xxv. 32); to a Net enclosing good and bad fish (Mtt. xiii. 47, 48); to a Vine with fruitful and unfruitful branches (Jn. xv. 1—6).

not only "Holy" but also "Catholic[1]." This term, indeed, is nowhere to be found in Scripture, but, as used by early Christian writers, it denotes "universal," *i. e.* "extending to all mankind." This the Jewish Church was not. It consisted only of one nation. Its sacrifices could be offered only in one temple, and in one place, Jerusalem. But our blessed Lord bade His Apostles *go forth into all the world* (Mk. xvi. 15), and gather into His Church from *every kindred and tongue and people* (Rev. v. 9; comp. Acts x. 34, 35). Wherever, therefore, there is "a congregation of faithful men, in the which the pure Word of God is preached, and the Sacraments duly administered according to Christ's ordinance[2]," there is a Branch of the one "Catholic," or "Universal" Church, of which He is the Head, and which He intended should not be limited to one people, or confined to one nation, but should "be disseminated through all nations, extended to all places, propagated to all ages[3]."

8. **The Church Militant.** By the nature of the case, then, so long as we live a mortal life, "the holiness of the Church is not yet full and perfectly finished." The Society of Christians, scattered over the world, forms a "Church Militant," whose mission is to be always in arms against sin and wickedness. But at the Last Day it shall be a Church Triumphant, "clothed

---

[1] From the Greek adjective καθολικὸs = *universal*, which is derived from the adverb καθόλου = *throughout*, and that from κατὰ and ὅλος = *whole*.

[2] Art. XIX. "As the main body of the sea being one, yet within divers precincts hath divers names; so the Catholic Church is in like sort divided into a number of distinct societies, every one of which is termed a Church within itself." Hooker, *E. P.* III. i. 14.

[3] See Pearson *On the Creed*, Art. IX. Hence the Church may be said to be Catholic in respect of *time* as well as of *place*.

with innocency and holiness, full and perfectly finished, as with a snowy white and most pure garment[1]," and Christ, who purchased it with His own blood, shall *present it to Himself a glorious Church, not having spot, or wrinkle, or any such thing* (Eph. v. 25—27).

PART II.

THE COMMUNION OF SAINTS.

1. **The First** of the four great privileges of the Christian Church is *The Communion of Saints*, and though this clause was one of the latest additions to the Western Creed, yet it is "in no way inferior in relation to the certainty of the truth thereof[2]."

2. **Saints.** The word "saints[3]" or "holy persons" is often applied in the New Testament to the whole body of baptized Christians in a city or district, just as the Israelites are frequently called by the prophets a "holy nation[4]," that is, a people separated from the rest of the world and dedicated to God's service. Thus we read of the Apostle Peter passing through all quarters, and coming down to *the saints which dwelt at Lydda* (Acts ix. 32). Thus the Apostle Paul speaks of the collection *for the poor saints at Jeru-*

---

[1] Noell's *Catechism;* Wordsworth's *Theophilus Anglicanus*, p. 14.
[2] Pearson *On the Creed*, Art. x.; Heurtley, p. 145.
[3] Sancti, contracted into sancti = *set apart*.
[4] "The penmen of the Old Testament do often speak of the people of Israel as of an holy nation, and God doth speak unto them as to a people holy unto Himself; because He had chosen them out of all nations of the world, and appropriated them to Himself. Although, therefore, most of that nation were rebellious to Him which called them, and void of all true inherent and actual sanctity; yet because they were all in that matter separated, they were all, as to that separation, called *holy*." Pearson *On the Creed*.

salem (Rom. xv. 26), and writes to *all the saints in Achaia* (2 Cor. i. 1), to *all the saints in Christ Jesus at Philippi* (Phil. i. 1), to *the saints at Ephesus* (Eph. i. 1). Thus too the Apostle Jude speaks of the *faith once delivered unto the saints* (Jude 3). In each of these places the term is applied to all who profess the name of Christ, and who are therefore called to walk in holiness. But as they were not *all Israel, which were of Israel* (Rom. ix. 6), and as *not every one that saith Lord, Lord, shall enter into the kingdom of heaven, but he that doeth the will of the Father which is in heaven* (Mtt. vii. 21), so the term "saints" is also applied in a more restricted sense to such as knowing that *God hath called them unto holiness* (1 Thes. iv. 7), seek, so far as is possible in this mortal life, to live up to their high vocation, and to be holy even as *He who called them is holy* (1 Pet. i. 15).

3. **The Communion of Saints.** Now the true members of the Church "militant here in earth," may be, and are, scattered and sundered from one another by divers and far distant times and places. But "in what nation soever, or in what land soever they be[1]," we believe that they have *communion* or *fellowship* with the Father[2], with the Son[3], with the Holy Ghost[4], and with the Holy Angels[5], who take delight in ministering for their benefit (Heb. i. 14). Again, we

---

[1] Noell's *Catechism;* Cranmer's *Catechism*, p. 124.
[2] 1 Jn. i. 3, *And truly our fellowship is with the Father.*
[3] 1 Jn. i. 3, *And truly our fellowship is...with His Son Jesus Christ.* Comp. also Jn. xiv. 23, *If a man love Me, he will keep My words; and My Father will love him, and we will come unto him, and make our abode with him.* Compare also Jn. xvii. 20—23; 1 Cor. i. 9; Rom. vi. 3—8.
[4] *The communion of the Holy Ghost be with you all,* 2 Cor. xiii. 14. Comp. Phil. ii. 1.
[5] Comp. Heb. xii. 22, *But ye are come to mount Sion, and unto the city of the living God, the heavenly Jerusalem, and to*

believe that, however scattered and sundered they may be now, they are knit together in communion and fellowship[1] one with another. They are all members incorporate in the same mystical Body, they are all united to the same Head (Eph. iv. 15, 16), and they have all one Faith, one Baptism, and one Hope of their calling[2].

4. **The Saints departed.** But the term "Saints" also includes those who have departed this life in the true faith and fear of God, and who having *finished their course* (2 Tim. iv. 7), have been "delivered from the burden of the flesh, and are in joy and felicity[3]." Now the author of the Epistle to the Hebrews says to the believers, to whom he was writing, that they were *come to the general assembly and Church of the firstborn, which are enrolled*[4] *in heaven, ... to the spirits of just men made perfect.* Hence we infer that the communion and fellowship, which the members of the Church have with their common Lord and with one another[5], is not broken up by the death of any. Death, which is no more than the separation of the soul from the body, does not separate the departed from the love

---

an innumerable company of angels. Compare also Mtt. xviii. 10, and the Collect for St Michael's Day. "Of angels we are not to consider only what they are and do in regard of their own being, but that also which concerneth them as they are linked into a kind of corporation amongst themselves, and of society or fellowship with men." Hooker, *E. P.* I. iv. 2.

[1] See the Collect for All Saints' Day, and the Prayer in the Post-Communion Service.

[2] *There is one body, and one Spirit, even as ye are called in one hope of your calling; one Lord, one faith, one baptism* (Eph. iv. 4, 5).

[3] See the Prayer in the Burial Service.

[4] See Heb. xii. 23, margin.

[5] The earliest writers who mention this Article of the Creed especially "understood it of the Communion which the saints on earth have with the saints departed." Heurtley, p. 146; Pearson *On the Creed*, Art. IX. note.

of God (Rom. viii. 39), *unto whom all live* (Lk. xx. 38), or from the love of Christ, who does not cease to be their Head, because they are removed from our sight. As we have communion with the Father, and the Son, so have they; as we look earnestly *for the adoption*, to wit, *the redemption of our body* (Rom. viii. 23), so do they, fellow-members of the same mystical body, long for the time when God's final Victory shall be revealed (Rev. vi. 9, 10), when we and they shall "have our perfect consummation and bliss in God's eternal and everlasting glory[1]."

CHAPTER XI.

ARTICLE X.

The Forgiveness of Sins.

1. **The Second** great privilege of the Church is *the Forgiveness of Sins*, and this Article occurs with hardly any variation in all the Creeds[2].

2. **Sin.** A mournful catalogue of words, based on a great variety of images, is employed in Scripture to describe the state of sinfulness which man inherits from his birth. Sometimes it is set forth as the missing of a mark or aim[3]; sometimes as the transgressing[4]

---

[1] See the Collect in the Burial Service, the Prayer *for the whole state of Christ's Church Militant here in earth*, and the Collect for All Saints' Day. Hence our Church has appointed special days for the commemoration of the saints of God, of which Hooker has said that "they are the splendour and outward dignity of our religion, forcible witnesses of ancient truth, provocations to the exercise of all piety, shadows of our endless felicity in heaven, and on earth everlasting records and memorials." *Eccl. Pol.* v. lxxi. 11.

[2] Heurtley, p. 146. The Nicene Creed mentions Baptism as the Sacrament of Remission.

[3] Ἁμαρτία, or ἁμάρτημα. Comp. Hom. *Il.* v. 287; ix. 501.

[4] Παράβασις, from παραβαίνω = *to transgress.* Compare

of a line; sometimes as disobedience to a voice[1]; sometimes as ignorance[2] of what we ought to have done; sometimes as a defeat or discomfiture[3]; sometimes as a debt[4]; sometimes as disobedience to law[5]. The last figure is employed in the most general definition of sin given in the New Testament, viz. *Sin is transgression of law* (1 Jn. iii. 4[6]).

3. **The Guilt of Sin.** For "whatsoever is done by man, or is in man, having any contrariety or opposition to the Law of God, is sin[7]." This Law was first broken by Adam, *by whom sin entered into the world, and death by sin* (Rom. v. 12). Hence "the fault and corruption of the nature of man[8]," who is the offspring of Adam, whereby he is inclined to act contrary to the law of God, is called *original sin*, and every yielding to this corrupt inclination, whether in thought, word, or deed, is *actual sin*. Now sin not only involves a breach

---

Cicero, *Peccare est tanquam transilire lineam*. The word occurs seven times in the N.T., and is twice applied to Adam's fall, Rom. v. 14, 1 Tim. ii. 14.

[1] Παρακοὴ, from παρακούειν = (1) *to hear beside*, (2) *to hear carelessly*, (3) *to take no heed of*. The word occurs three times, Rom. v. 19, 2 Cor. x. 6, Heb. ii. 2.

[2] Ἀγνόημα, which occurs once, Heb. ix. 7.

[3] Ἥττημα (Rom. xi. 12, 1 Cor. vi. 7), from ἡττᾶσθαι = *to be worsted, discomfited*. because, as Gerhard says, "a sinner yields to, is worsted by, the temptations of the flesh and of Satan." Compare the Latin *delictum*. Trench's *N.T. Synonyms*, p. 237, 2nd edit.

[4] Ὀφείλημα, from ὀφειλεῖν = *to owe*. Thus it occurs in Mtt. vi. 12, *Forgive us our debts as we forgive our debtors*.

[5] Ἀνομία, from ἀ *not* and νόμος = *a law*. The word occurs fourteen times in the N.T., and is generally translated in the E.V. by *iniquity* (Mtt. vii. 23, Rom. vi. 19, Heb. x. 17); once, by *unrighteousness* (2 Cor. vi. 14); and once, by *transgression of the law* (1 Jn. iii. 4): Trench's *Synonyms*, p. 232.

[6] See Alford *in loc*.

[7] Pearson *On the Creed*, Art. x.

[8] See the Ninth Article of the Church of England.

of the Law, but brings guilt upon the soul, and even its visible results are often of the most disastrous description. Of its ultimate and invisible consequences, however, experience can tell us nothing. But what the human conscience has more or less certainly anticipated[1], Revelation confirms, when it declares that *the wages of sin is death* (Rom. vi. 23; Jas. i. 15).

4. **The Forgiveness of Sin.** Now as experience testifies that mere sorrow and regret avail not to arrest the visible consequences of sin[2], so Revelation testifies that repentance alone, and by itself, cannot arrest its ultimate consequences. But what man's unaided efforts cannot do, that it declares[3] God in His infinite mercy has done for him. *The wages of sin is death, but the gift of God is eternal life through Jesus Christ our Lord* (Rom. vi. 23). For the only-begotten Son of God, whose very name JESUS testifies that He came *to save us from our sins*[4], and who Himself was without sin, *holy, harmless, and undefiled* (Heb. vii. 26), for us men and for our salvation came down from heaven[5], took upon Him our nature, and therein lived a life of spotless obedience to His Father, and yielded up His life *a ransom for many* (Mtt. xx. 28). He, who knew

---

[1] Compare the language of Socrates in Plato's *Gorgias*, 524 E, and in the *Republic*, IX. 579 D; also the words of Tacitus respecting Tiberius, *An.* VI. 6, and Cicero, *Off.* III. 21.

[2] See Butler's *Analogy*, Pt. II. ch. v.

[3] "In this darkness, or this light of nature, call it which you please, Revelation comes in, confirms every doubting fear which could enter into the heart of man, concerning the future unprevented consequence of wickedness,...but teaches us that God has mercifully interposed in such a manner as was necessary and effectual to prevent that execution of justice upon sinners which He had appointed should otherwise have been executed upon them." Butler's *Analogy*, Pt. II. ch. v.; comp. also Secker's *Lectures on the Catechism*, I. 239.

[4] See above, p. 23 and note.

[5] Nicene Creed.

no sin, *became a sin-offering for us* (2 Cor. v. 21), *bore our sins in His own Body on the tree* (1 Pet. ii. 24) and on the altar of His Cross made a full, perfect, and sufficient sacrifice, oblation, and satisfaction, not only for original guilt, but for all actual sins of men[1].

5. **Means and Conditions.** The Forgiveness of sins, then, is a free gift, which Christ, as our Paschal Lamb[2], purchased for us by His meritorious Cross and Passion, and which He commanded should be *preached to all nations in His Name* (Lk. xxiv. 47). All the reasons why His sufferings had this efficacy we cannot tell, but it is our wisdom thankfully to accept so great a benefit, and without disputing how it was procured on the part of our Redeemer[3], to enquire what are the means whereby, and the conditions on which it is offered to us. Now the means are (1) *Baptism*, wherein the promise of forgiveness is signed and sealed to us[4];

---

[1] See the Prayer of Consecration in the Communion Office, and the Second, Tenth, and Thirty-first Articles. The three great circles of images, which the Scriptures employ, when they represent to us the purport of the death of Christ, are (1) *a sin-offering or propitiation* (ἱλασμός, 1 Jn. ii. 2; iv. 10), (2) *reconciliation with an offended friend* (καταλλαγή = atonement, i.e. *at-one-moment*, Rom. v. 11, xi. 15; 2 Cor. v. 18, 19), (3) *redemption from slavery* (ἀπολύτρωσις, Rom. iii. 24; Eph. i. 7; Col. i. 14). See Grotii *Defensio Fidei Cath. de Satisfactione Christi*, Chap. I.; Trench's *N. T. Synonyms*, p. 276, 2nd edition.

[2] 1 Cor. v. 7; compare the Proper Preface in the Communion Office for Easter Day.

[3] See Butler's *Analogy*, Part II. ch. v., where he declares it to be the doctrine of the Gospel that our blessed Lord (1) rendered repentance of the efficacy which it is by what He did and suffered for us; (2) obtained for us the benefit of having it accepted unto eternal life; (3) put us into a capacity of salvation.

[4] Hence in the Nicene Creed we say we believe *in one Baptism for the remission of sins*, even as St Peter on the day of Pentecost bade the first Christians be baptized in the

(2) *Prayer*, in answer to which God has appointed forgiveness[1] at any time when it is sincerely sought; (3) *the Absolution of the Church*[2], which God has "given power and commandment to His ministers to declare and pronounce to His people;" (4) *the Sacrament of the Lord's Supper*, wherein we personally apply to ourselves the benefit of Christ's meritorious Cross and Passion. The conditions, on which we receive this inestimable benefit, are (1) that we sincerely *repent* us of our sins (Acts iii. 19), (2) that we *confess* them (1 Jn. i. 9), (3) that we *believe* that God *is faithful and just to forgive them, and to cleanse us from all unrighteousness* (1 Jn. i. 9; Rom. iii. 25).

CHAPTER XII.

ARTICLE XI.

The Resurrection of the Body.

1. **The Eleventh** Article of the Creed treats of *the Resurrection of the Body*[3], and fitly follows the pre-

Name of Jesus Christ *for the remission of sins* (Acts ii. 38), and Ananias bade the repentant Saul arise and be baptized, and *wash away his sins, calling on the name of the Lord* (Acts xxii. 16; comp. Acts x. 42—48; Eph. v. 25, 26, and the Baptismal Service). See Pearson *On the Creed;* Secker's *Lectures on the Catechism*, I. 242.

[1] Hence, in the Lord's Prayer, the Saviour has bidden us pray *Forgive us our trespasses as we forgive them that trespass against us* (Mtt. vi. 12; Lk. xi. 4), thereby teaching us that "as we through the frailty of our nature are always subject unto sin, so we should always exercise the acts of repentance, and for ever seek the favour of God." Pearson *On the Creed*, Art. x.

[2] Comp. Jn. xx. 22, 23; Mtt. xvi. 19; the Church of England has three forms of Absolution : (1) in the daily Morning and Evening Service, (2) in the Communion Service, (3) in the Visitation of the Sick, but they all presuppose Confession, Repentance, and Faith.

[3] In the Creed of the Church of Aquileia this Article was

ceding Article, as a third privilege of the Church and work of the Spirit.

2. **Even in the Old Testament** we find hopes expressed of a Resurrection. Thus Job says, *I know that my Redeemer liveth, and that He shall stand at the latter day upon the earth, and though after my skin worms destroy this body, yet in my flesh shall I see God* (Job xix. 25, 26). Again, Isaiah prophesies, *Thy dead men shall live, together with my dead body shall they arise* (Isai. xxvi. 19), and Daniel says yet more plainly, *Many of them that sleep in the dust of the earth shall awake, some to everlasting life, and some to shame and everlasting contempt* (Dan. xii. 2). The Sadducees, indeed, in the time of our Lord, denied the doctrine, as they also denied the existence of angels and spirits, but Martha without doubt expressed the hopes of her age, when she said of her brother Lazarus, *I know that he shall rise again in the resurrection at the last day* (Jn. xi. 24).

3. **But the New Testament** fully reveals what is only partially anticipated in the Old. *Verily, verily, I say unto you,* our Lord declared to the Jews, *The hour is coming, and now is, when the dead shall hear the voice of the Son of God...and shall come forth; they that have done good unto the resurrection of life, and they that have done evil unto the resurrection of condemnation* (Jn. v. 25, 28, 29). And when the Sadducees brought forward certain coarse objections to the doctrine, He declared that *they erred, not knowing the Scriptures, nor the power of God,* for a resurrection

entitled *The Resurrection of this flesh.* In the *Prymer* of A.D. 1538 it is expressed *The resurrection of the fleisch.* But in the *Necessary Doctrine and Erudition for any Christian Man,* A.D. 1543, this was altered to its present form, while the ancient formula still remains in the Baptismal Creed and the Visitation of the Sick. See Heurtley, pp. 100, 101.

was implied in the very name whereby God was pleased to reveal Himself, when He said, *I am the God of Abraham, and the God of Isaac, and the God of Jacob*[1], He was not *the God of the dead, but of the living* (Mtt. xxii. 30).

4. **Pledges of a Resurrection.** Not only, however, did He thus distinctly declare that there will be a resurrection, but He was pleased on more than one occasion to give proofs[2] of its possibility. Thus in the death-chamber He restored to life the daughter of Jairus[3]; on the way to the grave He raised the son of the widow of Nain[4]; and four days after death He called forth Lazarus from the tomb[5]. But the most signal instance was His own glorious conquest of death, when He arose triumphant from the grave, and *shewed Himself alive after His passion by many infallible proofs*[6] (Acts i. 3).

5. **The Resurrection of Christ.** And His Resur-

---

[1] "An assertion which could not be made of an annihilated being of the past." Alford *in loc.*

[2] Even as proofs had been given in Old Testament times: for we read there of the restoration to life,
  (a) Of the dead child of the widow of Zarephath (1 Kings xvii. 22);
  (b) Of the child of the Shunammite woman (2 Kings iv. 32—37);
  (c) Of the dead man who was cast into the grave of Elisha (2 Kings xiii. 21).

[3] Mtt. ix. 18—26; Mk. v. 22—43; Lk. viii. 41—56.

[4] Lk. vii. 12—15.

[5] Jn. xi. 39—44. We have also in the New Testament the instance of Tabitha or Dorcas (Acts ix. 38—45).

[6] See above, p. 37 and the notes. Observe the importance which St Paul attaches to *the historical proofs* of the Resurrection of Jesus Christ. *Illustrations* of the doctrine we may trace (1) in the resurrection of Spring from the icy sepulchre of Winter, (2) in the caterpillar passing into the butterfly, (3) in the uprising of the seed sown. See Pearson, on Art. XI. (1 Cor. xv. 36—39.)

rection is the pledge and earnest of the resurrection of humanity[1]. For as by virtue of our union with the first Adam we all die, even so by our union with the second Adam *shall we all be made alive* (1 Cor. xv. 22). *But every man in his own order*[2]. Christ, *the first fruit*, is risen; hereafter shall rise all *they that are Christ's at His coming* (1 Cor. xv. 23); for *if we believe*[3] *that Jesus died and rose again, even so them also which sleep in Jesus will God bring with Him* (1 Thess. iv. 14).

6. **The Resurrection of the Body.** And not only is His resurrection a pledge of our resurrection, but it also enables us to understand in some measure what is meant by a resurrection *of the body*. For while the intonations of His voice, and the marks in His hands and feet proved that the Body wherewith He rose, was the same Body in which He had died, yet there were not wanting proofs that it had undergone marvellous change. The risen Saviour was no longer subject to laws of time and space. He comes we know not whence. He goes we know not whither. Now He stands in the midst of the Apostles (Jn. xx. 19). Now He vanishes out of their sight (Lk. xxiv. 31); and at length He is received

---

[1] This was partially fulfilled when from the graves which opened at His death many *bodies of the saints which slept arose* after His resurrection, *and came out of their graves, and went into the Holy City, and appeared unto many* (Mtt. xxvii. 52, 53).

[2] Or, rather, "troop" or "rank," as in an army, $\dot{\epsilon}\nu\ \tau\hat{\wp}\ \dot{\iota}\delta\dot{\iota}\wp\ \tau\acute{\alpha}\gamma\mu\alpha\tau\iota$, 1 Cor. xv. 23, "as though the scene were presented of troop after troop appearing after their victorious general." Stanley *On the Corinthians;* and Barrow's Sermon *On the Resurrection.*

[3] "There is no shadow of uncertainty intended in the expression *if we believe.* It denotes, *as surely as it is a primary article of our Creed, that the Saviour first died, and then rose.* The resurrection of Christians is as sure as the resurrection of Christ." Vaughan *On* 1 *Thess.* iv. 14.

up into heaven[1] (Acts i. 9). So shall it be at the resurrection of the dead. The bodies with which they shall rise, shall so far be the same bodies, that every one shall have properly his own, and be truly the same person he was before[2]. But these bodies will be very different from our present bodies[3]. Sown in *corruption*, they shall be raised in *incorruption;* sown in *weakness*, they shall be raised in *power;* sown in *dishonour*, they shall be raised in *glory* (1 Cor. xv. 42—44); and, invested with new attributes and new properties, they shall be like unto Christ's glorious Body, according to the mighty *working whereby God is able to subdue all things unto Himself*[4] (Phil. iii. 21).

CHAPTER XIII.

ARTICLE XII.
The Life Everlasting. Amen.

1. **The Fourth** of our great privileges as members of the Church, is *the Life Everlasting.* This Article of

[1] "The Resurrection is not like any one of the recorded miracles of raising from the dead. It is not a restoration to the old life, to its wants, to its inevitable close, but the revelation of a new life, foreshadowing new powers of action and a new mode of being. It is not like any of the fabled apotheoses of the friends of the gods...it is the consecration of a restored and perfected manhood....The Body, which was recognised as essentially the same Body, had yet undergone some marvellous change, of which we can gain a faint idea by what is directly recorded of its manifestations." Westcott *On the Resurrection*, 154—160.

[2] Archbishop Secker *On the Catechism*, Vol. I. 271.

[3] The Apostle's analogy of the Seed-corn enables us in a measure to understand this. The grain of wheat, after being apparently destroyed, rises again, and the body with which it is raised may be called *its own body*. But still it is a new body, it is the old life reappearing in a higher form, with stem, and leaves, and fruit, &c. Robertson's *Lectures on the Corinthians*.

[4] See the Service for the Burial of the Dead.

the Creed[1] is to be taken in close connection with the one preceding. For as we believe that there shall be a resurrection of the dead, so we believe that the dead shall rise to life, and that this life will be everlasting.

2. **Everlasting Life.** True, indeed, it is that all shall rise again; *they that have done good, unto the resurrection of life; and they that have done evil, to the resurrection of condemnation* (Jn. v. 29). But in this Article is specially set forth "the most large gifts which God will give to them that be His[2]," and who depart hence "in His true faith and fear[3]."

3. **Present.** In one sense everlasting life may be regarded as a present gift, and as having its commencement on earth. For our blessed Lord says, *This is life eternal, to know the only true God, and Jesus Christ whom He has sent* (Jn. xvii. 3). Again, He saith, *He that heareth My word, and believeth on Him that sent Me, hath everlasting life, and shall not come into condemnation, but is passed from death unto life*[4] (Jn. v. 24); and this life He imparts through the grace of the Holy Ghost.

4. **Future.** But though begun on earth, everlasting life in all its fulness is a future gift, and will be only then perfectly realized, when it shall be shared by

---

[1] Wanting in some of the early Creeds, the Twelfth Article "can hardly be said to have been established in the Western formularies till the middle of the seventh century." Heurtley, p. 151.

[2] Noell's *Catechism;* see also Nicholson *On the Catechism*, p. 86, smaller Edn.

[3] See the Prayer *for the Church Militant* in the Communion Service.

[4] Compare also Jn. iii. 36; vi. 47. Hence we say in the second Collect in the Morning Prayer, that "our eternal life standeth," *i.e.* consisteth, "in the knowledge of God;" and in the Collect for St Philip and St James's Day, that "truly to know God is everlasting life."

the whole being of man, body, soul, and spirit, in the day of his complete redemption. Respecting the nature of this life, Revelation gives no exact or particular account, and that probably because our finite faculties are not capable of receiving it[1], for, as the Apostle Paul says, *Eye hath not seen, nor ear heard, neither hath it entered into the heart of man, to conceive the things which God hath prepared for them that love Him*[2] (1 Cor. ii. 9). Still some ideas are given us respecting "the life of the world to come[3]," and that (1) negatively and (2) positively[4], telling us what it will not and what it will have.

5. **Negatively.** In *the new heaven*, then, and *the new earth* (Rev. xxi. 1), we learn that there shall be neither *hunger*[5], nor *thirst*[5], nor *night*[6], nor *pain*[7], nor *sorrow*[8], nor *death*[9]. All that makes this life full of misery and trouble, of care and anxiety, shall be done away; for *God will wipe away all tears* from every eye (Rev. xxi. 4), and will *make all things new* (Rev. xxi. 5).

6. **Positively.** But Revelation also tells us something of what the life of the world to come will have. And we gather that not only will there be an absence of all painful toil, all distressing anxiety, all overwhelm-

---

[1] See Secker *On the Catechism*, Vol. I. p. 270, and Whately *On the Doctrine of a Future State*.
[2] Compare the Collect for the Sixth Sunday after Trinity.
[3] As this Article is expressed in the Nicene Creed.
[4] Nicholson *On the Catechism*, p. 86.
[5] Rev. vii. 16, and compare Isai. xlix. 10.
[6] Rev. xxii. 5, *There shall be no night there; and they need no candle, neither light of the sun; for the Lord God giveth them light;* comp. Rev. xxi. 23, 25.
[7] Rev. xxi. 4. The word for *pain* in the original also denotes *excessive toil, exhausting labour*, which also will have passed away.
[8] Rev. xxi. 4; comp. Isai. xxxv. 10.
[9] Rev. xxi. 4; 1 Cor. xv. 26.

ing sorrow, but the future life will be a state of *rest*[1], and *peace*[2], and *joy*[3]. Again, St Paul informs us, that our vile bodies[4] will be fashioned *like unto Christ's glorious Body* (Phil. iii. 21), which at His transfiguration *shone as the sun, and was white as the light* (Mtt. xvii. 2); St John tells us that *we shall be like unto God, for we shall see Him as He is* (1 Jn. iii. 2); and our Lord declares that we shall be *as the angels of God in heaven* (Mtt. xxii. 30). These words, whatever they may denote in all their depth and fulness, at least imply, that freed from all tendency to decay and disorder, our bodies will become fitting instruments for the noblest exertions, that our faculties will be infinitely exalted, and our understandings raised to their utmost capacities[5]; and that in a state of never-ending felicity, and ever-increasing progress and improvement[6], we shall be employed in executing the will of Him in whom *we live, and move, and have our being* (Acts xvii. 28).

7. **Amen.** Such are some of "the good things passing man's understanding, which God hath prepared for them that love Him[7]," and to this, and so to all the other Articles of the Creed, we reiterate our assent by solemnly adding, *Amen, i.e. So be it*[8].

---

[1] Or *Sabbath-keeping*, Heb. iv. 9.
[2] Isaiah lvii. 2.
[3] Mtt. xxv. 21, *Enter thou into the joy of thy Lord.*
[4] More literally, *the body of our humiliation*, τὸ σῶμα τῆς ταπεινώσεως ἡμῶν.
[5] St Paul tells us that we shall *know even as we are known* by God, 1 Cor. xiii. 12; see Secker's *Lectures on the Catechism.*
[6] See Whately's *Lectures on the Doctrine of a Future State;* and Isaac Taylor's *Physical Theory of Another Life.*
[7] See the Collect for the Sixth Sunday after Trinity.
[8] So ends the Creed in the Prymer of A.D. 1538, and an English Creed, circ. A.D. 1400. One of the xvth century concludes, *So mote it be, Amen.* See Heurtley, p. 99.

PART III.

THE COMMANDMENTS.

CHAPTER I.

You said, that your Godfathers and Godmothers did promise for you, that you should keep God's Commandments. Tell me how many there be? *Ten.*

Which be they? *The same which God spake in the twentieth Chapter of Exodus, saying, I am the Lord thy God, who brought thee out of the land of Egypt, out of the house of bondage.*

I. *Thou shalt have none other gods but me.*

II. *Thou shalt not make to thyself any graven image, nor the likeness of any thing that is in heaven above, or in the earth beneath, or in the water under the earth. Thou shalt not bow down to them, nor worship them: for I the Lord thy God am a jealous God, and visit the sins of the fathers upon the children, unto the third and fourth generation of them that hate me, and shew mercy unto thousands in them that love me, and keep my commandments.*

III. *Thou shalt not take the Name of the Lord thy God in vain: for the Lord will not hold him guiltless that taketh his Name in vain.*

IV. *Remember that thou keep holy the Sabbath-day. Six days shalt thou labour, and do all that thou hast to do; but the seventh day is the Sabbath of the Lord thy God. In it thou shalt do no manner of work, thou, and thy son, and thy daughter, thy man-servant, and thy maid-servant, thy cattle, and the stranger that is within thy gates. For in six days the Lord made heaven and earth, the sea, and all that in them is, and rested the seventh day; wherefore the Lord blessed the seventh day, and hallowed it.*

V. *Honour thy father and thy mother, that thy days may be long in the land which the Lord thy God giveth thee.*

VI. *Thou shalt do no murder.*

VII. *Thou shalt not commit adultery.*

VIII. *Thou shalt not steal.*

IX. *Thou shalt not bear false witness against thy neighbour.*

X. *Thou shalt not covet thy neighbour's house, thou shalt not covet thy neighbour's wife, nor his servant, nor his maid, nor his ox, nor his ass, nor any thing that is his.*

What dost thou chiefly learn by these commandments? I learn two things: my duty towards God, and my duty towards my Neighbour.

What is thy duty towards God? My duty towards God, is to believe in him, to fear him, and to love him with all my heart, with all my mind, with all my soul, and with all my strength; to worship him, to give him thanks, to put my whole trust in him, to call upon him, to honour his holy Name and his Word, and to serve him truly all the days of my life.

What is thy duty towards thy Neighbour? My duty towards my Neighbour, is to love him as myself, and to do to all men, as I would they should do unto me: To love, honour, and succour my father and mother: To honour and obey the Queen, and all that are put in authority under her: To submit myself to all my governours, teachers, spiritual pastors and masters: To order myself lowly and reverently to all my betters: To hurt no body by word nor deed: To be true and just in all my dealing: To bear no malice nor hatred in my heart: To keep my hands from picking and stealing, and my tongue from evil-speaking, lying, and slandering: To keep my body in temperance, soberness, and chastity: Not to covet nor desire other men's goods; but to learn and labour to get mine own living, and to do my duty in that state of life, unto which it shall please God to call me.

INTRODUCTION.

1. **The Ten Commandments.** Of the three vows made at our Baptism, the third, as we have already seen[1], is that of *Obedience*, or *to keep God's holy will and commandments, and walk in the same all the days of our life.* We have also seen that these Commandments are Ten in number, that they were given to the Israelites by God Himself, under circumstances of peculiar solemnity, that as containing the Moral Law they were not done away by our Lord, and

[1] See above, p. 15.

that "from obedience to them no Christian man whatsoever is free[1]."

2. **Their Division.** When first given to Moses they were written on two tables of stone[2] (Ex. xxxii. 15, 16), and were long preserved in the Ark (Deut. x. 5)[3]. How many Commandments were written on each Table is not certain. Some think Five were written on each[4]; others hold that Three were written on one and Seven on the other. Others, again, as is apparently the case in the Church Catechism, distribute them into Four and Six[5]. According to this division the First Table teaches us our *Duty towards God*[6], and the Second our *Duty towards our neighbour*.

3. **The Lord thy God.** To remind us, moreover, that the Ten Commandments are binding upon us, the preface to them contained in the twentieth Chapter of Exodus is also rehearsed in the Catechism[7]. For in answer to the question, *How many Commandments are there?* we reply, *Ten;* and in answer to the further

---

[1] See above, p. 16, and the note.
[2] And *on both their sides, on the one side and on the other side were they written* (Ex. xxxii. 15). "We know not their form or size. But we know the hard, imperishable granite out of which they were hewn; we know its red hue; the style of the engraving must have been such as can be still discerned in the Desert Inscriptions." Stanley's *Jewish Church*, Pt. I. p. 175.
[3] Comp. 1 Kings viii. 1, 9; Heb. ix. 4. Hence it was called *the Ark of the Testimony* (Numb. iv. 5).
[4] See Smith's *Dictionary of the Bible*, Art. *Ten Commandments*.
[5] See Noell's *Catechism*.
[6] And thus in effect our Lord divides them, see Mtt. xxii. 37—40.
[7] It is to be observed that the translation of the Decalogue used in the Communion Service, and in the Catechism, is not that of our present Version, but that of the Great Bible, A.D. 1539-40.

question, *Which be they?* we say, *The same which God spake in the twentieth Chapter of Exodus, saying, I am the Lord thy God, who brought thee out of the land of Egypt, out of the house of bondage.*

4. **Typical Condition of the Israelites.** For the circumstances of the Israelites at the time of the delivery of these Commandments were typical of our condition now (1 Cor. x. 6—11). and the grounds on which obedience to them was demanded of the chosen Nation, in a still deeper sense apply to all Christians. Thus, had the Israelites been set free, by a mighty hand and a stretched-out arm, from low and degrading bondage in Egypt? We have been delivered by the same infinite mercy, from a still worse thraldom, even that of sin, death, and Satan[1]. Had God made a solemn Covenant with the Israelites? He has made us partakers of a new and better Covenant[2]. Had they been *baptized unto*[3] *Moses in the cloud and in the sea?* (1 Cor. x. 2), we have been baptized into the Name of the Triune God Himself. Were they in a state of deliverance, and on the road amidst dangers and temptations to a Land of Promise? we also have been placed in a state of salvation, we are members of a Church Militant, and, amidst the temptations of the world, the flesh, and the Devil, are journeying through life towards a better and a heavenly inheritance (Heb. xi. 16).

5. **Principles of Interpretation.** Thus, then, were

---

[1] "Theirs was from the captivity of their bodies; ours from the bondage of our souls. Theirs from Egypt only, and the tyranny of man; ours from hell, and the tyranny of the devil. They were redeemed by strength of arm, by signs and wonders, without any price at all; but He bought and paid for us with His own blood" (1 Pet. i. 18, 19). Nicholson *On the Catechism*, p. 97. See also Noell's *Catechism*.

[2] See above, pp. 7, 8.

[3] That is, *into fealty or obedience to* Moses.

the circumstances of the Israelites typical of our own. Now, since God, the Author of these Commandments, is a Spirit (Jn. iv. 23, 24), His Law also is spiritual, and, unlike human laws, reacheth to *the thoughts and intents of the heart* (Heb. iv. 12). Hence, as our Lord's own exposition of certain of the Commandments teaches, every precept is to be regarded with great latitude, and we infer that when any duty is enjoined, the contrary sin is forbidden, and when any sin is forbidden, the contrary duty is enjoined[1].

SECTION I.

Duty towards God.

CHAPTER I.

THE FIRST COMMANDMENT.

FIRST COMMANDMENT.	DUTY TOWARDS GOD.
Thou shalt have none other gods but[2] Me.	*My duty towards God is to believe in Him, to fear Him, and to love Him with all my heart, with all my mind, with all my soul, and with all my strength.*

1. **The first Commandment** condemns and forbids idolatry, which, as we have already seen[3], gradually spread over the world through forgetfulness of the one true God, and unthankfulness to Him for common mercies[4]. Though men *knew God*, as St Paul says,

---

[1] See Nicholson *On the Catechism*, p. 92; Secker's *Lectures*, I. 287.
[2] Or, as it is in our version, *Thou shalt have no other gods before Me* (Exod. xx. 3).
[3] See above, p. 15.
[4] See *Class-Book of Old Testament History*, p. 22.

they glorified[1] *him not as God, neither were thankful; but became vain in their imaginations, and their foolish heart was darkened. Professing themselves to be wise, they became fools, and exchanged the glory of the incorruptible God for*[2] *an image made like to corruptible man, and to birds, and fourfooted beasts, and creeping things* (Rom. i. 21—23). Now all such worshipping of the creature rather than the Creator was solemnly forbidden to the Israelites. They were to have and acknowledge no other god beside the One true God, who had revealed Himself to them as the God of Abraham, Isaac, and Jacob, *merciful and gracious, longsuffering, and abundant in goodness and truth* (Ex. xxxiv. 6).

2. **The Sin forbidden.** Thus also we, as Christians, are forbidden to have or acknowledge any other god but that God of infinite mercy and holiness, who has revealed Himself to us in the person of His Son (Heb. i. 1), and into whose Name we have been baptized. And though we are not in danger of worshipping the gods of the heathen, there are other gods we are bidden to renounce, lest they usurp the place in our hearts due to God alone. Such gods men make for themselves when they ascribe all things to fate or chance; when they set their hearts on the accumulation of wealth[3]; when they are *lovers of pleasures*, or of *themselves*, more than *lovers of God*[4]*;* when they become devoted to *covetousness, which is idolatry*[5] (Col.

---

[1] That is, *they did not*, either in worship or conduct, *recognise the perfection of God's character*, as manifested in His works. Vaughan, *in loc.*

[2] Ἤλλαξαν...ἐν = *exchanged for.*

[3] Job xxxi. 24, 25; Mtt. vi. 24, *ye cannot serve God and Mammon.*

[4] 2 Tim. iii. 2, 4; Phil. iii. 19.

[5] *Avaritia maximè affigit ad terram.* Bengel *in loc.*

iii. 5), or to their own honour, their own glory, and their own advancement[1].

3. **The Duty enjoined.** While, however, this is the conduct forbidden, there is also a duty which this commandment enjoins. Our duty towards God, who has revealed Himself to us in His works and in His Word, is to *believe* in Him[2], and trust His providence and His superintending care; to *fear* Him as a Being of infinite power, knowledge, and holiness[3]; to *love* Him for all His goodness as manifested "in our creation, preservation, and all the blessings of this life, but above all for His inestimable love in the redemption of the world by our Lord Jesus Christ[4];" and this love and adoring gratitude we are to show forth not only with our lips, but in our lives, by giving up ourselves, and devoting all our powers and faculties, heart and mind, soul and strength, to His service, and that work in life which He has given us to do[5].

---

[1] "The second way of making goddes of creatures is when men put their hole confidence in other thinges than in God, and haue these or suche lyke thoughtes wythin themselfes—I woulde I hadde suche riches or landes, I woulde suche a man were my frende, then shoulde I be ryche, happye and blessed, then should I be sufficiently defended and armed against all chaunces that maye happen vnto me in this worlde. They that thinke thus, haue such riches landes and creatures for a god, although with their tongue they say not so, yea althoughe this affection lye hidde in our hearte so secretly, that we our selfes should scantly knowe of it." Cranmer's *Catechism*, pp. 10, 11.

[2] Heb. xi. 6.

[3] 1 Pet. v. 7; Phil. iv. 6.

[4] See the General Thanksgiving in the Morning and Evening Service.

[5] Mtt. xxii. 37; Mk. xii. 30; Luke x. 27.

CHAPTER II.
THE SECOND COMMANDMENT.

THE SECOND COMMANDMENT. *Thou shalt not make to thyself any graven image, nor the likeness of any thing that is in heaven above, or in the earth beneath, or in the water under the earth. Thou shalt not bow down to them, nor worship them: for I the Lord thy God am a jealous God, and visit the sins of the fathers upon the children, unto the third and fourth generation of them that hate Me, and shew mercy unto thousands in them that love Me, and keep my commandments.*

DUTY TOWARDS GOD. *My duty towards God is to worship Him, to give Him thanks, to put my whole trust in Him, to call upon Him.*

1. **Object of the Commandment.** As the first Commandment enjoined the Israelite to worship only the true God, so the second forbade his worshipping Him under any visible resemblance or form.

2. **As addressed to the Israelites.** Hence they were warned against making for themselves any graven image, or any likeness of anything *in heaven above*, as of the sun, moon, and stars, or *in the earth beneath*, as of men, birds, beasts, and creeping things, or *in the water under the earth*, as of fish and other marine animals (see Deut. iv. 15—19).

3. **Egyptian Idolatry.** The idolatrous objects here alluded to were chiefly those with which the Israelites had become acquainted in Egypt. There they had witnessed the gorgeous ceremonies which attended the worship of Ra[1] the "Sun-god," and of Isis and

---

[1] Hence "Pha-raoh," *the Child of the Sun*, "Potiphe-rah," *the Servant of the Sun*.

Osiris. There they had seen incense burnt three times every day in honour of the sacred black calf Mnevis at On[1], and of his rival the bull Apis at Memphis[2]. There they had seen religious honours paid to the sacred goat of Mendes; to the ram of Ammon; to the mighty Pharaoh, the child and representative of the Sun-god; to the Nile, "the life-giving father of all that exists;" to the cat, the dog and the serpent; to the hawk[3], the hippopotamus and the crocodile.

4. **Warnings against Idol-worship.** In this Commandment, therefore, God forbade the Israelites making any representation of such objects for the purpose of worship. To the command He also added a powerful motive why it should be obeyed. For He declared Himself to be *a jealous God*[4], i.e. full of zeal for His own glory, who would not let the honour, due only to Himself, be paid to any creature (Isai. xlii. 8), but for this sin would visit with punishment both the guilty person and his children *to the third and fourth generation*[5].

---

[1] Or Heliopolis, the *City of the Sun*. See Wilkinson's *Egyptians*, v. 315. "The molten calf in the wilderness, the golden calves of Dan and Bethel, were reminiscences, not to be wiped out of the national memory for centuries, of the consecrated calf of Ra, the god Mnevis." Stanley's *Jewish Church*, I. 90.

[2] See *Class-Book of Old Testament History*, p. 89 n.

[3] In the sanctuary of Heliopolis, "apart from all the surrounding chambers, underneath the carved figure of the Sun-god, sate in his gilded cage the sacred hawk." Stanley's *Jewish Church*, I. 90.

[4] By this word *jealousy* he declareth that he can abide no partner nor equal. See Exod. xxxiv. 14; Josh. xxiv. 19. Noell's *Catechism*.

[5] That is, if they persevered in the idolatrous iniquities of their fathers, see Ezek. xviii. 20. For examples compare the instances (1) of the Israelites when they worshipped the golden calf, Ex. xxxii. 4, 25—29; (2) of Jeroboam and his successors, 1 Kings xii. 28; xiii. 34; xiv. 10, 17; xv. 29,

At the same time He added that He would show mercy unto thousands, that is, to a thousand generations (Deut. vii. 9), of them that loved Him and showed forth their love by keeping His commandments.

5. **As addressed to us.** While this is the scope of the Commandment as addressed to the Israelites, in its application to us as Christians, it forbids our harbouring any unworthy conceptions of the Most High, or introducing any superstitious forms into our worship of Him. Moreover, it enjoins the positive duty of worshipping Him *in spirit and in truth* (Jn. iv. 23, 24), as revealed to us in the Person of His Son, who has become for us the Visible Image of the Invisible God; *of giving Him thanks* for His love and mercy; of *putting our whole trust in Him* amidst every event of our daily lives; and of *calling upon Him* in public and private prayer[1].

CHAPTER III.

THE THIRD COMMANDMENT.

THIRD COMMANDMENT.	DUTY TOWARDS GOD.
Thou shalt not take the Name of the Lord thy God in vain: for the Lord will not hold him guiltless that taketh His Name in vain.	*My duty towards God is... to honour His holy Name and His Word.*

1. **Object of the Commandment.** As originally addressed to the Israelites, the third Commandment forbade their taking, i. e. "taking up" in their mouth,

---

30; (3) Ahab, 1 Kings xxi. 29; (4) Manasseh, 2 Kings xxi. 10—15.

[1] Hence it includes the duty in the worship of God of using such ceremonies, as serve for (1) Decency, (2) Order, (3) Edification, 1 Cor. xiv. 30, 32, 40; Nicholson *On the Catechism*, p. 107.

or uttering the Name of the Lord their God to or upon a vain, false, or wicked thing[1]. It solemnly forbade, therefore, the application of the Name of the One true God to an idol[2], and the use of it in curses, false oaths, and blasphemous expressions, and affirmed that the Lord would not *hold him guiltless*, that is, would account him very guilty[3], that *took His Name in vain*.

2. **Its literal meaning.** In its first and most literal sense, therefore, as applicable to us, this Commandment forbids all false swearing or perjury, all profane oaths and blasphemy[4], all rash vows[5], and all use of the awful Name of God on light and trivial occasions.

3. **Its further meaning.** But the "Name" of God includes not only His own titles, but also everything, upon which He hath set His Name, as His Word, by which He hath revealed Himself to us, His House[6],

---

[1] Comp. Exod. xxiii. 1; Lev. xix. 11, 12; Deut. v. 11. The word לַשָּׁוְא = *to vanity*, probably = *for a falsehood*, though some, like the LXX, interpret it ἐπὶ ματαίῳ = *for a light and vain purpose*.

[2] Exod. xxxii. 3—5.

[3] A strong way of expressing the extreme contrary, as in Ps. v. 4; Eccl. viii. 13. Nicholson *On the Catechism*, p. 110.

[4] Levit. xxiv. 14—16; Mtt. v. 33—37, xxiii. 16—22. It does not, however, forbid the use of oaths in a court of justice, which (1) are directly commanded (Deut. vi. 13; Ex. xxii. 10, 11; comp. Heb. vi. 16); (2) are sanctioned by the example of our Lord (Mtt. xxvi. 63, 64), and of St Paul, who frequently in very weighty matters, calls God to witness, which is essentially taking an oath (comp. Rom. i. 9; 2 Cor. xi. 10, 31; xii. 19; Gal. i. 20; Phil. i. 8). The Thirty-Ninth Article says, the "Christian Religion doth not prohibit, but that a man may swear when the Magistrate requireth, in a cause of faith and charity, so it be done according to the Prophet's teaching (Jer. iv. 2), in justice, judgment, and truth."

[5] Matt. xiv. 7; James v. 12.

[6] Comp. also Isai. viii. 20; Acts xvii. 10, 11; Jn. v. 39; 2 Tim. iii. 15.

in which *His honour dwelleth* (Ps. xxvi. 8)[1], and the Sacraments and Ordinances ordained in His Church[2]. In this wider sense, therefore, this Commandment forbids severally all irreverence, levity, and thoughtlessness in regard to holy things, and enjoins the positive duty of honouring God's holy Name[3], of approaching Him with humility and awe, and treating His Word with reverence, docility, and faith.

CHAPTER IV.

THE FOURTH COMMANDMENT.

Fourth Commandment.	Duty towards God.
Remember that thou keep holy the Sabbath-day. Six days shalt thou labour, and do all that thou hast to do; but the seventh day is the Sabbath of the Lord thy God. In it thou shalt do no manner of work, thou, and thy son, and thy daughter, thy man-servant, and thy maid-servant, thy cattle, and the stranger that is within thy gates. For in six days the Lord made heaven and earth, the sea, and all that in them is, and rested the seventh day; wherefore the Lord blessed the seventh day, and hallowed it.	*My duty towards God is... to serve Him truly all the days of my life.*

1. **Institution of the Sabbath.** The Sabbath-day, or Day of *Rest*, as the word *Remember* seems to

---

[1] Comp. also Isai. lvi. 7; 1 Kings vi. 12, 13; Mtt. xxi. 13.
[2] Comp. 1 Cor. xi. 17—34.
[3] See Isai. lxvi. 1, 2; Col. iii. 16.

imply, was not improbably known to the Israelites before the giving of the Law. For a hallowing of the Sabbath by God is mentioned at the Creation (Gen. ii. 2, 3), and a trace of its observance may be found in the regulations respecting the collection of the manna in the wilderness before the Chosen people reached Sinai (Exod. xvi. 23, 30). The observance of it, however, was then definitely enjoined, (i) as a commemoration of the Creation (Exod. xx. 11); (ii) as an ordinance of humanity towards those employed in labour; (iii) as a national memorial of the deliverance from Egypt (Deut. v. 15); and (iv) as the sign of a perpetual covenant between God and the children of Israel for ever (Ex. xxxi. 16, 17; Ezek. xx. 12).

2. **Its observance amongst the Jews.** In accordance with the Divine command the Sabbath was observed by the Jews not as a fast, but as a day of rest from worldly occupations, and was shared by the whole people, their servants, the stranger within their gates, and even the animals (Ex. xx. 10; Deut. v. 14). All bodily labour was strictly prohibited, and wilful desecration of the Day was punished with stoning (Exod. xxxi. 14; Num. xv. 35).

3. **The Lord's Day.** Of this Commandment, then, the Moral part is that a certain time be set apart for the worship of the Most High, and this obligation is perpetual and eternal[1]. The Day observed by the Jews was the seventh day of the week, or our Saturday. But in very early times the *first* of every seven days became the Christian day of rest, for on it our Lord rose from the dead, and the first outpouring of the Holy Spirit was vouchsafed[2]. On this Day the first disciples were

---

[1] Nicholson *On the Catechism*, p. 116. Hammond's *Practical Catechism*, pp. 184, 185.
[2] See Article *Lord's Day* in Smith's *Dictionary of the Bible*.

wont to meet together (Jn. xx. 19, 26) to break the Bread, and join in holy worship (Acts xx. 7; 1 Cor. xvi. 1, 2), and in remembrance of the Saviour's resurrection to call it the *Lord's Day*[1] (Rev. i. 10).

4. **Its Obligation.** This, then, is the Christian Day of Rest, which we should *Remember to keep holy* by laying aside the ordinary occupations of the week, save such as are works of necessity or of charity[2], and as far as possible all worldly cares and pleasures (Isai. lviii. 13, 14); by joining in Church worship[3]; by devout meditation on God's word, and the performance of acts of charity and mercy. Such an observance of the Lord's Day is the best preparation for doing diligently and with all our might the proper work of the week, and by the due consecration of one day for truly serving God "all the days of our life[4]."

5. **Recapitulation.** Thus in these four Commandments is comprehended and set forth our Duty towards God. The *first* teaches us how we are to acknowledge Him and Him alone for our God; the *second* how, abhorring the adoration of all idols and images, we are to worship Him *in spirit and in truth;* the *third* how with the mouth we are to honour His holy Name and His word; the *fourth* how we are to consecrate His Day and so all days to His service[5].

[1] Ἡ ἡμέρα τοῦ Κυρίου, ἡ κυριακή, Dies Dominica, and sometimes simply Dominica. See Guericke's *Antiquities*, p. 124.

[2] Mtt. xii. 1—5, 12; Luke vi. 1—5. "As early as the end of the 2nd century all work and labour on the Sunday was regarded as a sinful tempting of God. In A.D. 321 the Emperor Constantine ordered a cessation on the day of all judicial and other public business, and subsequently forbade all such military exercises as would interfere with the public worship of the Christian, soldiers." Guericke's *Antiquities*, pp. 126, 127.

[3] Lk. iv. 16; Heb. x. 25.   [4] See the Catechism.

[5] Nicholson, p. 91; Hammond's *Catechism*, p. 184.

SECTION II.

Our Duty towards our Neighbour.

CHAPTER I.

THE FIFTH COMMANDMENT.

Fifth Commandment.
Honour thy father and thy mother, that thy days may be long in the land which the Lord thy God giveth thee.

Duty towards our Neighbour.
My duty towards my Neighbour, is to love him as myself, and to do to all men, as I would they should do unto me: To love, honour, and succour my father and mother: To honour and obey the Queen, and all that are put in authority under her: To submit myself to all my governors, teachers, spiritual pastors and masters: To order myself lowly and reverently to all my betters.

1. **Our Neighbour.** From the Commandments which teach us our Duty towards God, we pass on to those which teach us our Duty towards our neighbour[1], *i.e.*, all men with whom we have to deal. This Duty is thus generally described, *My duty towards my neighbour is to love him as myself, and to do to all men as I would they should do unto me.* Here our own selves are set for the rule towards our neighbour, and as *no*

---

[1] "Our Neighbour is every one, with whom we have at any time any concern, or on whose welfare our actions have any influence. For whosoever is thus within our reach, is in the most important sense near to us, however distant in other respects." Secker's *Lectures*, II. p. 1. "Our neighbour is that part of the universe, that part of mankind, that part of our country, which comes under our immediate notice, acquaintance, and influence, and with which we have to do." Bp. Butler *Upon the Love of our Neighbour.*

man hateth his own flesh, but nourisheth it and cherisheth it (Eph. v. 29), so[1] with that "truth of love" are we to love our neighbour, and *do to all men*, according to our Lord's golden rule, *as we would they should do unto us* (Mtt. vii. 12).

2. **Parental Authority.** The word "neighbour," then, including all men with whom we have to deal, comprehends superiors as well as equals, and as parental authority is the origin and type of all authority, the Fifth Commandment is placed at the head of the second Table, and treats of the honour due to *Father and Mother*.

3. **Enforced in the Mosaic Law.** The duty of showing honour to parents, as the authors of our being, which natural reason teaches, was strongly enforced in the Mosaic Law. Reverence for parents is the first duty after that appertaining to God Himself, and is the first and the only commandment to which a promise of long life and continuance in the Promised Land is definitely attached (Ex. xx. 12; Eph. vi. 2). The Mosaic Law, indeed, did not invest the father with the same boundless power as the Greek and Roman Laws, but it made the act of smiting father or mother a capital offence[2], and directed that unnatural and disobedient children should be put to death[3].

4. **And by Christ and His Apostles.** The duty

---

[1] The adverb *sicut*, 'as,' is not a note of parity, but similitude, and shows not the quantity, but the quality of our love. For no man is bound to love another equally, or so much as himself, but with that truth of love that he loves himself; the love then of man to man ought to be true, and not false; real, and not feigned nor adulterate. A man would be loath that other men should dissemble with him, neither may he then dissemble with them; *let love be without dissimulation* (Rom. xii. 9). Nicholson *On the Catechism*, p. 124.

[2] Ex. xxi. 15, 17; Lev. xix. 3, xx. 9.

[3] Ex. xxi. 17; Deut. xxi. 18—21.

of obedience of children towards their parents is also sanctioned by Christian teaching. For not only did our Lord go down with His earthly parents to Nazareth and live in subjection unto them (Lk. ii. 51), but when He hung upon the Cross, He commended His mother to the care of His favourite disciple St John (Jn. xix. 26). He also found great fault with those amongst the Jews who made this Law *of none effect* by certain traditions and exemptions (Mtt. xv. 3), and St Paul affirms obedience to parents to be at once *right* (Eph. vi. 1), and *well-pleasing unto the Lord* (Col. iii. 20), while he classes disobedience to them among the signs of *perilous times* (2 Tim. iii. 2).

5. **Earthly Authority.** But as the parental is the type and origin of all authority, and the family is the nursery of the State, the Catechism proceeds to include under the Fifth Commandment the duty not only of loving, honouring, and succouring[1] father and mother, but also of submission to all earthly authority. And this too is sanctioned by the teaching of Christ, who paid tribute (Mtt. xvii. 24—27), and enjoined others to *render unto Cæsar the things that are Cæsar's* (Mtt. xxii. 21), and of His Apostles, who taught the duty of rendering *tribute to whom tribute is due, fear to whom fear, honour to whom honour* (Rom. xiii. 7), and of subjection to *the higher powers* (Rom. xiii. 1—5; Tit. iii. 1; 1 Pet. ii. 13). Rightly, therefore, does the Catechism hold that the Fifth Commandment teaches us " to honour and obey the queen and all that are put in authority under her, to submit ourselves to all our governors, teachers, spiritual pastors and masters, and to order ourselves lowly and reverently to all our betters."

---

[1] To succour, from Latin *succurrere*, Fr. *secourir* = (1) *to run up to for the purpose of assisting;* (2) *to help;* (3) *to support.* Comp. 2 Sam. viii. 5, xxi. 17; 2 Cor. vi. 2; Heb. ii. 18. See *Bible Word-Book*, p. 464.

CHAPTER II.

THE SIXTH COMMANDMENT.

Sixth Commandment. *Thou shalt do no murder.*	Duty towards our Neighbour. *My duty towards my Neighbour is...To hurt no body by word or deed...To bear no malice nor hatred in my heart.*

1. **Right of Personal Security.** The previous Commandment treated of our duty towards superiors, the five following treat of our duty towards all men alike, whether superiors, inferiors, or equals. And first, we are taught our duty respecting *the life* of our fellow-man, that he possesses a right of personal security[1], and that we may not deprive him of his life, or commit wilful murder.

2. **Murder.** In accordance with this precept the wilful shedder of man's blood met with no compassion from the Mosaic code. The original law at Sinai and the subsequent repetition of it[2] made death the inevitable penalty of murder, even as it had been in the days of Noah; *Whoso sheddeth man's blood, by man shall his blood be shed* (Gen. ix. 6).

3. **The Sermon on the Mount.** But as interpreted by our Lord, we see that this Commandment has a deeper application than the mere committal of murder. *Ye have heard*, said He, *that it was said to*[3] *them of old time, Thou shalt not kill; and whosoever shall kill shall be in danger of the judgment. But I say*

---

[1] Whewell's *Elements of Morality*, I. 40.
[2] Comp. Ex. xxi. 12—14, with Deut. xix. 11—13.
[3] The Greek τοῖς ἀρχαίοις is better rendered *to them* than *by them of old time*.

unto you, that whosoever is angry with his brother without a cause[1] *shall be in danger of the judgment; and whosoever shall say to his brother, Raca*[2], *shall be in danger of the Council; but whosoever shall say Thou fool*[3], *shall be in danger of hell fire*[4] (Mtt. v. 22). Whence it is clear that while the letter of this precept forbids only the *act*, the spirit of it forbids all those vindictive passions, which tend to murder, revenge, envy, hatred, provoking words, malice, and illwill. (See Eph. iv. 26, 31.)

4. **The Positive Duty.** But while, in the words of

---

[1] The received Version adds here εἰκῆ = *without a cause*, but the word is wanting in many MSS. and is omitted by Tischendorf.

[2] Raca = *empty, brainless*, a term of contempt. See Tholuck's *Sermon on the Mount*, p. 178.

[3] In Greek μωρέ = either (1) *thou fool* (comp. Mtt. xxiii. 17, 19); or (2) = a Hebrew word signifying *rebel* (comp. *Hear now, ye rebels*, Num. xx. 10); or (3) = ἄθεος, *atheist*. Tholuck, p. 180. "He addresses himself," says Luther, "not to the hand, but to the whole person. Hence it is that *Thou shalt not kill*, expresses as much as if He had said, Whatever members you have, and however you may kill, whether by hand, or heart, or tongue, or gesture; whether you look fiercely, and refuse with your eyes to let your neighbour live, or whether you mean with your ears to kill, and hate to hear him praised, all is condemned; for then is your heart and all within you so disposed as to wish him dead."

[4] "There were among the Jews three well-known degrees of guilt, coming respectively under the cognizance of the local and the supreme courts (See Deut. xvi. 18); and after these is set the γέεννα τοῦ πυρός, the end of the malefactor, whose corpse, thrown out into the valley of Hinnom, was devoured by the worm or the flame (comp. 2 Kings xxiii. 10; Jer. vii. 31). Similarly in the spiritual kingdom of Christ, shall the sins even of thought and word be brought into judgment and punished, each according to its degree of guilt, but even the least of them before no less a tribunal than the judgment-seat of Christ." Alford *On Mtt. v. 22*.

the Catechism, the precept thus forbids our hurting anybody "by word or deed," or bearing any "malice or hatred in the heart," it also enforces the positive duty of cultivating a forgiving disposition [1], of praying for and relieving the wants of our enemies [2], of contributing to the necessities of those in need [3], and generally of being merciful even as our Father in heaven is merciful (Lk. vi. 36).

CHAPTER III.
THE SEVENTH COMMANDMENT.

Seventh Commandment.	Duty towards our Neighbour.
Thou shalt not commit adultery.	*My duty towards my Neighbour is...To keep my body in temperance, soberness, and chastity.*

1. **The relation of Husband and Wife.** As the last Commandment proclaimed the sanctity of human life, so the present proclaims the sanctity of marriage. The institution of marriage, the parent of civil society [4], is "an honourable estate" ordained by God Himself [5], "adorned and beautified [6]" by the presence and first

---

[1] *If ye forgive men their trespasses, your heavenly Father will also forgive you: but if ye forgive not men their trespasses, neither will your Father forgive your trespasses* (Mtt. vi. 14); *forgiving one another, even as God for Christ's sake hath forgiven you* (Eph. iv. 32).

[2] *Pray for them which despitefully use you and persecute you* (Mtt. v. 44). *If thine enemy hunger, feed him; if he thirst, give him drink* (Rom. xii. 20).

[3] *Whoso hath this world's goods, and seeth his brother have need, and shutteth up his bowels of compassion from him, how dwelleth the love of God in Him?* (1 Jn. iii. 17).

[4] Cicero calls marriage *Principium Urbis et quasi seminarium reipublicæ*, *De Off.* I. xvii. 54.

[5] Gen. ii. 24, quoted by Christ Mtt. xix. 4, 5; Mk. x. 6—9.

[6] Jn. ii. 1—11. See the Marriage Service.

miracle of His blessed Son, and declared by St Paul to be a type of "the mystical union that is betwixt Christ and His Church[1]."

2. **Adultery.** All offences, therefore, against so honourable an estate are of a very heinous character, and the sin of adultery has in all ages and amongst all nations been severely punished. In the Mosaic code it ranked next to murder, and the punishment for both parties was death by stoning[2].

3. **Duty of Purity.** But like the last, this Commandment also has been explained by our Lord. *Ye have heard,* said He, *that it was said to them of old time, Thou shalt not commit adultery: but I say unto you, That whosoever looketh on a woman to lust after her, hath committed adultery with her already in his heart* (Mtt. v. 27, 28). From which we learn that this Precept goes far beyond the mere *act* of adultery, and forbids the dominion of sensual desires and the indulgence of every kind of wantonness in act, speech, or thought[3].

4. **Specially incumbent on Christians.** Hence the Catechism traces to this Commandment the positive duty of keeping[4] the body in temperance[5] soberness,

---

[1] Eph. v. 23—32. See the Marriage Service.
[2] Comp. Levit. xviii. 20; xx. 10; Deut. xxii. 22.
[3] See Gal. v. 19, where St Paul classes *adultery, fornication, uncleanness, lasciviousness* among *the works of the flesh,* and Eph. v. 3, where he declares that *fornication and all uncleanness ought not to be once named* amongst Christians, *neither filthiness, nor foolish talking, nor jesting, which are not convenient.* Comp. also 1 Cor. vi. 9; Col. iii. 5.
[4] Or as St Paul expresses it, 1 Cor. ix. 27, *keeping under.* ὑπωπιάζω μου τὸ σῶμα καὶ δουλαγωγῶ, literally, *I beat my body black and blue and lead it about as a slave.*
[5] *Temperance* (Acts xxiv. 25; Gal. v. 23; 2 Pet. i. 6) has lately assumed almost exclusively the meaning of moderation in the matter of drink; its original sense was that of

and chastity. For every other *sin that a man doeth is without the body* (1 Cor. vi. 18), but he that is impure sinneth against his own body which is *a temple of the Holy Ghost* (1 Cor. vi. 19), and *if any man destroy the temple of God, him shall God destroy* (1 Cor. iii. 17).

CHAPTER IV.
THE EIGHTH COMMANDMENT.

Eighth Commandment.	Duty towards our Neighbour.
Thou shalt not steal.	*My duty towards my Neighbour is...To be true and just in all my dealing...To keep my hands from picking and stealing.*

1. **Rights of Property.** Besides his right to life and personal security, every man has a just title to somewhat which he may call his own, whether his title ariseth by just acquisition, or inheritance, or gift, or contract[1]. This right has been protected by all laws, and not least by the Mosaic law, which denounced all robbery, and enacted that the thief should not go unpunished[2].

self-restraint (Gr. ἐγκράτεια, Latin *temperantia*) or *self-control*. Comp. Latimer, *Rem.* p. 378, "Doctor Barnes, I hear say, preached this day a very good sermon, with great moderation and *temperance* of himself;" also Bacon's *Essays*, v. 17, "The vertue of prosperitie, is *temperance*, the vertue of adversity, is fortitude." The *Bible Word-book*, p. 478.

[1] Nicholson *On the Catechism*, p. 137. "The Right of Property is requisite as a condition of the Free Agency of Man." Whewell's *Elements of Morality*, II. 22.

[2] Direct theft was punished by *restitution*. If the stolen goods were found in the hands of the thief, he was to restore twofold. But a still heavier fine was exacted if he had sold, or injured the stolen property. If unable to pay, he was to be sold into slavery to a Hebrew master, and serve him till he could pay (Ex. xxii. 1—4, Comp. 2 Sam. xii. 6). See *Class-Book of Old Testament History*, pp. 165, 166.

2. **Picking and Stealing.** But according to the principle of interpretation, which has been applied to the other Commandments, it is clear that, as explained in the Catechism, this also forbids, besides open robbery, all kinds of dishonesty[1], all "picking[2]" and stealing, all unfairness and trickery in buying or selling[3], borrowing or lending, in fact every species of fraud and extortion[4].

3. **Truth and Justice.** And while the Commandment forbids such sins, it enjoins the positive duty of being "true and just in all our dealings," of using every honest means to get our own living[5], of giving and paying every man his due, and, instead of taking what is another's, of being ready to distribute[6] from our own

---

[1] "And here note that this worde, thefte, dothe not onely signifie open robberies, extorcions, and manyfest poollyng but also all manner of craftes, and subtile wayes, by the whiche we conuey our neyghbours goodes from him, contrary to his knowledge or wytt, althoughe the gyle haue neuer so fayre a coloure of vertue and honesty." Cranmer's *Catechism*, p. 73.

[2] Picking = *pilfering* or *petty thieving*. "I had of late occasion to speak of *picking* and stealing, where I shewed unto you the danger wherein they be that steal their neighbours' goods from them." Latimer's *Sermons*, p. 452, quoted in the *Bible Word-book*, p. 368.

[3] *Ye shall do no unrighteousness...in meteyard, in weight, or in measure. Just balances, just weights, a just ephah, and a just hin, shall ye have*, Lev. xix. 35, 36. Comp. Deut. xxv. 13—16; Prov. xi. 1, xvi. 11.

[4] *I have written unto you not to keep company if any man that is called a brother be......an extortioner*, 1 Cor. v. 11. *Thieves......shall not inherit the Kingdom of God*, 1 Cor. vi. 10. Comp. Ezek. xxii. 29; Hos. iv. 2, 3.

[5] *Let him that stole steal no more: but rather let him labour, working with his hands the thing which is good, that he may have to give to him that needeth.* Eph. iv. 28; Comp. 1 Thess. iv. 11; 1 Tim. v. 8.

[6] *Charge them that are rich in this world...that they do good, that they be rich in good works, ready to distribute.* 1 Tim. vi. 17, 18; Comp. Rom. xii. 13; Heb. xiii. 16; 1 Jn. iii. 17.

wealth to the wants and necessities of those that lack[1].

CHAPTER V.
THE NINTH COMMANDMENT.

NINTH COMMANDMENT.	DUTY TOWARDS OUR NEIGHBOUR.
Thou shalt not bear false witness against thy Neighbour.	*My duty towards my Neighbour is...To keep my tongue from evil-speaking, lying, and slandering.*

1. **The Character.** The Ninth Commandment treats of our duty respecting our neighbour's *character* and reputation, which are as precious as his life and property[2].

2. **False Witness.** The crime, therefore, at which the Commandment first and most expressly points, is giving false witness in a court of justice. And as in such cases evidence is always given upon oath, this Precept, like the third, forbids perjury, which there is regarded as impiety against God, here as injurious to man[3]. The Mosaic Law, like all other laws, regarded perjury as one of the most heinous of crimes, and

---

[1] "Also thys precepte wylleth us to be so farre absent from takynge awaye an other manne's good, that it byddeth us to gyue parte of our owne riches to them that lacke and desire it, according to the commaundment of Christ, whiche sayeth, *Gieue to every man that doeth aske the.*" Cranmer's *Catechism*, p. 79.

[2] "Forasmuche as our riches standeth not onelye in possession of landes, tenementes, cattell, or money, but also in our good name, fame and estimation, (which farre passeth al gold syluer and precious stones,) therfore foloweth this commaundment, *Thou shalt beare no false witnes agaynst thy neyghbour.*" Cranmer's *Catechism*, p. 80.

[3] *A good name is rather to be chosen than great riches*, Prov. xxii. 1. *A good name is better than precious ointment*, Eccl. vii. 1 ; see Secker's *Lectures on the Catechism*, II. p. 96.

enacted that *if a false witness rose up against any man* he should be brought before the priests and judges, and if, after diligent inquisition, the charge was established, then should be done unto him *as he had thought to have done unto his brother*[1] (Deut. xix. 16—21).

3. **Evil speaking.** But this Commandment extends to false witness, not merely in judicial proceedings, but also in common conversation. For a man's reputation may be, and too often is, seriously injured by calumny, misrepresentation, imputing bad motives, and spreading false and slanderous reports. Hence, the Israelites were forbidden to allow *any to go up and down as a talebearer among the people* (Lev. xix. 16), and were directed to keep *from a false matter* (Ex. xxiii. 7); for whoso *privily slandered his neighbour him would God destroy* (Ps. ci. 5). Hence also our Lord instructs us, *condemn not, and ye shall not be condemned, judge not, that ye be not judged* (Lk. vi. 37; Mtt. vii. 1), and St Paul enjoins us to *put away all evil-speaking* (Eph. iv. 31), for true Christian love *thinketh no evil* (1 Cor. xiii. 5).

4. **Lying and Slandering.** Thus, as explained in the Catechism, this Commandment enjoins the duty of "keeping the tongue from evil-speaking, lying, and slandering." For detraction and calumny generally lead to lying, which is one of the seven things that are described as *an abomination unto the Lord* (Prov. vi. 17), and including, as it does, equivocation, exaggeration, and false colouring, strikes at the very root of that mutual trust and confidence which is the foundation of society. Again and again therefore in the New Testament is the Christian exhorted to put away lying as being unworthy of

---

[1] For examples of false witness see 1 Kings xxi. 9, 10; Mtt. xxvi. 59—61.

his profession[1], and his membership of Christ's Church[2], as being worthy only of the Evil One[3], and entailing future condemnation[4].

CHAPTER VI.

THE TENTH COMMANDMENT.

TENTH COMMANDMENT.	DUTY TOWARDS MY NEIGHBOUR.
Thou shalt not covet thy neighbour's house, thou shalt not covet thy neighbour's wife, nor his servant, nor his maid, nor his ox, nor his ass, nor any thing that is his.	*My duty towards my neighbour is...not to covet nor desire other men's goods; but to learn and labour truly to get mine own living, and to do my duty in that state of life, unto which it shall please God to call me.*

1. **Scope of the Commandment.** The tenth Commandment deals not with the act or speech, but with the thoughts and motions of the heart. As addressed to the Israelites it strikingly anticipates the teaching of our Lord in the Sermon on the Mount, for it cuts to the quick, and shews that God's law takes hold on the first and inmost intentions and motions to evil[5] (Rom. vii. 7).

2. **The sin forbidden.** The sin, which this Commandment forbids, is covetousness, or concupiscence.

---

[1] *All liars shall have their part in the lake which burneth with fire and brimstone; which is the second death.* Rev. xxi. 8; xxii. 15.

[2] *Lie not one to another, seeing that ye have put off the old man with his deeds.* Col. iii. 9.

[3] *Putting away lying, speak every man truth with his neighbour: for we are members one of another.* Eph. iv. 25; comp. Rom. xii. 5.

[4] *When he speaketh a lie, he speaketh of his own: for he is a liar, and the father of it.* Jn. viii. 44.

[5] Nicholson *On the Catechism*, p. 141.

§ II.]   *THE TENTH COMMANDMENT.*   99

The original word thus translated[1] in our Bibles has the force not merely of to desire, which may be natural, but "to set the heart upon," to "desire immoderately," and is generally used in a bad sense, as denoting "evil concupiscence." It may, therefore, include various objects of immoderate desire, and may assume the form of fleshly lust[2], or of covetous longing for another's property[3], or of the love of money[4]. But whatever may be its precise object, closely allied as it is with envy and discontent, *when it hath conceived, it bringeth forth sin, and sin, when it is finished*[5], *bringeth forth death* (Jas. i. 14, 15).

3. **And denounced.** Hence the sin of covetousness is again and again condemned in the Bible. *Take heed and beware of covetousness* is one of the Lord's warnings (Lk. xii. 15); *the covetous man*, writes St Paul to the Ephesians, *is an idolater*[6], *and hath no inhe-*

---

[1] Ἐπιθυμία, sometimes translated *desire* (Lk. xxii. 15, Phil. i. 23), sometimes *lust* (Mk. iv. 19, Rom. i. 24, &c.), sometimes *concupiscence* (Rom. vii. 8; Col. iii. 5). It is rarely used in a good, much oftener in a bad sense, not only as = *concupiscentia*, but *mala concupiscentia*. Our English word *lust* once meant mere strong desire, and was not always employed in an evil sense as now. See Trench's *Synonyms*, p. 311; *Bible Word-Book*, p. 302, and p. 552.

[2] *Thou shalt not covet thy neighbour's wife*, as in the case of David (2 Sam. xi. 1—5), who verily was *drawn away by his own lust and enticed* (Jas. i. 14), and so fell into adultery and murder.

[3] As in the case of Ahab and the vineyard of Naboth (1 Kings xxi. 4. 19).

[4] As in the instances of (1) Achan, (Josh. vii. 1—26), (2) Balaam (2 Pet. ii. 15), (3) Gehazi (2 Kings v. 20—27), (4) Judas Iscariot (Mtt. xxvi. 14, 15).

[5] Ἀποτελεσθεῖσα, *consummatum, adultum robur nactum: id quod celeriter fit.* Bengel in loc.

[6] For he worships Mammon instead of God (Mtt. vi. 24) see Ellicott on Eph. v. 5. *Avaritia est summa defectio a Creatore ad creaturam, et summe violat præceptum de dili-*

ritance in the kingdom of Christ and of God (Eph. v. 5); *the love of money*, he says to Timothy, *is the root of all evil* (1 Tim. vi. 10); and on account of *evil concupiscence*, he says to the Colossians, *the wrath of God cometh on the children of disobedience* (Col. iii. 5, 6).

4. **The Duty Enjoined.** Now for this sin the great antidote is the grace commended in the Catechism, viz. Contentment[1]. This virtue, when united with godliness, is truly *great gain* (1 Tim. vi. 6), and teaches us, who *brought nothing into this world*, and who *it is certain* will *carry nothing out* (1 Tim. vi. 7), instead of coveting or desiring other men's goods, to "learn and labour truly to get our own living[2], and to do our duty in that state of life[3] unto which it shall please God to call us."

gendo proximo, quod simile est præcepto de diligendo Deo. Bengel in l. c. Comp. 1 Cor. vi. 10; Col. iii. 5, 6.

[1] *Let your conversation be without* COVETOUSNESS; *and be* CONTENT *with such things as ye have; for He hath said, I will never leave thee, nor forsake thee.* Heb. xiii. 5; and comp. Phil. iv. 11.

[2] *Study...to do your own business, and to work with your own hands.* 1 Thess. iv. 11, and comp. Acts xx. 34; Eph. iv. 28.

[3] "God calls us to our state of life: there let us rest, and do our duty in it. In it, whatever it be, is safety, usefulness, true dignity: beyond it, outside of it, lies the unknown, the untried, perhaps the dangerous, certainly the disappointing." Vaughan, *On Confirmation*, p. 39.

PART IV.

THE LORD'S PRAYER.

My good child, know this, that thou art not able to do these things of thyself, nor to walk in the Commandments of God, and to serve him, without his special grace; which thou must learn at all times to call for by diligent prayer. Let me hear therefore, if thou canst say the Lord's Prayer?

Our Father, which art in heaven, Hallowed be thy Name. Thy kingdom come. Thy will be done in earth, As it is in heaven. Give us this day our daily bread. And forgive us our trespasses, As we forgive them that trespass against us. And lead us not into temptation; But deliver us from evil. Amen.

What desirest thou of God in this Prayer?

I desire my Lord God our heavenly Father, who is the giver of all goodness, to send his grace unto me, and to all people; that we may worship him, serve him, and obey him, as we ought to do. And I pray unto God, that he will send us all things that be needful both for our souls and bodies; and that he will be merciful unto us, and forgive us our sins; and that it will please him to save and defend us in all dangers ghostly and bodily; and that he will keep us from all sin and wickedness, and from our ghostly enemy, and from everlasting death. And this I trust he will do of his mercy and goodness, through our Lord Jesus Christ. And therefore I say, Amen, So be it.

INTRODUCTION.

1. **Need of Grace.** Having explained the Baptismal vow of *renunciation, faith, and obedience,* the Catechism proceeds to remind us that we are not able to keep it of ourselves, nor "to walk[1] in the command-

---

[1] Compare Cranmer's *Catechism,* p. 128.

ments of God, and to serve Him, without His special grace[1], which we must learn at all times to call for by diligent prayer."

2. **The frailty of our Nature.** That of ourselves we are unable to do these things is sadly brought home to us by daily experience. For no one ever made a sincere effort to do his duty towards God and man without finding that "through the weakness of his mortal nature[2]" "he is sore let and hindered in running the race that is set before him[3]," that the *good he would he does not, and the evil which he would not that he does* (Rom. vii. 19); that *the flesh lusteth against the Spirit, and the Spirit strives*[4] *against the flesh* (Gal. v. 17); that he may *delight in the law of God after the inward man;* but sees *another law in his members, warring against the law of his mind, and*

---

[1] Compare the words of the Catechism, "And I pray unto God to give me His grace (spiritual aid), that I may continue in the same (state of salvation) unto my life's end." Grace, from the Latin *gratia*, (i) in its literal denotes *favour*, as in Ruth ii. 2, 10, and in Shakspeare 2 *Hen. IV.* IV. 4,
    Blunt not his love,
 Nor lose the good advantage of his *grace*,
 By seeming cold or careless of his will.
(ii) Hence in the Scriptures it denotes God's *free favour* in (*a*) the redemption of the world by His Son, (*b*) the forgiveness of our sins; (*c*) the promise of everlasting life. Comp. Rom. iv. 4; v. 16; xi. 6; Eph. i. 6, 7; ii. 8; 2 Tim. i. 9; Titus ii. 11—14; iii. 7. (iii) But, as the favour of God is never an idle feeling, but an active expression of love, it further denotes a spiritual gift, and especially the gift of such "spiritual aid as may enable a man both to *will* and to *do* according to what God has commanded." See Waterland's *Works*, Vol. IV. p. 666.

[2] See the Collect for the First Sunday after Trinity.

[3] See the Collect for the Fourth Sunday in Advent.

[4] "As ἐπιθυμεῖν cannot apply to the Spirit some other verb must be supplied in the second clause." Lightfoot on Gal. v. 17.

bringing him into captivity[1] *to the law of sin* (Rom. vii. 22, 23).

3. **Necessity of Prayer.** Because, then, the frailty of man without God, cannot but fall[2], and we have no power of ourselves to help ourselves[3], we must seek help of Him, of whom alone cometh our strength. To this end Prayer, which is an instinct of the human soul, and the key that opens the gate of heaven[4], is the ordained means.

4. **Example of our Lord.** This is specially taught us by the example of our blessed Lord. For, while He was upon earth, though He was God of God, and Light of Light, yet He was in the constant habit of engaging in prayer to His Father in heaven. Sometimes we read of His retiring *into a solitary place a great while before day* (Mk. i. 35) for the purpose of prayer, sometimes of His *continuing all night in prayer to God*[5] (Lk. vi. 12). Moreover, we find that all the most momentous events in His life, The descent of the Holy Ghost at His Baptism[6], His choice of the Apostles[7], His Transfiguration[8], His Betrayal to be

---

[1] Αἰχμαλωτίζοντά με = *leading me captive in its chains.* Comp. Lk. xxi. 24; 2 Cor. x. 5; 2 Tim. iii. 6.

[2] See the Collect for the Eighteenth Sunday after Trinity.

[3] Collect for Second Sunday in Lent.

[4] *Cœli clavis oratio: ascendat oratio, ut descendat gratia.* Nicholson *On the Catechism*, p. 155.

[5] Compare also Mtt. xiv. 23; Mk. vi. 46; Lk. v. 16.

[6] *Now...it came to pass, that Jesus also being baptized,* AND PRAYING, *the heaven was opened* (Lk. iii. 21). *Sæpe preces Jesu commemorat Lucas in rebus maximis,* Bengel.

[7] *And it came to pass that in those days, He went out into a mountain* (τὸ ὄρος = the mountain-range) *to pray, and continued all night in* PRAYER *to God; and when it was day, He called unto Him His disciples, and of them He chose twelve* (Lk. vi. 12). "Magnum hac nocte negotium inter Deum et Mediatorem!" Bengel.

[8] *And it came to pass about an eight days after these sayings, He took Peter and John and James, and went up into a*

crucified[1], were either preceded by or accompanied with prayer and supplication.

5. **His Precepts.** Moreover, we find that what He was in the habit of doing Himself, He bade His disciples do likewise. On one occasion, He said to them, *Ask, and it shall be given you; seek, and ye shall find; knock, and it shall be opened unto you* (Mtt. vii. 7); on another, *What things soever ye desire, when ye pray, believe that ye receive them, and ye shall have them*[2] (Mk. xi. 24); on another, *Whatsoever ye shall ask in My Name*[3], *that will I do, that the Father may be glorified in the Son* (Jn. xiv. 13); on another, *Verily, verily*[4], *I say unto you, Whatsoever ye shall ask the Father in My Name, He will give it you* (Jn. xvi. 23).

6. **Apostolic Precepts.** What, therefore, their Master thus taught at once by His own example and precept, the Apostles also were careful to inculcate. Writing to the Thessalonians, St Paul says, *Pray without ceasing* (1 Thess. v. 17); to the Romans, *continue instant*[5] *in prayer* (Rom. xii. 12); to the Ephesians,

---

mountain to PRAY, *and as He* PRAYED, *the fashion of His countenance was altered*, &c. Lk. ix. 28, 29.

[1] *Then cometh Jesus with them unto a place called Gethsemane, and saith unto the disciples, Sit ye here, while I go and* PRAY *yonder*, on which followed the agony and the thrice-repeated prayer. Mtt. xxvi. 36, and compare the parallels.

[2] Comp. also Mtt. xxi. 22.   [3] Comp. Jn. xv. 7, 16.

[4] *Asseveratio gravissima, Ei propria, qui per se ipsum et per veritatem suam asseverat: et a dignitate personæ loquentis æquipollet juramento, præsertim ubi geminatur*, Bengel.

[5] Προσκαρτεροῦντες = *adhering steadfastly to, persevering in.* Comp. Acts i. 14; ii. 42. "Instant," (from the Latin instare = *to urge, press upon*,) occurs in our Version also in Lk. xxiii. 23, and 2 Tim. iv. 2. As applied (i) to prayer, it = *importunate, persevering;* (ii) to business, it = *earnest, diligent*. Comp. *I preached in Kent also, at the instant request of a curate*. Latimer's *Rem*. p. 324, quoted in the *Bible Word-Book*, p. 269.

Pray always with all prayer and supplication in the Spirit (Eph. vi. 18); to the Colossians, *Continue in prayer, and watch in the same with thanksgiving* (Col. iv. 2). Again, St James writes, *If any of you lack wisdom, let him ask of God, that giveth to all men liberally, and upbraideth not, and it shall be given him* (Jas. i. 5); and St John tells us, that this is the confidence that we have concerning God, that *if we ask anything according to His will, He heareth us: and if we know that He hear us, whatsoever we ask, we know that we have the petitions that we desired of Him*[1] (1 Jn. v. 14, 15).

CHAPTER I.

STRUCTURE OF THE LORD'S PRAYER.

1. **Need of a Form of Prayer.** We require, however, not only to be encouraged to pray, but also to be taught how and for what to pray, and this need our blessed Lord, who knows our necessities before we ask, and our ignorance in asking[2], has graciously supplied.

2. **Supplied by our Lord.** For in His Sermon on the Mount, after warning His disciples against hypocrisy in prayer (Mtt. vi. 5), and using *vain repetitions* like the heathen (Mtt. vi. 7), He proceeded to teach them a Form of supplication, after the model of which they were to pray (Mtt. vi. 9—13). Again, at a later period of His public ministry, we read that, as *He was praying in a certain place*[3], *when He ceased, one of*

---

[1] Comp. also Heb. iv. 16; 1 Pet. iv. 7; 1 Jn. iii. 22.
[2] See the Collects at the close of the Communion Office.
[3] The place is not pointed out by St Luke, but "it seems probable that this lesson of prayer was given in the same place as the preceding lesson of faith (Lk. x. 38—42), viz. Bethany." Oosterzee on Lk. ix. 1.

His disciples, speaking probably in the name of the rest, *said unto Him, Lord, teach us to pray, as John also taught His disciples*[1] (Lk. xi. 1). Whereupon He again instructed them to use the same form, which He had already delivered to the multitudes, and the general body of His disciples[2] on the Mount of Beatitudes.

3. **The Lord's Prayer.** The Form thus impressively taught us, and which has not for its author any one of the patriarchs, prophets, or apostles, nay, not an angel from heaven, but which was given and commanded to be used by the Eternal Son[3], who with the Father and the Holy Ghost is God and our Lord, has ever been known as *the Lord's Prayer*[4].

4. **Its structure.** In reference to the structure of this incomparable Prayer, it may be divided into four parts.

(i) The Address or Invocation.   *Our Father which art in heaven:*

(ii) Three petitions for God's glory.
1. *Hallowed be Thy Name;*
2. *Thy kingdom come;*
3. *Thy will be done in earth, as it is in heaven:*

---

[1] That John taught his disciples to pray is also implied in Lk. v. 33.

[2] "Formulam incomparabilem alio tempore Matthæus populo pluribus verbis; alio Lucas discipulis rogantibus brevius præscriptam recenset." Bengel on Lk. xi. 1. See also Tholuck's *Sermon on the Mount*, p. 25.

[3] Stella, quoted in Denton's *Commentary on the Lord's Prayer*, p. 26. "Though men should speak with the tongues of angels, yet words so pleasing to the ears of God, as those which the Son of God Himself hath composed, were not possible for men to frame. He which made us to live hath also taught us to pray, to the end that, speaking to the Father in the Son's own prescribed form, without gloss of ours, we may be sure that we utter nothing which God will either disallow or deny." Hooker's *Eccl. Pol.* v. xxxv. 3.

[4] See Bingham's *Works*, IV. 480—493.

(iii) Four petitions for ourselves.
1. *Give us this day our daily bread:*
2. *And forgive us our trespasses, as we forgive them that trespass against us;*
3. *And lead us not into temptation;*
4. *But deliver us from evil:*

(iv) A Doxology.
For Thine is the Kingdom, the Power, and the Glory, for ever and ever, Amen.[1]

CHAPTER II.
THE INVOCATION.

THE LORD'S PRAYER.	EXPLANATION.
Our Father which[2] *art in heaven.*	*I desire my Lord God, our heavenly Father, who is the giver of all goodness.*

1. **Our Father.** The first point deserving of notice in this Invocation is the title, whereby our blessed Lord bids us address *the King eternal, immortal, invisible, the only*[3] *God* (1 Tim. i. 17). We might have imagined that He would have bidden us employ some term that would express the greatness, or the power, or the majesty of Him, *in whom we live, and move, and have our being* (Acts xvii. 28). But this He has not

---

[1] The Doxology does not occur in St Luke's Gospel, and is omitted from St Matthew's Gospel by Lachmann, Tischendorf, and Tregelles. But see Scrivener's *Supplement to the Authorized English Version of the New Testament*, and Denton *On the Lord's Prayer*, pp. 206—216.

[2] *Which*, commonly used for the relative *who*, and applied to persons, from the A.-S. *huilc*, Mœso-Goth. *hvéleiks*, literally, *who-like*. Comp. Latimer's *Sermons*, p. 338, "Whosoever loveth God, will love his neighbour, *which* is made after the image of God." See the *Bible Word-Book*, p. 528.

[3] The word σοφῷ, *wise*, does not occur here in the best MSS.

done. *When ye pray*, He told His disciples, *say, Our* FATHER *which art in heaven*.

2. **The Fatherhood of God.** Now it is indeed true that the idea of God as a Father was not unfamiliar to the world[1]. For Isaiah says, *Thou, O Lord, art our Father, our Redeemer, Thy Name is from everlasting* (Isai. lxiii. 16), and Malachi asks, *Have we not all one Father? Hath not one God created us?* (Mal. ii. 10). It is true also that the ancient Greeks[2] and Romans[3], our Saxon ancestors[4], and many other heathen nations, had dim convictions of the existence of a "Father of gods and men," an "All-Father," whose offspring we are (Acts xvii. 28). But not till our blessed Lord appeared upon this earth did we know that God was our Father, not only by creation but redemption, having given His own Son to die for us, and bestowed on us *power to become the sons of God*[5] (Jn. i. 12).

---

[1] See above, p. 21.

[2] By the Greeks Zeus was emphatically called Πατήρ, Πατὴρ Ζεύς; hence the expression Πατὴρ ἀνδρῶν τε Θεῶν τε, so common in Homer; comp. Æsch. *Theb*. 512; Pind. P. IV. 275, 344.

[3] Jupiter, Diumque hominumque pater rex. "Wherever God hath been acknowledged, He hath been understood and worshipped as a Father," Pearson *On the Creed*.

[4] "Who is first and eldest of the gods?" it is asked in the *Edda*, and the answer is, "He is called Allfadir in our tongue. He made heaven and earth, and the *lift*, that is, the sky, and all that belongs to them, and, what is most, He made man, and gave him a soul that shall live and never perish, though the body rot to mould, or burn to ashes."

[5] See above, p. 21: "He made us, and is our Father by *creation;* He preserves us, and is our Father by His *providential care;* He has in His mercy taken us into His family, and is therefore our Father by *adoption;* He has redeemed us by His infinite love from the yoke of our sin and from bondage to Satan, and is our Father by *redemption*." Maldonatus, quoted in Denton, *On the Lord's Prayer*, p. 49.

3. **A ground of Confidence.** We may well believe, then, that the Saviour made choice of this name to encourage us when we draw near to *the throne of grace* (Heb. iv. 16). While it is the glory of earthly princes to be known by names which express their power, their descent, or the extent of their rule, "Christ, the natural Son of God, and best acquainted with His Father's mind[1], assures us that it is God's will to be called by the sweetest name in earth, by that name alluring us to Himself, that we should without fear come to Him, taking away all doubting of His fatherly heart and good will," and reminding us that *if we, who are evil, know how to give good things to our children, much more will our Father which is in heaven give good things to them that ask Him* (Mtt. vii. 11).

4. **Our.** But there is another point respecting this title which is deserving of notice. When, during His agony in the Garden of Gethsemane, the Saviour prayed, three times using the same words, He said, *O* MY *Father, if it be possible, let this cup pass from Me* (Mtt. xxvi. 39). Again, when He spoke of His Ascension, He said, *I ascend unto* MY *Father, and your Father, to* MY *God, and your God* (Jn. xx. 17). Thus He could speak with all possible propriety, for He is the only begotten of the Father. But when He bids us pray, He would have us call God OUR Father in common, rather than severally MY Father. And hereby He reminds us that we ought to think not merely of ourselves, but of one another[2], and bear in mind those

---

[1] Noell's *Catechism.* Compare also Cranmer's *Catechism,* p. 134: "Christ our Lorde knewe most certenly the will of His heuenly Father, that is to say, that He would be oure moste swete and louyinge Father, for els He woulde not haue taught vs this title, *Our Father.*"

[2] Hence the explanation in the Catechism, "I desire my Lord God...that He will send His grace unto me *and to all people.*"

common bonds, which knit us together as men and as Christians in that mystical Body, of which He has made us "very members incorporate[1]."

5. **Which art in heaven.** Again, to the title *Our Father*, He has joined the words *which art in heaven*, and thereby reminds us that "we are to look for God, not in ourselves, but out of and above ourselves[2]," that we lift up our hearts from earth and earthly things to the high and holy place, where He sitteth in majesty ineffable, amidst *the light which no man can approach unto* (1 Tim. vi. 16). Moreover, He would remind us of the reverence and humility, with which we should draw near to Him, that *He is in heaven, and we upon earth*, and therefore that we should not be *rash with our mouth, or let our hearts be hasty to utter any thing before Him*[3] (Eccl. v. 2).

[1] Hence also in the petitions that concern ourselves He has taught us each to say, "*Give us this day our daily bread;*" "*Forgive* us our *trespasses; lead* us *not into temptation; but deliver* us *from evil.*" "Every godly man may, I grant, lawfully call God his own; but such ought to be the community and fellowship of Christian men together, and such clear love and goodwill ought every one to bear to all, that no one of them, neglecting the rest, care for himself alone, but have regard to the public profit of all." Noell's *Catechism*. Hence St Augustine calls the Lord's Prayer "the fraternal prayer," "Oratio fraterna est; non dicit, *Pater meus*, tanquam pro se tantùm orans, sed *Pater noster*, omnes videlicet unâ oratione complectens, qui se in Christo fratres esse cognoscunt." *De Serm. Dom. in Mon.* II. c. 4.

[2] Trench's St Augustine, *On the Sermon on the Mount*, p. 93.

[3] "We are, by these words, admonished not to ask anything unmeet for God; but as speaking to our heavenly Father, to have our hearts raised from earth, high and looking upward, despising earthly things, thinking upon things above and heavenly, and continually to aspire to that most blessed felicity of our Father, and to heaven as our inheritance by our Father." Noell's *Catechism;* see also Nicholson *On the Catechism.*

CHAPTER III.

THE FIRST PETITION FOR GOD'S GLORY.

The Lord's Prayer.	The Explanation.
Hallowed be Thy Name.	*I desire my Lord God, who is the giver of all good, to send His grace unto me, and to all people, that we may worship Him...as we ought to do.*

1. **Thy Name.** From the Address or Invocation, which we have considered in the last Chapter, we pass on to the first petition[1] contained in the Lord's Prayer, *Hallowed be Thy Name.* The name of a person, as we have seen above[2], marks him out as an individual, presents him to the mind, or expresses something peculiar to him. The name of God, therefore, may be defined to be that summary of His nature and character, or that revelation of Himself, which He has been pleased to vouchsafe to us His creatures.

2. **The Name** of God is thus frequently spoken of in the Bible. Thus David says, *O Lord, how excellent is Thy* NAME *in all the earth, who hast set Thy glory above the heavens* (Ps. viii. 1), and he bids men praise *the* NAME *of the Lord, for His Name only is excellent, and His glory above heaven and earth* (Ps. cxlviii. 13). Again, Isaiah bids the man that fears the Lord, *Trust*

---

[1] "Our Pater Noster," says one of old, "for the most part begins at *Give us this day our daily bread,* and our prayers are much like Jacob's vow, If God will give us bread to eat and raiment to put on, then shall He be our God; but our Lord bids us *seek first the kingdom of God and His righteousness,* and assures us that all things necessary *shall be added unto us.*"

[2] See above, pp. 2, 3.

in the NAME *of the Lord, and stay upon his God* (Isai. l. 10). Again, on a memorable occasion[1] in the life of our blessed Saviour, His prayer to His heavenly Father was, *Father, glorify Thy* NAME[2]; whereupon there came a *voice from heaven, saying, I have both glorified it, and will glorify it again* (Jn. xii. 28).

3. **Names of God.** It has been observed "that the great epochs of the history of the Chosen People are marked by the several names by which in each the Divine Nature is indicated[2]." In the Patriarchal age the word by which the most general idea of the Divinity was expressed was "El," "Elohim," *the Strong One, the Strong Ones.* When by the vision of the Burning Bush Moses was summoned to deliver the Israelites from bondage in Egypt, *Behold,* he said, *when I shall come to the children of Israel, and shall say unto them, The God of your fathers hath sent me unto you, and they shall say, What is His* NAME? *what shall I say unto them? And God said unto Moses,* I AM THAT I AM—*Thus shalt thou say unto the children of Israel,* I AM JEHOVAH[4], (*the Eternal, the Self Existent*) *hath sent me unto you* (Ex. iii. 13, 14). At a later period, when the monarchy was established, the idea of the "Leader of the armies of heaven and earth" was en-

---

[1] In one of the courts of the Temple after the visit of the enquiring Greeks. See *Class-Book of New Testament History,* pp. 273, 274.

[2] Σοῦ τὸ ὄνομα=nomen tuum paternum, quod est in Me. Bengel.

[3] Stanley's *Jewish Church,* Pt. I. p. 112.

[4] Compare Ex. vi. 2, 3, *And God spake unto Moses, and said unto him, I am* JEHOVAH: *and I appeared unto Abraham, unto Isaac, and unto Jacob, by the name of El-Shaddai* (*God Almighty*), *but by my name* JEHOVAH *was I not known unto them.* The word LORD, by which we have rendered JEHOVAH, is the translation of Κύριος in the LXX, which is the translation of the Hebrew Adonai, the word used by the later Jews, out of excessive reverence, in place of JEHOVAH.

shrined in the name JEHOVAH SABAOTH, the *Lord of Hosts*[1]. When the Jewish economy had run its course, and He had finished His work, of whose coming Moses and the prophets had written (Jn. v. 46), He bade His Apostles baptize all nations *into the Name of the Father, and of the Son, and of the Holy Ghost* (Mtt. xxviii. 19). And this is the last revelation we have received of the Name of HIM, *in whom we live, and move, and have our being*.

4. **Hallowed be Thy Name.** When, then, we pray that God's Name may be hallowed[2], it is plain that that Name cannot in itself "be made either greater by increase, or lesser by decrease, it changeth not with any addition or diminishing, as our earthly things do[3]." But our prayer is that the Name of God, and that Revelation of His nature and Attributes, which we have received, may be made known in all the world, that "we and all people may worship[4] Him as we ought to do," look up to Him, as a Father, serve and obey Him as His children, and so let our light shine forth, that all may *see our good works, and glorify our Father which is in heaven* (Mtt. v. 16).

[1] Compare the words of Daniel to the Philistine, *Thou comest to me with a sword, and with a spear, and with a shield: but I come to thee in the Name of* THE LORD OF HOSTS, *the God of the armies of Israel, whom thou hast defied* (1 Sam. xvii. 45; and comp. Josh. v. 14, 15).

[2] Ἁγιάζειν = (1) *to set apart for sacred purposes, to consecrate* (Jn. x. 36; xvii. 19); (2) *to treat a holy thing as holy, to hold sacred, to honour* (see Pet. iii. 15; and comp. Ex. xx. 8; Lev. xxi. 8; Numb. xx. 12; Deut. xxxii. 51). See Tholuck's *Sermon on the Mount*, p. 332.

[3] Noell's *Catechism*. Compare S. Augustine, *de Serm. Dom.* LVII. 4. "Pro nobis rogamus, non pro Deo. Non enim bene optamus Deo, cui nihil mali potest aliquando accidere. Sed optamus nobis bonum, ut sanctificetur sanctum nomen ejus: quod semper sanctum est, sanctificetur in nobis."

[4] Hence this Prayer is that we may keep the Second and Third Commandments; see above, pp. 82—84.

CHAPTER IV.

THE SECOND PETITION FOR GOD'S GLORY.

The Lord's Prayer.	The Explanation.
Thy Kingdom come.	*I desire my Lord God, who is the giver of all goodness, that He will send His grace unto me, and to all people...that we may serve Him...as we ought to do.*

1. **Connection.** Having in the previous petition prayed that the "Name of God," or that revelation of His Character and Attributes, which He has been pleased to make known to us, may be "hallowed," we are next taught to pray that His kingdom may come," or, as the petition is explained in the Catechism, that He will "send His grace to us and to all people, that we may *serve* Him as we ought to do."

2. **The Kingdom of God.** The expression *Kingdom of God*, or *Kingdom of Heaven*[1], is of frequent occurrence in the New Testament. Thus, when John the Baptist appeared on the banks of Jordan as the forerunner of the Saviour, his message to the multitudes who gathered round him was, *Repent ye, for the kingdom of heaven is at hand* (Mtt. iii. 2). Again, when our Lord commenced His public ministry, and *went about all Galilee teaching in the synagogues*, the theme of His preaching was the Glad Tidings *of the kingdom of heaven* (comp. Mtt. iv. 17, 23). When He

---

[1] The expression ἡ βασιλεία τῶν οὐρανῶν is peculiar to St Matthew, and was probably grounded on the prophecy of Daniel ii. 44, respecting the establishment of a Kingdom *by the God of heaven, which should never be destroyed.* Compare also Dan. vii. 13, 14, 27.

rose from the dead and *shewed Himself alive after His passion* to His Apostles, the great subject of His converse with them was *the things pertaining to the kingdom of God* (Acts i. 3). When He describes the scene of the last Judgment, He tells us He will say to those on His right hand, *Come, ye blessed of my Father, inherit the kingdom prepared for you from the foundation of the world* (Mtt. xxv. 34).

3. **The Kingdom of Grace.** The passages quoted illustrate some of the senses in which the expression is used. Sometimes it denotes the visible Church, or Kingdom of Grace (Eph. iii. 2), which the Baptist proclaimed as at hand, and which Christ established on earth (Heb. ii. 3, 4), and described in various parables its slight and despised beginning[1], its hidden, its mysterious working[2], and its final assured triumph[3]. In this sense the Kingdom of God has come, and we pray in the Lord's Prayer that it may be extended throughout the world[4], that *the earth may be filled with the knowledge of the glory of the Lord, as the waters cover the sea* (Hab. ii. 14), that its ministers may be

---

[1] In the Parable of the "Mustard Seed," Mtt. xiii. 31, 32; Mk. iv. 30—32; see Trench *On the Parables*, pp. 107, 108; Tristram's *Natural History of the Bible*, pp. 472, 473.

[2] In the parable of the "Hidden Leaven," Mtt. xiii. 33; Lk. xiii. 20, 21; Trench, p. 111; and of the "Seed growing secretly," Mk. iv. 26—29, the only Parable peculiar to St Mark, Trench, p. 282.

[3] "The 'Mustard Seed' and the 'Leaven' declare the victorious might,—the first, the *outward*, and the second, the *inward* might of the Kingdom; and therefore implicitly prophecy of its development in spite of all the obstacles set forth in the Parable of 'the Tares' (Mtt. xiii. 24—30), and its triumph over them." Trench, p. 142.

[4] In opposition to *the Kingdom of God* is *the Kingdom of Satan* (Mtt. xii. 26), with "its 'Principalities,' its 'Powers,' its 'World-rulers of darkness,' its 'Spiritual Hosts of evil in the heavenly regions.'" See Bp. Ellicott on Eph. vi. 12.

multiplied[1] (Mtt. ix. 37, 38), that all men being delivered from the power of darkness (Col. i. 13) may be won to its holy company, may serve God as they ought to do, and "having strength and steadfastness by His divine power, restraining corrupt and crooked affections, subduing and taming lusts, conquering, vanquishing, putting to flight, and chasing away all vices, may increase and enlarge His heavenly commonweal[2]."

4. **The Kingdom of God in the heart.** Again, the Kingdom of God sometimes denotes the personal rule of Christ in the hearts[3] of His followers, and is described as being *within us*[4] (Eph. ii. 22; iii. 17), as not consisting *in meat and drink*, but in *righteousness, and peace, and joy in the Holy Ghost* (Rom. xiv. 17). In reference to the Kingdom of God in this sense, we pray that we and all who profess and call themselves its subjects, may be so not in name[5], but in deed, not in pretence, but in reality; we pray that every member of His Church, in his vocation and ministry, may truly and

---

[1] "Christianity is very particularly to be considered as a *trust*, deposited with us in behalf of others, in behalf of mankind, as well as for our own instruction." See Bp. Butler's *Sermon for the Society for the Propagation of the Gospel*.

[2] Noell's *Catechism*, p. 195.

[3] Ἐντὸς ὑμῶν in Lk. xvii. 21 is better rendered *among you*, as in the margin of our Version. "*Intra*, non respectu cordis singulorum Pharisæorum (tametsi revera Christus habitat in corde suorum Eph. iii. 17) sed respectu totius populi Judaici." Bengel *in loc*.

[4] The Kingdom of God, as not merely a general but an *individual thing*, is set forth in the Parables of (*a*) *the Hid Treasure* (Mtt. xiii. 44), and (*b*) *the Pearl of great price* (Mtt. xiii. 45, 46), which were addressed, not to the multitude, but to the more immediate disciples. See Trench, p. 118.

[5] On the awful danger of having only a *name to live*, see Rev. iii. 1, and Archbp. Trench's Commentary, *Epistles to the Seven Churches*, p. 155; compare the Parable of the *Barren Fig-Tree* (Lk. xiii. 6—9).

godly serve Him[1], may eschew[2] those things that are contrary to their profession, and follow all such things as are agreeable to the same[3], to His honour and glory.

6. **The Kingdom of Glory.** Again, the Kingdom of God sometimes denotes not the Kingdom of Grace now established upon earth, and chequered and marred with sin and infirmity, but that perfect Kingdom of glory[4], which shall hereafter be established over and in this earth, when the present order of things shall be closed, and having *put down all rule and all authority and power*, Christ shall *deliver up the kingdom to God, even the Father* (1 Cor. xv. 24). Respecting this Kingdom[5], we pray that it may please God shortly to accomplish the number of His elect, and to hasten its coming[6], that the Kingdoms of the world may indeed become *the kingdoms of God and of His Christ* (Rev. xi. 15), that we, with all those who are departed this

---

[1] See the Collect for Good Friday. "Hoc desideras, hoc cupis orando, ut sic vivas, quomodo ad regnum Dei, quod est omnibus sanctis dandum, pertineas, ergo ut bene vivas, tibi oras, cum dicis, *Veniat regnum tuum.*" S. Aug. *de Serm. Dom.* LVI. 6. "Cum ergo dicimus, *Veniat regnum tuum*, oramus ut nobis veniat. Quid est, ut nobis veniat? Ut bonos nos inveniat. Hoc ergo oramus, ut bonos nos faciat; tunc enim nobis veniet regnum ejus." *De Serm. Dom.* LVIII. 3.

[2] *Eschew* (Job i. 1, 8; 1 Pet. iii. 11; Ps. xxxiv. 14) comes from the old Norman *eschiver*, Ital. *schivare* = to *flee from, shun, avoid*). *Bible Word-Book*, p. 182, and compare Cranmer's *Catechism*, p. 143, "to be swift and redye to do all thinges that maye please God, and to eschewe those things that maye displease Hym."

[3] See the Collect for the Third Sunday after Easter.

[4] See Mtt. xxv. 34; Eph. v. 27; and see above, p. 58.

[5] "Venturum est ipsum regnum, cum facta fuerit resurrectio mortuorum; tunc enim veniet ipse." *De Serm. Dom.* LVII. 5.

[6] See the Prayer in the Burial Service; Noell's *Catechism*, p. 196.

life in His true faith and fear, may see Him for ever and ever in His eternal and everlasting glory (Rev. xxii. 17, 20).

CHAPTER V.

THE THIRD PETITION FOR GOD'S GLORY.

The Lord's Prayer.	The Explanation.
Thy will be done in earth, as it is in heaven.	*I desire my Lord God, our heavenly Father, who is the giver of all goodness, to send His grace unto me and to all people, that we may ... obey Him, as we ought to do.*

1. **The Third Petition** in the Lord's Prayer is closely connected with the two preceding petitions[1]. For if God's Name is to be hallowed, and His Kingdom come, His will must be done and obeyed by us, even as our Lord Himself has warned us, saying, *Not every one that saith unto me, Lord, Lord, shall enter into the kingdom of heaven, but he that doeth the will of my Father which is in heaven* (Mtt. vii. 21).

2. **God's secret will.** Now the will of God sometimes denotes His secret will[2], or the secret Purpose, whereby He originally created and ever ordereth and determineth *all things in the army of heaven, and among the inhabitants of the earth, so that none can stay His hand, or say unto Him, What doest thou?* (Dan. iv. 35). But this will is hid from us; it is *unsearchable and past finding out* (Rom. xi. 33), and when we pray to God, *Thy will be done,* we pray that we may be enabled, after the example of His blessed Son[3], to

---

[1] The Third petition is wanting in the best MSS. of Lk. xi. 2. See Tischendorf's *Greek Test.*

[2] "Voluntas absoluta." See Denton *On the Lord's Prayer*, p. 104.

[3] Compare the Prayer of our Lord in the Garden of Gethsemane, *O my Father, if it be possible, let this cup pass*

resign ourselves cheerfully to whatever He may order for us, to humble ourselves *under His mighty hand* (1 Pet. v. 6), and receive and suffer whatever be His will concerning us, not only with contented, but also with gladsome hearts[1], remembering that all things are appointed and continued by infinite wisdom and goodness.

3. **God's Revealed Will.** But that which is mainly alluded to here[2] is the revealed will of God, made known to us by precepts and prohibitions of His written word, and *teaching us that, denying ungodliness and worldly lusts, we should live soberly, righteously, and godly in this present world* (Titus ii. 12), and also by the example[3] of our blessed Lord. For *as He who hath called us is holy*, so should we *be holy in all manner of conversation* (1 Pet. i. 15; 1 Thess. iv. 3).

4. **Thy will be done.** When, therefore, we pray *Thy will be done*, we pray for grace to enquire *what

from me; nevertheless, not my will, but thine be done (Mtt. xxvi. 39, and Lk. xxii. 42). To this same will Job also referred when he said, *the Lord gave, and the Lord hath taken away; blessed be the name of the Lord* (Job i. 21).

[1] Noell's *Catechism*, p. 197. "Resignation to the will of God is the whole of piety, it includes in it all that is good, and is a source of the most settled quiet and composure of mind ... it is a temper particularly suitable to our mortal condition, and what we should endeavour after for our own sakes in our passage through such a world as this, where there is nothing upon which we can rest or depend, nothing but what we are liable to be deceived and disappointed in." Bp. Butler, Serm. XIV, *Upon the Love of God;* see also his Sermon *On the Ignorance of Man.*

[2] Secker's *Lectures on the Catechism*, II. 174.

[3] See the Collect for the Second Sunday after Easter, where we pray that God, "Who hath given His only Son to be unto us both a sacrifice for sin, and also *an ensample of godly life*, will give us grace...to daily endeavour ourselves to follow the blessed steps of His most holy life."

the good, and acceptable, and perfect will of God is (Rom. xii. 2), and as His blessed Son came *not to do His own will, but the will of Him that sent Him*[1] (Jn. vi. 38), so we may make His will the rule of our actions, and His commandments[2] the rule of our lives. We pray also that He, who alone can "order the unruly wills and affections of sinful men[3]," will so "change and fashion our wills to the meaning and will of His majesty, that we may will or wish nothing, much less do anything that His Divine will misliketh[4]," but may obey Him in all things, as we ought to do.

5. **As it is in heaven.** Not only, however, are we to pray that God's will may be done by us on earth, but that it may be done in earth, *as it is in heaven*[5]. For the *heavens declare the glory of God, and the firmament showeth His handywork* (Ps. xix. 1), and *fire and hail, snow and vapours, wind and storm, fulfil His word* (Ps. cxlviii. 8). In heaven, moreover, God hath ordained and constituted the services of angels and archangels in a wonderful order[6]. In that blest abode they *do His commandments, hearkening unto the voice of His word* (Ps. ciii. 20), and render unto Him perfect, ready, willing, and constant service[7]. As, then, in heaven

---

[1] Comp. also Jn. iv. 34, *My meat is to do the will of Him that sent me, and to finish His work.*

[2] See Cranmer's *Catechism*, p. 150.

[3] See the Collect for the Fourth Sunday after Easter; and the conclusion of that for the First Sunday after Trinity.

[4] Noell's *Catechism*, p. 197. The petition, then, offered up is for the grace of perfect *obedience.*

[5] Γενηθήτω τὸ θέλημά Σου ὡς ἐν οὐρανῷ καὶ ἐπὶ γῆς (Mtt. vi. 10) = *Thy will be done, as in heaven, so on earth.* Some would refer the words *in earth as it is in heaven* to the three petitions which have gone before. See Bengel on Mtt. vi. 10; Denton, pp. 110, 111.

[6] See the Collect for Michaelmas Day.

[7] Comp. (1) Isai. vi. 2, 3; (2) Heb. i. 14; (3) Lk. i. 19, ii. 8—14; (4) Acts xii. 6—11.

there is perfect obedience, so we pray that in earth the same ready and willing service may be rendered by us, that here as there one will may be loved, and one will may be done[1].

CHAPTER VI.

THE FIRST PETITION FOR OUR OWN NEEDS.

THE LORD'S PRAYER.	THE EXPLANATION.
Give us this day our daily bread.	*I pray unto God, that He will send us all things that be needful both for our souls and bodies.*

1. **Connection with the preceding Petitions.** The first three Petitions of the Lord's Prayer relate, as we have seen, to the glory and sovereignty of God, and are therefore expressed in general and impersonal forms. The four remaining petitions relate to our own wants and our own daily necessities. Hence they are expressed in our own name as four personal entreaties. *Give* us *this day* our *daily bread; forgive* us *our trespasses; lead* us *not into temptation: deliver* us *from evil*[2].

2. **The life of the body.** Of our daily necessities the first and most obvious is the preservation of life[3],

---

[1] Respecting the plan and inner coherence of the Lord's Prayer, St Augustine observes of the first three petitions, that "God's Name, at His coming in the flesh, began to be hallowed; since then His kingdom has been ever coming, as it is in part come; hereafter it will be a perfected kingdom, at His Second Advent, from which time His will will be done here as perfectly as in heaven." Trench's *Sermon on the Mount*, from St Augustine, p. 108.

[2] See Denton *On the Lord's Prayer*, p. 123.

[3] " Restant petitiones pro ista vita peregrinationis nostræ: ideo sequitur, *Panem nostrum quotidianum da nobis hodie.* Da æterna, da temporalia. Promisisti regnum, noli negare

which depends on a due supply of food, and both on the good-will of our heavenly Father[1] (Ps. cxlv. 15, 16). Therefore our Lord has taught us to pray for bread, which *strengtheneth man's heart* (Ps. civ. 15), and is sometimes put for the whole sustenance of man, bodily food, clothing and shelter, and "all competent means and outward blessings, that shall be meet for our necessity, for our Christian and sober delight[2]."

Our daily bread. But He has bidden us pray not for our sustenance generally throughout our lives, but to say, *Give us this day* (Mtt. vi. 11), or *day by day* (Lk. xi. 3), the bread required for our subsistence[3].

subsidium. Dabis apud te sempiternum ornamentum, da in terra temporale alimentum." S. Augustine, *de Serm. Dom.* LVII. 7.

[1] "When we saye, Gyue us thys daye oure daylye breade, we praye to God, that as through His great mercye and goodnesse, He dydde create vs, so He wyl lykewise nouryshe and feade vs." Cranmer's *Catechism*, p. 155.

[2] Nicholson *On the Catechism*, p. 168. Compare the Church Catechism "all things that be needful for our bodies." "When we desyer God to gyue vs oure dayly breade, thynke not that our heauenly Father wyl gyue vs only a morsell of bread, and nothing besyde, but under the name of breade be all thynges conteyned, which be necessarie to the maintenance of our lyfe, as meate, drynke, apparell, house, landes, cattell, and moneye, according to the saynge of sainte Paule, God gyveth all thynge to our vse richely and aboundantly." Cranmer's *Catechism*, p. 158.

[3] Τὸν ἄρτον ἡμῶν τὸν ἐπιούσιον δὸς ἡμῖν σήμερον. The word ἐπιούσιον, which occurs nowhere else, has caused great difficulty. It is capable of two derivations, (i) from ἐπί and ἰέναι, (ii) from ἐπί and εἶναι.

i. If we derive it from ἐπί and ἰέναι, we must connect it with either (*a*) the feminine participle ἡ ἐπιοῦσα, sc. ἡμέρα = *give us this day our bread for to-morrow*, which would be direct contrary to the precept in Mk. vi. 34; or (*b*) the participle masculine ὁ ἐπιών, sc. χρόνος = "Give us this day, and every day to come, the bread which we need in the present and in the future," which it is difficult to explain side by side with σήμερον.

Hereby He teaches us moderation in our desires[1], and warns us against allowing ourselves in anxious and distracting cares about the morrow, which may not come, and making luxurious provision for the flesh and for its lusts. It is for bread, simple fare, He would have us pray, and that the bread of to-day[2].

4. **The life of the soul.** But man doth not, like the beasts that perish, *live by bread only* (Deut. viii. 3), nor is it his body only that requires to be sustained. There is the life of the soul also, and in this Prayer we pray unto God that He will send us all things that be needful for our souls as well as for our bodies[3]. Of the life of the soul Christ is the Sustainer. *I am the Bread of life*, He tell us; *he that cometh to me shall never hunger; and he that believeth on me shall never thirst* (Jn. vi. 35).

5. **Needs of the soul.** This spiritual life He supplies through the study of the revealed word of God,

---

ii. If we derive it from ἐπί and εἶναι, we must refer it either (*a*) directly to the participle, like παρουσία, μετουσία, or (*b*) to the substantive οὐσία, which = (1) *existence*, (2) *subsistence* (comp. Lk. xv. 12), and translate it *the bread of our existence*, or better, *the bread required for our subsistence*. See Tholuck's *Sermon on the Mount*, 341—353.

[1] See Prov. xxx. 8, 9; Mtt. vi. 34; 1 Tim. vi. 8; and above, p. 100. "Christ hath not taught vs to aske sustinaunce for fyfty or three score yeare, nor yet for one yeare, no nor for one moneth or weake, but He hath wylled us to aske our dayly breade; and He saieth, *Be not careful for to morowe, for to morow bringeth care enough of it selfe.*" Cranmer's *Catechism*, p. 186.

[2] "Impudentia est ut a Deo petas divitias: non est impudentia ut petas panem quotidianum. Aliud est unde superbias, aliud est unde vivas." August. *de Serm. Dom.* LVI. 10. "Pereat avaritia, et dives est natura." *Ib.* LVIII. 5.

[3] See the Catechism. "Quidquid animæ nostræ et carni nostræ in hac vita necessarium est, quotidiano pane concluditur." August. *de Serm. Dom.* VIII. 5.

which is *perfect, converting the soul, enlightening the eyes, a lamp unto the feet, and a light unto the path*[1] (Ps. xix. 7, 8; cxix. 105), through the steady use of the appointed means of grace[2], public and private prayer, and especially the reception of the Eucharist, wherein we "spiritually eat the flesh of Christ, and drink His Blood; we dwell in Christ, and Christ in us; we are one with Christ, and Christ with us[3]."

CHAPTER VII.

THE SECOND PETITION FOR OUR OWN NEEDS.

The Lord's Prayer.	The Explanation.
And forgive us our trespasses, As we forgive them that trespass against us.	*I pray unto God...that He will be merciful unto us, and forgive us our sins.*

1. **Connection.** Having prayed unto God to give us the food necessary for this life, we supplicate Him that with this He will bestow upon us this greater mercy, and forgive us our trespasses against Himself, the bountiful Giver of all good gifts.

2. **Trespasses.** A great variety of words, as we have already seen[4], are employed in Scripture to describe

---

[1] *Man doth not live by bread only, but by every word that proceedeth out of the mouth of God doth man live.* (Deut. viii. 3). *The words that I speak unto you, they are spirit and they are life* (Jn. vi. 63). Compare the Collect for the Second Sunday in Advent, "read, mark, learn, and *inwardly digest* them."

[2] "Quod vobis tracto, panis quotidianus est: et quod in Ecclesia lectiones quotidie auditis, panis quotidianus est: et quod hymnos auditis et dicitis, panis quotidianus est." August. *de Serm. Dom.* LVII. 7.

[3] Jn. vi. 47—65. See the Exhortation in the Ante-Communion Service, and the Second Prayer in the Post-Communion Service; and see Alford's note on Mtt. vi. 11.

[4] See above, pp. 61, 62, and the notes.

the state of sinfulness we inherit from our birth, and the offences we daily commit. Two of these occur in the Lord's Prayer. *Forgive us our debts*, we read in St Matthew[1]; *forgive us our sins*, we read in St Luke[2]; and when our Lord in the Sermon on the Mount repeats His precepts respecting forgiveness, He uses the word *trespasses*[3]. By the use of these words we confess not only that our nature is sinful, and that we come very far short of the obedience God expects of us, but that by our sins we have contracted *debts* which we are not able to pay, and by wandering from the narrow road, which leadeth unto life (Mtt. vii. 14), have *trespassed* into forbidden paths.

3. **Forgiveness.** But with this confession we join the prayer that God will be merciful unto us, and forgive us our sins, debts, and trespasses. The promise[4] of this forgiveness is, as we have seen, signed and sealed to us in Baptism, and God is ever ready to fulfil it, and to *cleanse us from all unrighteousness* (1 Jn. i. 9) for

---

[1] Mtt. vi. 12: Ἄφες ἡμῖν τὰ ὀφειλήματα ἡμῶν; see above, p. 62, n. 4; comp. 1 Cor. vi. 19 20; Rom. vi. 23.

[2] Lk. xi. 4: ἄφες ἡμῖν τὰς ἁμαρτίας ἡμῶν, the figure being taken from missing a mark or aim; see above, p. 61, n. 3.

[3] Ἐὰν ἀφῆτε τοῖς ἀνθρώποις τὰ παραπτώματα αὐτῶν, ἀφήσει καὶ ὑμῖν ὁ Πατὴρ ὑμῶν ὁ οὐράνιος, Mtt. vi. 14. The word παράπτωμα should have been added to those cited above, pp. 62, 63. It denotes (1) *a falling beside, falling from the right way.* Polybius, IX. 10. 6, uses it for *a blunder, a mistake in judgment;* and our translators have rendered it by (1) *fault* in Gal. vi. 1; Jas. v. 16; (2) *offence* in Rom. iv. 25; v. 15, 17, 18, 20; (3) *fall* in Rom. xi. 11, 12; (4) *trespass* in Mtt vi. 14, 15; Mk. xi. 25, 26; 2 Cor. v. 19; Eph. ii. 1; Col. ii. 13; (5) *sins* in Eph. ii. 5; Col. ii. 13.

[4] "Remissio peccatorum una est, quæ semel datur; alia, quæ quotidie datur. Remissio peccatorum una est, quæ semel datur in sancto Baptismate; alia, quæ quamdiu vivimus hic, datur in Dominicâ oratione." S. Aug. *de Serm. Dom.* LVIII. 6.

the sake of Jesus Christ our only Mediator and Intercessor.

4. **As we forgive.** But while our Lord teaches us to ask for forgiveness of our sins with as little doubt as for our daily bread, He adds to it a condition and proviso[1], of which we should never lose sight. *Forgive us our trespasses*, He teaches us to say[2], *As we forgive*[3] *them that trespass against us.* This condition He solemnly enforced, saying, *If ye forgive men their trespasses, your heavenly Father will also forgive you: but if ye forgive not men their trespasses, neither will your Father forgive you your trespasses*[4] (Mtt. vi. 14, 15). The stress which the Saviour lays upon it, ought to remind us of the supreme importance of cultivating a forgiving disposition, of being *kind one to another, tender-hearted, forgiving one another*[5], if we hope that *God, for Christ's sake, will forgive us* (Eph. iv. 31, 32).

---

[1] "Sponsionem facimus cum Deo, pactum et placitum. Hoc tibi dicit Dominus Deus tuus: *Dimitte, et dimitto—non dimisisti; tu contra te tenes, non ego.*" S. Aug. *de Serm. Dom.* LVI. 13.

[2] Ὡς καί = *like as we also*, implying in the two actions a similarity of kind, not a comparison of degree. We may forgive each other *a hundred pence*, but God forgives us *ten thousand talents*, Mtt. xviii. 23—34. See Trench *On the Parables*, p. 147, and the notes.

[3] Or rather *have forgiven*, ἀφήκαμεν, according to the better reading. Comp. Mtt. v. 23, 24. The forgiveness is supposed to be *completed before we approach* the throne of grace. Alford *in loc.*

[4] Compare also Mk. xi. 25, 26. *And when ye stand praying, forgive, if ye have ought against any: that your Father also which is in heaven may forgive you your trespasses: but if ye do not forgive, neither will your Father which is in heaven forgive your trespasses.* The same truth is set forth in the Parable of the "Unmerciful Servant," Mt. xviii. 23—35.

[5] And that *from our hearts*, ἀπὸ τῶν καρδιῶν, Mtt. xviii. 35. Comp. Col. iii. 12, 13.

"A forgiving spirit is absolutely necessary, if we hope for pardon of our own sins, if ever we hope for peace of mind in our dying moments, or for the Divine Mercy in that Day when we shall most stand in need for it[1]."

CHAPTER VIII.

THE THIRD PETITION FOR OUR OWN NEEDS.

The Lord's Prayer.	The Explanation.
And lead us not into temptation.	*I pray unto God that ... it will please Him to save and defend us in all dangers ghostly and bodily.*

1. **Connection.** Having prayed for present support, and for the forgiveness of past transgressions and of daily shortcomings, we proceed in the next petition to pray for future protection from the temptations of the world, the flesh, and the devil, the enemies, against which we have promised to fight manfully[2], but which are ever assailing us.

2. **Temptation.** The word temptation is used in Scripture in two senses, to denote (i) *trial* or *probation*, (ii) *seduction* or *ruin*[3]. In the first sense God is said to tempt, that is, to prove His children, either for the purpose of making trial of their faith, as in the case of Abraham (Gen. xxii. 1, 2); or of testing their patience, as in that of Job (Job i. 11, 12); or of humbling them, and of discovering what is in their hearts, as in the case

---

[1] Butler's Sermon *Upon forgiveness of Injuries.* Comp. Ecclus. xxviii. 1—4.

[2] See the Vow of Renunciation, above, pp. 10—12.

[3] Nicholson *On the Catechism*, p. 172. "Intelligimus duas esse tentationes, unam quæ decipit, alteram quæ probat: secundum eam quæ decipit, Deus neminem tentat: secundum eam quæ probat, tentat vos Dominus Deus vester, ut sciat si diligitis eum." St Augustine *in Evang. Joh.* Tract. XLIII.

of the Israelites (Deut. viii. 2; xiii. 3); or of checking self-conceit and showing the perfection of His grace, as in the case of St Paul (2 Cor. xii. 7, 9). In the second sense the word is specially applicable to the wiles and snares which the Devil[1] employs to pervert to evil what in itself is designed for good, and to draw men on to their destruction. Hence he is emphatically termed the Tempter[2] (1 Thess. iii. 5), and we read of his tempting Eve (Gen. iii. 1—5), David (1 Chr. xxi. 1), the Apostle Peter (Lk. xxii. 31), and especially our Lord Himself (Mtt. iv. 1—11).

3. **Lead us not into temptation.** In the Petition, therefore, *lead us not into temptation*[3], we do not simply and absolutely ask of God that we may be freed from temptation, for St James bids those, to whom he wrote, *count it all joy when they fell into divers temptations, knowing that the trying of their faith worked patience* (Jas. i. 2, 3). But we pray out of a deep sense of our own infirmity that we may not be brought into their power, as to be overcome by them[4]. We pray that even

---

[1] But he cannot tempt us without the permission of God, and then only through our own corrupted nature.

[2] See above, p. 11, and note.

[3] In Cranmer's *Catechism* the Petition runs, *and suffer us not to be led into temptation;* and in the French version of De Saci, *Et ne nous abandonnez point à la tentation*, or, as he renders it at the foot of the page, *Et ne nous laissez point succomber à la tentation.* See Cranmer's *Catechism*, p. 167; Denton *On the Lord's Prayer*, p. 162, n. St Augustine alludes to this reading of the Petition in numerous Latin MSS. *De Dono Persev.* c. VI. 12; Opp. Tom. X. p. 1401.

[4] Καὶ μὴ εἰσενέγκῃς ἡμᾶς εἰς πειρασμόν, Mtt. vi. 13. Comp. Mtt. xxvi. 41; where, "Intrare in tentationem, significat ita involvi illecebris aut periculis ut non extriceris." Grotius. "Temptatio semper est in medio: unde rogamus, non ut ne sit, sed ut ne nos ea tangat aut vincat." Bengel. Thus our Lord said to St Peter that Satan had desired to *sift* him and his fellow Apostles (ὑμᾶς, Lk. xxii. 31) *as wheat,* but that He had prayed for him, that his faith might

the trials sent for our improvement may not be too great (1 Cor. x. 13), that we may be approved not condemned by them[1]. We pray that in all the dangers ghostly and bodily, to which we may be exposed, we may not be without God's gracious help[2], that He "who knows us to be set in the midst of so many and great dangers, that by reason of the frailty of our nature we cannot always stand upright, will grant to us such strength and protection, as may support us in all dangers, and carry us through all temptations[3]."

4. **The Duty implied.** But if we would make this petition a reality instead of a mockery, we must attend to the Duty which it implies, of *maintaining a habit of humility, watchfulness, and prayer*. An absence of humility betrays us into self-confidence, and self-confidence, as in the instance of St Peter (Mtt. xxvi. 33—35), brings about many a fall. An absence of watchfulness exposes us to the wiles and snares of the Wicked One, and renders us ready victims to his assaults. An absence of prayer sends us to trial unprepared, and to battle without armour. *Watch and pray*, said the Saviour to the three Apostles in the Garden of Geth-

---

not *utterly fail* (ἐκλείπῃ, Lu. xxii. 32), that he might not be *completely* overcome.

[1] "Da ut per tentationes probemur, non reprobemur." Peter Abelard.

[2] The idea of such a petition for help in ghostly danger expressed in the Catechism is well brought out by St Augustine: "Pugna, pugna; quia qui te regeneraverit, Judex est; proposuit luctum, parat coronam. Sed quia sine dubio vinceris, si Illum adjutorem non habueris, si te deseruerit; ideo proponis in Oratione, *Ne nos inferas in tentationem.*" *De Serm. Dom.* LVII. 9. "Petimus ne deserti Ejus adjutorio alicui tentationi vel consentiamus decepti, vel cedamus afflicti." *Ep.* 130 *ad Probam*.

[3] See the Collect for the Fourth Sunday after Epiphany, and compare 2 Pet. ii. 9.

semane, *lest ye enter into temptation*[1]. And, lastly, if we would do as we would be done by, while avoiding all needless danger ourselves, we must be very careful that we do not lead others into temptation[2], and cause them to fall, when we ourselves have prayed that we may be enabled to stand.

CHAPTER IX.

THE FOURTH PETITION FOR OUR OWN NEEDS.

The Lord's Prayer.	The Explanation.
But deliver us from evil.	*And...I pray unto God... that He will keep us from all sin and wickedness, and from our ghostly Enemy, and from everlasting death.*

1. **Connection.** The last petition of the Lord's Prayer differs from the preceding one. Temptation, as we have seen, is not in itself necessarily evil, unless it prevails, and we are overcome by it; for it may prove the means of bringing out, and through the conflict, of strengthening what is good in men, to their everlasting gain. But there is evil around us in the world, and from it we pray that God would deliver and rescue[3] us.

---

[1] Mtt. xxvi. 41; Lk. xxii. 40. "Christ knew that hour in the Garden was a precious opportunity for laying in spiritual strength. He struggled and fought *then:* therefore there was no struggling afterwards—no trembling in the Judgment-hall—no shrinking on the Cross, but only dignified and calm victory; for He had fought the Temptation on his knees beforehand, and conquered all in the Garden. The battle of the Judgment-hall, the battle of the Cross, were already fought and over, in the Watch and in the Agony." Robertson's *Sermons,* II. 330.

[3] See Secker's *Lectures on the Catechism,* II. 210.

[2] 'Ρῦσαι ἡμᾶς ἀπὸ τοῦ πονηροῦ. 'Ρύεσθαι = (1) *to draw to oneself;* (2) *to draw out of danger, to rescue* (comp. Hom. *Od.* XII. 107; Eurip. *Orest.* 1563); (3) *to shade, screen, protect,*

2. **Evil.** The evil around us is of many kinds. (i) There is moral evil, sin, and wickedness, in the world[1] (1 Jn. v. 19), and in ourselves[2], for *out of the heart proceed evil thoughts, murders, adulteries, fornications, thefts, false-witness, blasphemies*[3] (Mtt. xv. 19). (ii) There is the original Author, and the constant Promoter of evil[4], the Evil One[5], our "ghostly[6] Enemy," whom we

used especially of (*a*) guardian deities, (Hom. *Il.* xv. 257, 290), of (*b*) princes and chiefs, (Hom. *Il.* IX. 396). Hence in the New Testament we find it applied to the *rescue of Lot from Sodom* (2 Pet. ii. 7); to the delivery of St Paul from *great trouble* (2 Cor. i. 10), from *persecutions* and *afflictions* (2 Tim. iii. 11), and from *imminent peril* (2 Tim. iv. 17, 18); to the delivery of mankind by Christ from *the power of darkness* (Col. i. 13), from *the wrath to come* (1 Thess. i. 10); to deliverance from *the hand of enemies* (Lk. i. 74), from *wicked men* (2 Thess. iii. 2), from *temptations* (2 Pet. ii. 9). The title ὁ ῥυόμενος = the *Deliverer* is specially applied to Christ, Rom. xi. 26.

[1] See above, pp. 11, 12.
[2] Hence St Augustine observes that the Petition is for deliverance from ourselves: "Libera me ab homine malo, a me ipso." Serm. XLIV. 3.
[3] Comp. Ps. xix. 12; Jer. xvii. 9; Gal. v. 19—21.
[4] See above, p. 11.
[5] Hence some would translate the petition, *deliver us from the Evil One.* The title ὁ πονηρός, *the Evil* or *Wicked One,* is applied to the Tempter by our Lord in Mtt. xiii. 19, *then cometh the Wicked One;* in Mtt. xiii. 39, *the children of the Wicked One;* in Jn. xvii. 15, *I pray not that Thou shouldest take them out of the world, but that Thou shouldest keep them from the Evil One;* by St Paul, Eph. vi. 6, *the fiery darts of the Wicked One;* by St John, *ye have overcome the Wicked One* (1 Jn. ii. 13, 14); *Cain was of the Wicked One* (1 Jn. iii. 12); *the Wicked One toucheth them not* (1 Jn. v. 18).
[6] From the Anglo-Saxon gástlíc = *spiritual.* Compare Latimer's *Sermons,* p. 66, "For as the body wasteth and consumeth away for lack of bodily meat, so doth the soul pine away for default of *ghostly* meat." Compare also Shakespeare, *Rom. and Jul.* II. 2.
  Hence will I to my *ghostly* father's cell.
Bible Word-Book, 225.

have promised to renounce, but who is powerful and ever seeking *to get an advantage of us* (2 Cor. ii. 11; 1 Pet. v. 8). (iii) There are the wages, or consequences of evil, and of yielding to the seductions of the Evil One, everlasting death (Rom. vi. 23).

3. **Deliver us from evil.** Thus set in the midst of many and great dangers, and having no power of ourselves to help ourselves[1], we pray to God, who is a most strong Tower to all them that put their trust in Him, to stretch forth His right hand, and save and defend us from the power of evil in the world and in ourselves (Rom. vii. 24), from the crafts and assaults of the Devil[2], and from the evil that follows these, eternal death. We pray that God will not withdraw His grace from us, or leave us to ourselves, to our own counsels and lusts, but will "raise up His power, and come among us, and with great might succour us[3]," that we may be enabled to withstand the temptations of the world, the flesh and the devil, and with pure hearts and minds to follow Him the only God[4], and to obey His blessed will.

4. **Victory.** In effect, therefore, the Petition is not merely for deliverance from evil, but to have power and strength to have victory and to triumph[5] against the enemies we promised at our Baptism to renounce; to have grace to endure[6] (Rev. ii. 3), to persevere unto

---

[1] See the Collect for the Second Sunday in Lent.

[2] See the Prayer in the Litany, and the Prayer in the Burial Service.

[3] See the Collect for the Fourth Sunday in Advent.

[4] See the Collect for the Eighteenth Sunday after Trinity.

[5] See the Baptismal Service.

[6] Ὑπομενεῖν. Ὑπομονή, *patience*, as we have rendered it, is not so much *patientia* as *perseverantia*, "a beautiful word, expressing the *brave* and persistent endurance of the Christian; βασιλὶς τῶν ἀρετῶν, as Chrysostom does not fear to call it." Trench, *Epistles to the Seven Churches in Asia*, p. 20.

the end, and to overcome, remembering what glorious promises are held out to *him that overcometh*[1] in this life-long battle (Rev. ii. 7).

CHAPTER X.
THE DOXOLOGY.

Close of the Lord's Prayer.	Close of the Explanation in the Catechism.
For Thine is the Kingdom, the Power, and the Glory, for ever and ever. Amen.	*And this I trust He will do of His mercy and goodness, through our Lord Jesus Christ. And therefore I say, Amen, so be it.*

1. **The Doxology**, as has been already remarked[2], does not occur in St Luke's Gospel, it is absent from some MSS. of St Matthew[3], and is not given or explained in the Catechism[4], which closes its explanation of what we desire of God in the Lord's Prayer, with the expression of a confident hope that He will of His mercy and goodness, through our Lord Jesus Christ, do for us what we ask of Him. As, however,

---

[1] Comp. Rev. ii. 11, 17, 26; iii. 5, 12, 21; xii. 11; xxi. 7. The use of νικᾶν, as expressive of moral victory over sin and temptation, while it occurs in Rom. xii. 21, is of frequent occurrence in St John, and "constitutes an interesting point of contact between the language of the Apocalypse and of his Gospel and his Epistles:" comp. Jn. xvi. 33; 1 Ep. ii. 13, 14; v. 4, 5. Trench, *Epistles*, pp. 90, 91.

[2] See above, p. 107.

[3] It does not occur in Wiclif's version of Mtt. vi. 13.

[4] It is wanting also in Cranmer's, but is given and explained in Noell's *Catechism*, where it is called "Dominicæ precationis appendix quædam." It was not added to the Lord's Prayer in the Prayer Book till the year A.D. 1661, when it was directed to be used at the beginning of Morning and Evening Service and in the Post-Communion Service. See Procter *On the Book of Common Prayer*, p. 212.

ascriptions of praise are a suitable conclusion of all prayers, and are warranted by Holy Scripture[1], and since this Doxology expresses several attributes of God, which are "so many props to our faith, so many assurances that we shall be heard[2]," it may be well to take note of them.

2. **For Thine is the Kingdom.** We express, then, in this Doxology our trust that God will do for us what we ask, because to Him belongs *the Kingdom, the Power, and the Glory, for ever and ever.* When we thus assert that to God belongs the Kingdom, we mean that to Him belongs the Dominion over all creation[3], and that though there is a kingdom of Satan[4], and divers kingdoms of men, yet *the Kingdom* belongeth to Him, that He is *exalted as Head over all* (1 Chr. xxix. 11), and is the *blessed and only Potentate, the King of kings, and Lord of lords* (1 Tim. vi. 15).

3. **And the Power.** The second reason why we trust that our Petitions will be heard, is because to God belongs not only the Right but *the Power* to do as seemeth Him fit. As we express it in the Creed, He is Omnipotent[5]; He can do all things, *and none can stay His hand, or say unto Him, What doest Thou?* (Dan. iv. 35); He is all-sufficient, the Source of all strength and might. But not only does He by His never-failing Providence order all things both in heaven and earth[6], but He declares His Almighty power most

---

[1] See 1 Chron. xxix. 11. *Thine, O Lord, is the Greatness, and the Power, and the Glory, and the Victory, and the Majesty; all that is in the heaven and in the earth is Thine; Thine is the Kingdom, O Lord, and Thou art exalted as Head above all;* and compare 1 Tim. i. 17; Jude 25; Rev. iv. 11; v. 13.

[2] Nicholson *On the Catechism*, p. 175.

[3] See Ps. xxii. 28; xcv. 3; ciii. 19; Dan. iv. 25.

[4] See above, p. 115, n.

[5] See above, p. 21.

[6] Collect for the Eighth Sunday after Trinity.

chiefly in showing mercy and pity[1], He is *able to do exceeding abundantly above all that we ask or think* (Eph. iii. 20), and is always more ready to hear than we to pray, and wont to give more than either we desire or deserve[2]. On Him, therefore, to whom *the Power* belongeth, and from whom all other powers are derived, we may well depend, to help us in the hour of need.

4. **And the Glory.** Moreover, as the *blessed and only Potentate, the King of kings and Lord of lords,* and the Source of all power and might, to Him belong *the Glory and the Majesty* (1 Chr. xxix. 11), and to Him are due *the Honour and the Praise* from every order of created beings. *Glory to God in the highest* was part of the Angels' Song at the Incarnation of our blessed Lord (Lk. ii. 14). *Father, glorify Thy Name,* was one of His prayers on earth (Jn. xii. 28). *Glory, honour, and thanks to the Lord God Almighty,* is the perpetual ascription of *ten thousand times ten thousand and thousands of thousands* of the hierarchy of heaven (Rev. iv. 3—11; v. 11—14). "When, therefore, we put God in mind of His glory, we have little cause to doubt of audience[3]," for we make mention of that which He loves, and which *He will not give to another* (Isai. xlii. 8), and we need not fear, if it be for His glory, but that our request shall be granted.

5. **For ever and ever.** Moreover, the Kingdom, the Power, and the Glory belong to Him *for ever and ever. His kingdom is an everlasting kingdom, and His dominion endureth throughout all generations* (Ps. cxlv. 13); *before the mountains were brought forth, or ever the earth and the world were made, He*

---

[1] Collect for the Eleventh Sunday after Trinity.
[2] Collect for the Twelfth Sunday after Trinity.
[3] Nicholson *On the Catechism*, p. 177; Noell's *Catechism*, pp. 204, 205.

is God from everlasting, and world without end[1] (Ps. xc. 2). As, therefore, He changeth not, and with Him *is no variableness, neither shadow of turning* (Jas. i. 17), as He is *the same yesterday, to-day, and for ever* (Heb. xiii. 8); ever a King, and so ready to help His subjects; ever a Potentate, and so able to do that which seemeth Him right; we may trust that what we have heard with our ears, and our fathers have declared unto us, of the noble works that He did in their days, and in the old time before them[2], our heavenly Father will do also for us, "if not always according to our wish, will, and desire[3]," yet as it shall promote our salvation and His glory (Rom. viii. 32, 38, 39).

6. **Amen.** Therefore we say at the close of the Lord's Prayer, *Amen*[4], which expresses not only *So be it*, but also *So it is*[5]. As *So be it*, it denotes our own hope and trust that God will of His mercy and goodness do for us according to our petitions[6]. As *So it is*,

---

[1] The Prayer-Book Version.

[2] Ps. liv. 1, and compare the clause in the Litany.

[3] Nicholson *On the Catechism*, p. 179.

[4] Amen literally =*firm, true,* and, as a substantive, *that which is true, truth.* It "was the proper response of the person to whom an oath was administered (1 Chr. xvi. 36; Neh. v. 13; viii. 6); and the Deity, to whom appeal is made on such occasions, is called the God of *Amen* (Isai. lxv. 16), as being a witness to the sincerity of the implied compact." Compare its use in (i) Deut. xxvii. 15—26; (ii) 2 Cor. i. 20; (iii) Rev. iii. 14. Smith's *Bibl. Dict.*

[5] "Fratres mei, Amen vestrum subscriptio vestra est, consentio vestra est, adstipulatio vestra est." S. Augustin. *Serm. Dom.* LVII.

[6] "And this the Lorde's Prayer we must ever ende with this worde *Amen*. Whiche is asmuche to say, *as surely I trust it shall be so.* And it is not ynough to say *Amen* with our tongue onely, but also *Amen* must be in our harte, and continew and tarry there, that is to saye, we ought to believe suerly and constantlye that our prayer is hearde, and that our heauvenly Father wyll grant vs our petitions." Cranmer's *Catechism*, p. 180.

it expresses our faith, our full assurance, and confidence that the attributes ascribed really belong to Him, that as He is the *Amen, the faithful and true* (Rev. iii. 14), He will also do according to that He hath promised (1 Thess. v. 24).

PART V.

THE SACRAMENTS.

How many Sacraments hath Christ ordained in his Church?—*Two only, as generally necessary to salvation, that is to say, Baptism, and the Supper of the Lord.*

What meanest thou by this word *Sacrament?*—*I mean an outward and visible sign of an inward and spiritual grace given unto us, ordained by Christ himself, as a means whereby we receive the same, and a pledge to assure us thereof.*

How many parts are there in a Sacrament?—*Two; the outward visible sign, and the inward spiritual grace.*

What is the outward visible sign or form in Baptism?—*Water; wherein the person is baptized In the Name of the Father, and of the Son, and of the Holy Ghost.*

What is the inward and spiritual grace?—*A death unto sin, and a new birth unto righteousness: for being by nature born in sin, and the children of wrath, we are hereby made the children of grace.*

What is required of persons to be baptized?—*Repentance, whereby they forsake sin; and Faith, whereby they stedfastly believe the promises of God made to them in that Sacrament.*

Why then are Infants baptized, when by reason of their tender age they cannot perform them?—*Because they promise them both by their Sureties; which promise, when they come to age, themselves are bound to perform.*

Why was the Sacrament of the Lord's Supper ordained?—*For the continual remembrance of the sacrifice of the death of Christ, and of the benefits which we receive thereby.*

What is the outward part or sign of the Lord's Supper?—*Bread and Wine, which the Lord hath commanded to be received.*

What is the inward part, or thing signified?—*The Body and Blood of Christ, which are verily and indeed taken and received by the faithful in the Lord's Supper.*

What are the benefits whereof we are partakers thereby?— *The strengthening and refreshing of our souls by the Body and Blood of Christ, as our bodies are by the Bread and Wine.*

What is required of them who come to the Lord's Supper? —*To examine themselves, whether they repent them truly of their former sins, stedfastly purposing to lead a new life; have a lively faith in God's mercy through Christ, with a thankful remembrance of his death; and be in charity with all men.*

SECTION I.

The Number and Nature of the Sacraments.

CHAPTER I.

NUMBER OF THE SACRAMENTS.

1. **Connection.** Having treated of the Creed, the Ten Commandments, and the Lord's Prayer, the Catechism proceeds to speak of the Sacraments, whereby God doth "present, exhibit, and seal[1]" to us the blessed effects of the Redemption wrought for us men by His Only-begotten Son.

2. **Number of the Sacraments.** Its first question, therefore, relates to the *number* of the Sacraments ordained by Christ in His Church. And it teaches us to say that He ordained *two only*[2] *as generally neces-*

---

[1] Nicholson *On the Catechism*, pp. 182, 188.

[2] See Article XXV. The Church of Rome holds that there are five other Ordinances, which may be called Sacraments, "that is to say, *Confirmation, Penance, Orders, Matrimony,* and *Extreme Unction.*" These, however, "have grown partly of the corrupt following of the Apostles, partly are states of life allowed in the Scriptures; but yet have not like nature of Sacraments with Baptism and the Lord's Supper, for that they have not any visible sign or ceremony ordained of God."

sary to salvation, that is to say, Baptism, and the Supper of the Lord.

3. **Proved from the Gospels.** That our blessed Lord ordained but two Sacraments is clear from the Gospel narrative. There we find that shortly before He ascended up to heaven He bade His Apostles *Go, and make disciples of all nations, baptizing them into the Name of the Father, and of the Son, and of the Holy Ghost* (Mtt. xxviii. 19). There too we find that on the same night that He was betrayed[1], at a Paschal[2] Feast, He took Bread; and when He had given thanks, He brake it, and gave it to His disciples, saying, *Take, eat; This is my Body which is given for you: Do this in remembrance of Me.* Likewise He took the Cup, and when He had given thanks, He gave it to them, saying, *Drink ye all of this; for this Cup is my Blood of the New Testament, which is shed for you and for many for the remission of sins: Do this, as oft as ye shall drink it, in remembrance of Me* (Mtt. xxvi. 26—28).

4. **Generally necessary to Salvation.** These two Sacraments, and these two only[3], did He ordain as

---

[1] See the Prayer of Consecration in the Communion Office.

[2] On the vexed and extremely difficult question whether the meal of which the Saviour now partook was (1) the Passover, or (2) an anticipation of it, see Ebrard's *Gospel History*, pp. 395—405; Lange's *Life of Christ*, IV. 158—271; the Article Passover in Smith's *Bib. Dict.*, and Bp. Ellicott's *Hulsean Lectures*, p. 322.

[3] As there were in the Jewish Church two Ordinances, Circumcision, whereby the Jew was admitted into the old covenant, and the Passover, wherein he commemorated the deliverance of his nation from Egyptian bondage, so did Christ ordain two Sacraments, Baptism, whereby we have our admission and entrance into the Church, and the Lord's Supper, wherein we commemorate His Redemption of the whole world. See Hooker, *Eccl. Pol.* v. lxvii.

generally necessary to salvation, that is to say, as necessary for men in general, for the race of man taken as a whole, bidding His Apostles *go into all the world* (Mk. xvi. 15), *make disciples of and baptize all nations*[1] (Mtt. xxviii. 19), and enjoining them, wherever they went, to celebrate the Lord's Supper *in remembrance of Him*[2] (Lk. xxii. 19; 1 Cor. xi. 24, 25).

[1] Compare the exhortation in the Baptismal Service; "Forasmuch as *all men* are conceived and born in sin; and that our Saviour Christ saith, *None* can enter into the kingdom of God, except he be regenerated and born anew of water and of the Holy Ghost."

[2] The Latin of this answer in the Catechism, "Duo tantum, quæ quidem *in genere* necessaria sint ad salutem consequendam," is a key to its meaning. The expression *in genere* clearly points to the *race* (genus) of mankind. For the use of "generally" as = "universally" compare

    (a) *Therefore I counsel that all Israel be* GENERALLY *gathered unto thee, from Dan even to Beersheba*, 2 Sam. xvii. 11; here the LXX has πᾶς 'Ισραήλ, and the Vulgate *universus Israel*.

    (b) *There shall be lamentation* GENERALLY *upon all the housetops of Moab*, Jer. xlviii. 38; here the LXX has ἐπὶ πάντων τῶν δωμάτων Μωάβ, and the Vulgate *super omnia tecta Moab*.

    (c) *This kingdom* IN GENERAL, in the Prayer for the High Court of Parliament, where the Latin is *pro hoc regno universo*.

    (d) *The General Thanksgiving* in the Morning and Evening Service, where the Latin is *Gratiarum actio generalis*.

    (e) "Then shall this *General Confession* be made, in the name of *all those* that are minded to receive the Holy Communion." See *The Communion Service*.

    (f) *We must receive God's promises in such wise as they be* GENERALLY *set forth to us in Holy Scripture*, Art. XVII., where *generally* is the translation not of *plerumque* but of *generaliter*, i. e. to Christians as a class, genus, *collectively*, not *individually*.

    (g) "*The promises of Christ are* GENERAL, *they pertain to all mankind*." Latimer's *Sermon on the Parable of the King's Son*.

CHAPTER II.

NATURE OF A SACRAMENT.

1. **Connection.** Having stated the number of the Sacraments ordained by Christ Himself, the Catechism proceeds to enquire the meaning of the word Sacrament itself.

2. **Classical usage.** The word "Sacrament" comes from the Latin Sacramentum, which denotes (1) *The sum of money that the parties to a suit deposited with the judge, as a* SIGN *or* PLEDGE *that they would proceed with the trial*[1]; (ii) *The* OATH, *whereby the newly enlisted soldier bound himself to obey his commander*[2].

3. **Ecclesiastical usage.** The earliest application of the word to anything Christian occurs in the celebrated letter of Pliny the younger to the emperor Trajan, where he says of the Christians, that "they were wont to meet on a certain fixed day before sunrise, to sing hymns to Christ as to God, and to bind themselves

---

(h) *From all these coasts,* IN GENERAL, *full fifty sail were sent.* Chapman's *Homer,* II. 439.
See Blunt's *Annotated Book of Common Prayer,* p. 249, n. The *Bible Word-Book,* p. 223.

[1] Probably because the money was deposited in a sacred place. See Cic. *in Verrem,* II. i. 9. 26.

[2] Comp. Cæsar, *B. C.* I. 23. 5, and the phrases milites *sacramento* rogare, Cæsar, *B. G.* VI. 1; milites *sacramento* adigere, Liv. VII. 11; aliquem *sacramento* tenere, Cæsar, *B. C.* II. 32. 9. Hence it came to mean *a solemn engagement* generally; comp. Hor. *Od.* II. xvii. 10, Non ego perfidum dixi *sacramentum:* ibimus, ibimus. Petr. LXXX. 4. Amicitiæ *sacramentum* delevi.

by a sacrament not to commit any sort of wickedness[1]." Tertullian again, speaking of the Christian's baptismal vow, says that "he is called to the warfare of the living God, and makes answer to the words of *the Sacrament*[2]." More commonly, however, it was used as the Latin translation[3] of the Greek word Μυστήριον, *a Mystery*[4], and denoted "anything whereby an holy thing is signified[5]," and so could be used (i) generally of any sacred rite of the Church, or (ii) specially of some particular sacred ordinance.

4. **Defined in the Catechism.** In this higher and more special signification the word Sacrament is used in the Catechism, and is defined to be *an outward and visible sign*[6] *of an inward and spiritual grace given unto us, ordained by Christ Himself, as a means*

---

[1] "Affirmabant autem hanc fuisse summam vel culpæ suæ, vel erroris, quod essent soliti, stato die, ante lucem convenire, carmenque Christo quasi Deo dicere; seque *sacramento* non in scelus aliquod obstringere, sed ne furta, ne latrocinia, ne adulteria committerent, ne fidem fallerent, ne depositum appellati abnegarent." Plin. *Epist.* XCVII.

[2] Tertullian *ad Mart.* 3. See Bp. Browne *On the Articles*, p. 577, n.

[3] Thus Tertullian *de Jejuniis*, cap. III., translates μέγα μυστήριον in Eph. v. 2, by *magnum sacramentum*.

[4] Μυστήριον = (i) *a religious mystery*, like those of Eleusis, into which men were initiated; (ii) *a secret* (comp. Mtt. xiii. 11; 1 Cor. xv. 51; Rev. xvi. 25); (iii) a *symbolic representation* or *emblem* (comp. Rev. xvii. 5, 7). For the use of *Mystery* as applied to the Lord's Supper, see the Exhortation in the Communion Office, and Noell's *Catechism*.

[5] "Sacramentum, id est sacrum signum." S. Aug. *de Civ. Dei*, x. 5; and see the Homily on *Common Prayer and Sacraments*.

[6] "As for the number of these, if they should be considered according to the exact signification of a Sacrament, namely, for the visible signs, expressly commanded in the New Testament, whereunto is annexed the promise of free forgiveness of our sin, and of our holiness and joining in Christ, there be but two; namely, Baptism, and the Supper of the Lord." See the Homily of *Common Prayer and Sacraments*.

whereby we receive the same, and a pledge to assure us thereof[1].

5. Essentials of a Sacrament. To the constitution then of a Sacrament, it is essential

(i) That there be an outward and visible sign of an inward and spiritual grace given unto us; and that

(ii) This outward and visible sign should have been ordained by Christ Himself, as (1) a *means* whereby we receive that spiritual grace, and (2) a *pledge* to assure us thereof[2].

CHAPTER III.
THE PARTS OF A SACRAMENT.

1. **Connection.** In a Sacrament, then, there are two parts, *the outward and visible sign*, and *the inward and spiritual grace*.

2. **The outward visible sign.** The first part is the outward and visible sign, which is sometimes called the "matter[3]," and sometimes the "element[4]," that is, the material used in the Sacrament.

---

[1] "This definition does not exclude Confirmation, Penance, Orders, Matrimony, from being *in some sense* Sacraments; but it excludes them from being such Sacraments as Baptism and the Lord's Supper. No other ordinances but Baptism and Communion have an express sign ordained by Christ Himself, and annexed thereat the promise of free forgiveness of sins, and of inward and spiritual grace given unto us." Bp. Browne *On the Articles*, p. 582.

[2] Compare the Definition of a Sacrament in Noell's *Catechism;* and see Hooker, *Eccl. Pol.* v. lviii. 2.

[3] Compare the question *With what* MATTER *was this Child baptized?* in the Office of Private Baptism of Children.

[4] Compare the first prayer in the Office for Adult Baptism; and Noell's *Catechism.*

"*M.* Of how many parts consisteth a Sacrament?

"*S.* Of two parts: *the outward element*, or visible sign, and invisible grace."

3. **Use of material things as signs and pledges.**
In all ages God, who knoweth *whereof we are made* (Ps. ciii. 14), "that we are not endued with mind and understanding so heavenly and divine, that His graces do appear clearly of themselves to us, as it were to angels[1]," has condescended to use material things as *signs and pledges*. Thus:—

> (1) *The Rainbow* was a sign and pledge to Noah that the world should no more be destroyed by a flood (Gen. ix. 13—15).
>
> (2) *Circumcision* was a sign and pledge to Abraham of the Covenant betwixt himself and God (Gen. xvii. 11; Rom. iv. 11).
>
> (3) *The miracles* Moses was to perform before Pharaoh were signs and pledges of his divine mission (Ex. iv. 1—9).
>
> (4) *The Fleece*, wet while all the ground around was dry, dry while the ground was wet, was a sign and pledge to Gideon that the Lord would give him victory in the battle against the Midianites (Judg. vi. 36—40).
>
> (5) *The return of the shadow* ten degrees on the sun-dial of Ahaz was a sign and pledge to Hezekiah that the Lord would have mercy upon him (2 Kings xx. 8—11).

4. **Use of material things as supernatural means.** But God has condescended to use material things, not only as signs and pledges, but also as *supernatural means* of grace[2]. Thus

> (1) When the Israelites were dying from the bites of the fiery serpents, He bade Moses

---

[1] Noell's *Catechism;* and comp. Hooker, *Eccl. Pol.* v. lvii. 2.

[2] See *The Catechist's Manual*, p. 223.

set up a brazen serpent on a pole, *and it came to pass, that if a serpent had bitten any man, when he beheld the serpent of brass, he lived* (Num. xxi. 6—9).

(2) When Naaman, afflicted with leprosy, came to Elisha, he was bidden to go and dip himself seven times in the Jordan, and he went *according to the saying of the man of God, and his flesh came again like unto the flesh of a little child, and he was clean* (2 Kings v. 14).

(3) When our Lord was upon earth He saw a man blind from his birth, *and He spat on the ground, and made clay of the spittle, and He anointed the eyes of the blind man with the clay,* and bade him *Go, wash in the pool of Siloam, and he went, and washed, and came seeing* (Jn. ix. 1—7);

(4) Again, when one that was deaf and had an impediment in his speech was brought to Him, *He took him aside from the multitude, and put His fingers into his ears, and He spit, and touched his tongue, and looking up to heaven, He sighed, and saith unto him, Ephphatha, that is, Be opened; and straightway his ears were opened, and the string of his tongue was loosed, and he spake plain* (Mk. vii. 33—35).

5. **Use in the Sacraments.** Now in the two great Sacraments of the Gospel these three methods of using material things are combined[1]. For

(1) They are outward and visible *signs* of inward and spiritual grace;

---

[1] See *The Catechist's Manual*, p. 225.

(2) They are *pledges* of God's love[1], and of His willingness to confer grace upon us;

(3) They are appointed *means*, whereby He imparts grace to all faithful recipients.

SECTION II.

The Sacrament of Baptism.

CHAPTER I.

THE OUTWARD SIGN IN BAPTISM.

1. **Connection.** Of the two Sacraments, then, ordained by Christ in His Church, the first is Baptism, and its outward and visible sign and form is *Water, wherein the person is baptized, In the Name of the Father, and of the Son, and of the Holy Ghost.*

2. **The Use of Water** for ceremonial purification has been familiar to all nations from the earliest times. With the Egyptians[2], the Greeks[3], and the Romans,

---

[1] "He hath instituted and ordained holy mysteries as *pledges of His love;*" Exhortation in the Communion Service, and compare the xxvth Article, "Sacraments ordained of Christ be not only badges or tokens of Christian men's profession: but rather they be
 (1) Certain sure witnesses (*testimonia*) and effectual signs (*efficacia signa*) of grace and God's good will towards us.
 (2) By the which He doth work invisibly in us, and doth not only quicken, but also strengthen and confirm our faith in Him."

[2] Herodotus tells us that the Egyptian priests bathed twice in the day and twice in the night to fit them for their sacred functions. Hdt. II. 37. Compare the ceremonies of the Greeks at the Eleusinian Mysteries. Smith's *Dict. Antiq.* p. 453, b.

[3] Compare Hom. *Od.* IV. 758—761:
ἣ δ' ὑδρηναμένη, καθαρὰ χροΐ εἵμαθ' ἑλοῦσα,

solemn ablutions formed a necessary preliminary to all acts of devotion, especially prayer[1] and sacrifice[2], and were essential to the removal of all ceremonial pollution[3], and of the guilt of homicide[4], whether accidental or intentional.

3. **Amongst the Jews** similar lustrations were equally frequent. When Jacob was returning with his family to Bethel, he *said unto his household and to all that were with him, Put away the strange gods that are among you, and be clean, and change your garments* (Gen. xxxv. 2). When the Lord was about to deliver the Law on Sinai, He commanded Moses to sanctify the people, and to *let them wash their clothes* (Ex. xix. 10). Before the passage of the Jordan, Joshua bade the people *sanctify themselves*, for on the morrow the Lord would do wonders among them (Josh. iii. 5). When Aaron and his sons were consecrated to their office, they were brought to the door of the Tabernacle, and *washed with water*, and whenever they entered the sanctuary they were directed *to wash their hands*

εἰς ὑπερῷ' ἀνέβαινε σὺν ἀμφιπόλοισι γυναιξίν,
ἐν δ' ἔθετ' οὐλοχύτας κανέῳ, ἠρᾶτο δ' Ἀθήνῃ.

[1] Ov. *Fast.* v. 679:
Spargit et ipse suos lauro rorante capillos,
Et peragit solita fallere voce *preces.*
Pers. *Sat.* II. 15:
Hoc *sancte ut poscas*, Tiberino in gurgite mergis
Mane caput bis terque, et noctem flumine purgas.

[2] Eo lavatum, ut *sacrificem*. Plaut. *Aulular.* III. 6. 43; Cic. *de Legibus*, II. x. 23.

[3] Comp.
Me, bello e tanto digressum et cæde recenti,
Attrectare nefas, *donec me flumine vivo*
Abluero. Virg. *Æn.* II. 718.
Dic corpus properet *fluviali spargere lympha*,
Et pecudes secum et *monstrata piacula* ducat.
Virg. *Æn.* IV. 635.

[4] Compare Soph. *Ajax*, 654—656.

and their feet, that they died not[1] (Ex. xxx. 19, 20). When Solomon built the Temple, he made ten lavers *to wash such things as they offered for the burnt-offering,* and a molten Sea[2] *for the priests to wash in* (2 Chron. iv. 6).

4. **Baptism of Proselytes.** At a later period these *divers washings* (Heb. ix. 10) were considerably multiplied. They preceded all great religious observances[3]; they accompanied all meals (Mk. vii. 3) and many of the most ordinary avocations of daily life[4]. Moreover by Baptism, together with circumcision and sacrifice, all Israelites were admitted into covenant with God, and whenever a Gentile proselyte desired to enter into the covenant of Israel, and to take the yoke of the law upon him, Baptism was one of the necessary ceremonies, so that it was a common axiom, *No man is a proselyte until he be circumcised and baptized*[5].

5. **The Baptism of John.** Hence, when John the Baptist, who came to prepare the way of the Lord and

---

[1] Comp. also Ex. xl. 30—32. The Law directed the purification by water of all ceremonial pollutions, as (*a*) touching a dead body (Lev. xxii. 46), or that which died of itself (Lev. xvii. 15); (*b*) the burning of the skin of the bullock used in the sin-offering (Lev. xvi. 27); (*c*) the release of the scape-goat (Lev. xvi. 26).

[2] See *Class-Book of O. T. History,* pp. 377, 378.

[3] Comp. Jn. xi. 55, *And the Jews' Passover was nigh at hand: and many went out of the country up to Jerusalem before the Passover, to purify themselves.* Compare the *six water-pots of stone, after the manner of the purifying of the Jews,* at Cana of Galilee, Jn. ii. 6. Hence Proseuchæ were generally near running water; see Acts xvi. 13, and *Class-Book of New Testament History,* p. 442.

[4] For the spiritual significance of such ceremonial washings comp. (*a*) Ps. xxvi. 6; li. 2, 7; lxxiii. 13; (*b*) Isai. i. 16; iv. 4; Jer. iv. 14; Ezek. xxxvi. 25—27; Zech. xiii. 1.

[5] See Lightfoot, *Hor. Heb.* on Mtt. iii. 6; Vol. II. p. 55; Wall's *History of Inf. Baptism,* Introduction; Godwyn's *Moses and Aaron,* I. 3; Art. *Baptism* in Smith's *Bibl. Dict.*

§ II.] *THE OUTWARD SIGN IN BAPTISM.* 149

announce the advent of the Messiah, declared the whole nation to be spiritually unclean, and demanded that the chosen people themselves should be baptized, if they would have any place in *the Kingdom of heaven*, the Jews, who knew that Baptism implied admission into a new covenant or faith, were not struck with his proceeding as something unintelligible. They flocked forth unto him *from Jerusalem, and all Judæa, and all the region round about* (Mtt. iii. 5), and were baptized by him *confessing their sins*[1] (Mk. i. 5), for it was a common belief that the sins of Israel delayed the coming of the Messiah, while their repentance would hasten it[2].

6. **Baptism of our Lord.** But John had not been long engaged in this preparatory mission, before the Saviour Himself came from Nazareth, and was baptized by him in the Jordan, thus submitting to the ordinances of the Law[3] (Mtt. iii. 15), inaugurating His public ministry and His office as Redeemer[4], and "sanctifying water to the mystical washing away of sin[5]."

---

[1] On the questions put to proselytes to test the sincerity of their conversion, see Lightfoot, *Hor. Heb.* II. 61.

[2] Lightfoot, *Hor. Heb.* on Mtt. iii. 2; Godwyn's *Moses and Aaron*, I. 3.

[3] As the Jewish high-priest was consecrated by (1) *baptism* (Ex. xxix. 4—14), (2) *unction*, (3) *sacrifice* (Lev. viii. 1—30), so our Lord was consecrated as our High-priest (1) by *baptism* in the Jordan; (2) by the *unction of the Holy Ghost* (Mtt. iii. 16, comp. Acts x. 38); (3) by the *sacrifice* of Himself. See Heb. vii. 28. Smith's *Bibl. Dict.* Art. *Baptism.*

[4] "The answer of our Lord to John may have meant that He who had taken upon Him the form of a servant and was born under the Law was desirous of submitting to every ordinance of God. He had been circumcised in His infancy; He had been subject to His mother and Joseph, He would now go through the transitional dispensation, being baptized by John in preparation for the Kingdom." Smith's *Bibl. Dict.* Art. *Baptism.*

[5] See the first prayer in the Office for Publick Baptism of Infants.

With this element of water also our Lord baptized (Jn. iii. 22, 28; iv. 1), either in Person or by the hands of His disciples, and with the same element He commanded that they should everywhere baptize[1], and so admit proselytes or converts from Judaism or heathenism into the covenant of Grace, as circumcision had admitted to the covenant of works[2].

7. The Mode of Administration of this Sacrament of initiation into the Christian Church was in the earliest times undoubtedly by immersion, which St Paul uses as a lively figure of the Christian's *burial*[3] *with Christ by baptism into death*, and his *rising again to a new life* (Rom. vi. 4; Col. iii. 12). In the East and in warm countries this mode would be easy, especially where the recipients were chiefly adults, but there are not wanting indications that baptism by sprinkling may have been practised in Apostolic times[4], and when the Gospel spread into colder climes sprinkling was deemed sufficient[5].

---

[1] The Scripture types of Baptism are (1) the delivery of Noah and his family in the ark from perishing by water (1 Pet. iii. 21); (2) the passage of the Israelites through the Red Sea, *when they were baptized unto Moses in the cloud and in the sea* (1 Cor. x. 1, 2). See the first Prayer in the Baptismal Service.

[2] Bp. Browne *On the Articles*, p. 622.

[3] Compare the Collect for Easter Eve, the afternoon of which day was one of the most favourite times in the early Church for baptizing, Guericke's *Antiquities*, p. 149, n.

[4] Thus we read of the baptism of the family of the gaoler at Philippi on the night of their conversion (Acts xvi. 33), and of the baptism of three thousand at Pentecost *immediately* after their profession of repentance (Acts ii. 41). In neither of which cases is it likely that immersion would have been possible. Certainly the baptism of the sick by sprinkling was defended as valid and sufficient as early as the time of Cyprian. See Guericke's *Antiquities*, p. 232.

[5] By the rule of our own Church baptism may be ad-

8. **The Formula** addressed directly to the person baptized, is that directed by Christ Himself, *in*, or rather, *into the Name of the Father, and of the Son, and of the Holy Ghost* (Mtt. xxviii. 19). This never was and never may be omitted[1], for it is a sacramental declaration of the Christian's union with the nature of each Person in the blessed Trinity (Gal. iii. 27 and comp. Num. vi. 27).

CHAPTER II.

THE INWARD AND SPIRITUAL GRACE OF BAPTISM.

1. **Connection.** Having treated of the outward and visible sign or form in Baptism, and the mode of administration, we pass on to consider "the inward and spiritual grace" therein given unto us. Much that bears upon this point has been already anticipated, and it will chiefly be necessary to exhibit it at one view here.

2. **Man by Nature.** All men, then, as we have seen above[2], who are naturally engendered of the offspring of Adam, are born in sin. In consequence of the original fault and corruption which infect their nature, they are of themselves disinclined to please God, they are "very far[3] gone from original righteousness," and *the*

ministered either by immersion or sprinkling. See the Rubric for the Baptism of Infants, and also for Adults.

[1] Comp. the Questions in the Office for Private Baptism,
   With what matter was this Child baptized?
   With *what words* was this Child baptized?
And see the quotations from Tertullian and Cyprian in Bingham's *Antiquities*, Vol. IV. p. 26.

[2] See pp. 62, 102.

[3] *Quam longissimè;* See Art. IX., and Compare (*a*) Ps. li. 5; Eccl. vii. 20; Isai. liii. 6; Jer. xvii. 9; (*b*) Mtt. xix. 17; Jn. ii. 24, 25; Mtt. xv. 18, 19; (*c*) Rom. iii. 19, 23; v. 12; viii. 5—9; Eph. ii. 1—5; Col. ii. 13.

carnal mind[1] that is in them *is enmity against God, it is not subject to the law of God, neither indeed can be* (Rom. viii. 7). As, therefore, God is a Being of infinite holiness, and of purer eyes than to behold iniquity, and must of necessity hate all evil, men are truly said to be by nature not only born in sin[2], but also *the children of wrath*[3] (Eph. ii. 3). Hence, as our Lord said to Nicodemus, in their natural condition they *cannot see the kingdom of God*[4]. For entrance into His kingdom it is necessary that they *be born again*, or *from above*[5], that they *be born of water and of the Spirit* (Jn. iii. 3, 5).

3. **Man by Adoption and Grace.** Of this new birth, this translation from a state of nature into a state of adoption and grace[6], Baptism is the ordained instrument[7]. For, first, as circumcision admitted the Jew to the privileges of the Old Covenant, so Baptism admits to the privileges of *the new and better* Covenant, which

---

[1] Τὸ φρόνημα τῆς σαρκός, "which some do expound the wisdom, some sensuality, some the affection, some the desire, of the flesh." See Art. IX.

[2] Compare the first address in the Baptismal Service.

[3] Ὀργή has here its proper meaning, and denotes not τιμωρία or κόλασις itself, but the moving principle of it, God's holy hatred of sin, which reveals itself in His punitive justice, Rom. i. 18. Bp. Ellicott, *in loc.*

[4] On the various meanings of the Kingdom of God, see above, pp. 114—17.

[5] Οἱ μέν, ἐκ τοῦ οὐρανοῦ, φασιν, οἱ δέ, ἐξ ἀρχῆς. S. Chrysost. '*Born afresh* would be a better rendering than *born again*, being closer to the meaning of ἄνωθεν = *from the very beginning*. Comp. Luke i. 3;" Alford *in loc.* See Stier, IV. 381, &c.

[6] See the Collect for Christmas Day, and Waterland's *Works*, IV. 433.

[7] "Tanquam per instrumentum," Art. XXXVII. "Bucerus agnoscit sacramenta rectè dici *instrumenta*, organa et canales gratiæ," *Retract. in Mtt.* "Insuper ibi etiam *quasi instrumento quodam* operatur et perficit plenam nostri innovationem." See other illustrations in Archd. Hardwick's *History of the Articles*, p. 393; and Comp. Hooker, *Eccl. Pol.* V. lx. 2.

God has ratified with the whole world in the blood of the Mediator, His only-begotten Son, Jesus Christ. For His sake, of His bounteous mercy, God grants to us in Baptism that "which by nature we cannot have[2]," and on His part promises[3] (1) *the forgiveness of our sins*[4], (2) *the assistance of the Holy Spirit*,[5] and (3), if we do not forfeit it by neglecting our part of the Covenant, *everlasting life*[6].

4. **Baptism admits into the Church.** Again, by Baptism we are grafted into the universal Church, which is "the blessed company of all faithful people," and which is termed sometimes the *Body of Christ*[7], some-

---

[1] Heb. viii. 7—13; ix. 12. See above p. 8.

[2] See the Baptismal Service.

[3] Compare the address in the Baptismal Service. "Ye have brought this child here to be baptized, ye have prayed that our Lord Jesus Christ would vouchsafe to receive him, (1) to release him of his sins, (2) to sanctify him with the Holy Ghost, (3) to give him the kingdom of heaven, and everlasting life. Ye have heard also that He *hath promised to grant* all these things that ye have prayed for."

[4] *Repent and be baptized every one of you in the name of Jesus Christ*, said St Peter to the multitudes pricked in their heart on the day of Pentecost, *for the remission of sins* (Acts ii. 38). *Arise, and be baptized*, said Ananias to Saul of Tarsus, *and wash away thy sins* (Acts xxii. 16). See Waterland's *Works*, IV. 433.

[5] *Be baptized every one of you for the remission of sins, and ye shall receive the gift of the Holy Ghost* (Acts ii. 38), and compare Acts xix. 2, 6.

[6] *He that believeth and is baptized shall be saved*, saith our Lord (Mk. xvi. 15, 16), and salvation implies eternal life, as we have seen above pp. 69—72. "Yet it is evident from the whole tenour of Scripture that the promise of eternal life, though sure on God's part, may be made of none effect by us; so that, *a promise being left us of entering into His rest, we may come short of it;*" Bp. Browne *On the Articles*, p. 628; and see Waterland, *Works*, IV. 433.

[7] See above, p. 8, and p. 55, "As by an instrument, they that receive Baptism rightly are grafted into the Church." Art. XXVII.

times the *Family or Household of God*[1]. Grafted into this mystical Body, and adopted into this Household, we become, as we have already seen[2], (1) members of Christ[3], (2) children of God[4], and (3) inheritors of the Kingdom of Heaven[5].

5. **The Grace of Baptism.** Now the Jews were wont to say of proselytes admitted to their Baptism that they were "as one new born[6]", that they entered on a new life, and it is probable that our Lord was alluding to this, when he was conversing with Nicodemus. But with far greater truth are we said to be new born in Christian Baptism, and its inward and spiritual grace is defined to be a "death unto sin[7] and a new birth

---

[1] *Now therefore ye are...fellow citizens with the saints, and of the household of God,* οἰκεῖοι τοῦ Θεοῦ, Eph. ii. 19. Comp. Eph. iii. 15; Gal. vi. 10.

[2] See above, pp. 8, 9.

[3] See above, p. 8. *Ye are the Body of Christ,* St Paul writes to the Corinthians, *and members in particular,* ἐκ μέρους =*individually* (1 Cor. xii. 27); *by one Spirit we were all baptized* (ἐβαπτίσθημεν) *into one Body* (1 Cor. xii. 13); *As many of you,* he writes to the Galatians, *as were baptized* (ἐβαπτίσθητε) *into Christ, did put on Christ* (Gal. iii. 27).

[4] See above, p. 9, and compare the Baptismal Service.

[5] See above, p. 9, and compare Bp. Browne *On the Articles,* p. 630.

[6] "The Gentile that is made a proselyte, and the servant that is made free, behold, he *is like a child new born.*" "*If any one become a proselyte, he is like a child new born.*" Lightfoot *Hor. Heb.* on Jn. iii. 3. "The Jews called the admission or reception of proselytes by the name of *regeneration,* or *new birth;* as it was somewhat like the bringing them into a *new world.*" Waterland's *Works,* IV. 429. See also Wall *On Infant Baptism,* Introduction, p. 95. "Even Repentance was generally compared to the being *born again as children.*" Stier's *Words of the Lord Jesus,* IV. 384.

[7] *Know ye not,* St Paul asks the Romans, *that so many of us as were baptized into Jesus Christ were baptized into His death? we were buried, therefore, with Him by baptism into death, that, like as Christ was raised from the dead by the glory*

unto righteousness." For whereas by nature we were born in sin and the children of wrath, we are hereby translated from our natural state in Adam into a spiritual state in Christ; by this *laver of regeneration*[1] (Tit. iii. 5) we are new born into the Church and Family of God; we have His promises signed and sealed to us; the corruption of our nature is, as it were, *buried with Christ into death* (Rom. vi. 4); and by virtue of His Resurrection the first germ of spiritual grace is given unto us

---

of the Father, so we also should walk in newness of life (Rom. vi. 3, 4). The Aorists here point to a particular time and act. "Baptism (in the case of a penitent and believing convert) was a moment of actual transition from a life of sin to a life of holiness, and is constantly referred to in Scripture as such;" Dr Vaughan *On the Romans*.

[1] Regeneration, in Greek παλιγγενεσία, was a term not unknown to classical writers. (I) Thus (a) Plutarch applies it to the transmigration of souls, to their being born again into a new world; (b) Marcus Antoninus applies it to the revival of nature in spring-time from its winter sleep; (c) Cicero in a letter to Atticus (*ad Att.* VI. 6) applies it to his restoration from exile to the dignities and honours of life at Rome. (II) With this sense of renewal, revival, restoration, the word passes into the writings of the New Testament, and there it occurs twice, and twice only. (a) In Mtt. xix. 28, we read how in reply to a question of St Peter our Lord said, *Verily I say unto you, that ye which have followed Me in the* REGENERATION (παλιγγενεσία) *when the Son of Man shall sit in the throne of His glory, ye also shall sit upon twelve thrones, judging the twelve tribes of Israel;* (b) in Titus iii. 5, St Paul says that we are saved by *the laver of* REGENERATION (παλιγγενεσίας). In the former of these passages the word denotes *the new birth of the whole creation*, the restitution of all things at the last day (comp. Acts iii. 21); in the latter it denotes in a narrower sense the new birth, not of the whole creation, but of a single soul, "the free act of God's mercy and power, whereby he translates the sinner out of the kingdom of darkness into that of light, out of the state of nature into a state of grace," the ἄνωθεν γεννηθῆναι of Jn. iii. 3. See Trench's *Synonyms*, New Edition, p. 63.

"to be newly formed unto a new life, and to obey the righteousness of God[1]."

CHAPTER III.

THE REQUIREMENTS FOR BAPTISM.

1. **Connection.** Having defined what is the inward and spiritual grace of Baptism, the Catechism proceeds to ask *What is required of those who would be baptized?*

2. **Examination of Jewish Proselytes.** For, at the baptism of proselytes[2] to Judaism it was always usual to enquire into the spirit and motives of professed converts, before they were admitted to the rite of initiation.

3. **Preparation of the Soul.** And hence, when St Peter, after speaking of the delivery of Noah and his family from the deluge, says that the *antitype of that*[3], *even Baptism, doth now save us*, lest any should imagine that it acts as a charm or incantation[4], he adds, *not the putting away of the filth of the flesh, but the*

---

[1] See the answer in Noell's *Catechism* to the question "Whence have we regeneration?" The distinction between παλιγγενεσία and ἀνακαίνωσις (Tit. iii. 5; Rom. xii. 2), between "regeneratio" and "renovatio," between "regeneration" and "renewal," is well brought out in the Collect for Christmas Day, where we pray that "we being regenerate, and made God's children by adoption and grace, may daily be renewed (ἀνακαινισθῶμεν) by His Holy Ghost." "The regeneration is contemplated as past, as having found place once for all, while the 'renewal' or 'renovation' ought to be ever going forward in Him, who, through the new birth, has come under the transforming powers of the world to come." (Rom. xii. 2; Eph. iv. 23; 2 Cor. iv. 6). Trench's *Synonyms*, p. 62. Compare also Waterland's *Works*, IV. 435.

[2] See Lightfoot's *Hor. Heb.* on Mtt. iii. 6.

[3] Ὃ καὶ ὑμᾶς (a better reading than ἡμᾶς) ἀντίτυπον νῦν σώζει βάπτισμα = literally *the antitype of which is now saving you also.*

[4] *Ex opere operato*, as it is termed.

§ II.] *THE REQUIREMENTS FOR BAPTISM.* 157

answer of a good conscience toward God[1] (1 Pet. iii. 21). Thereby he reminds us that the mere outward washing with water does not save the soul. Baptism is a Sacrament ordained by Christ Himself for grafting us into the body of His Church, for bringing us into covenant with God, and so into a "state of salvation[2]." The promises therein signed and sealed God for His part "will surely keep and perform[3]," but there must be a corresponding preparation of the conscience and the soul on the part of the recipient, if his Baptism is to be to him a truly saving ordinance[4].

4. **Teaching of our Lord.** In what this needful preparation consists is clear from the words of our Lord and his Apostles. For when after His resurrection He was conversing with the two disciples on the road to Emmaus[5], and opening to them the Scriptures, He said that *it behoved Christ to suffer and to rise from the dead the third day, and that repentance and remission of sins should be preached in His Name among all nations* (Lk. xxiv. 46, 47). Again, when just before His Ascension He bade His Apostles *go into all the world and preach the Gospel to every creature,* He added, *he that believeth*[6] *and is baptized shall be saved* (Mk. xvi. 15, 16).

---

[1] Οὐ σαρκὸς ἀπόθεσις ῥύπου, ἀλλὰ συνειδήσεως ἀγαθῆς ἐπερώτημα εἰς Θεόν = *not the putting away of the filth of the flesh, but the enquiry of a good conscience after God,* or *the pledge of a good conscience toward God.* For the first meaning here given to ἐπερώτημα εἰς Comp. 2 Kings xi. 7, and Comp. Alford *in loc.;* for the second Comp. Beza's translation *Stipulatio bonæ conscientiæ apud Deum,* and Bingham's *Antiquities,* XI. vii. 3, and the note.
[2] Compare the Catechism, and see above, p. 17, n.
[3] See the Baptismal Service.
[4] See Bp. Browne on the XXVIIth Article, Sect. II.
[5] See *Class-Book of N. T. History,* p. 327.
[6] Ὁ δὲ ἀπιστήσας κατακριθήσεται. "Qui non credebant non suscipiebant. Privatio baptismi non damnat, nisi *per*

5. **Teaching of the Apostles.** Thus instructed by the Lord in the things concerning His kingdom (Acts i. 3), when on the day of Pentecost the multitudes were *pricked in their heart*, and enquired of St Peter and the rest of the Apostles what they should do, he replied, *Repent*[1] *and be baptized*[2] *every one of you in the name of Jesus Christ for the remission of sins* (Acts ii. 38)[3]. Again, when the Philippian gaoler, alarmed by the sudden earthquake, anxiously enquired of the Apostle Paul *what he should do to be saved*, he was told to *believe on the Lord Jesus Christ*, and the same night he was baptized, he and all his household (Acts xvi. 30—33).

6. **Repentance.** These passages sufficiently establish that what is required of those who would be baptized is (1) *Repentance*, and (2) *Faith*[4]. First, there must be on the part of the recipient *Repentance*. By repentance[5], however, is intended not mere sorrow

---

incredulitatem. Circumcisionis neglectæ pœna expressius indicata." Gen. xvii. 14. Bengel *in loc.*

[1] Μετανοήσατε, not μετανοεῖτε as in Matt. iii. 2, iv. 17. The aorist denotes a definite, immediate act; the present, a more gradual one, or a habit. See *Class-Book of N. T. History*, p. 348, n.

[2] *Loquitur, ut de re jam omnibus nota.* Bengel *in loc.*

[3] The answer of Philip the deacon to the Ethiopian eunuch in Acts viii. 37 can hardly be quoted here, as it is wanting in the best MSS., and is omitted by Lachmann and Tischendorf. See *Class-Book of N. T. History*, p. 378, n.

[4] "Doubt ye not therefore, but earnestly believe, that He will favourably receive these present persons *truly repenting*, and coming unto Him by *faith*." Baptismal Service for such as are of Riper Years.

[5] Μετανοία, *repentance*, denotes (1) *after-knowledge* (as πρόνοια = *fore-knowledge*); (2) *the change of mind* consequent on this after-knowledge; (3) *regret for the past* arising from this change of mind; (4) a change of conduct *for the better* in future, arising from all this, or "such a virtuous alteration of the mind and purpose as begets a like virtuous change in the life and practice." See Trench's *Synonyms*, new ed., pp. 246—249.

§ II.] *THE REQUIREMENTS FOR BAPTISM.* 159

and compunction for sin, but a real and sincere resolve to renounce[1] and forsake it. It denotes a hearty endeavour to act up to that profession which Baptism doth represent unto us[2], and implies that as He, into whose death *we are buried by baptism* (Rom. vi. 4), died and rose again for us, so we, dying to sin[3] and rising again unto righteousness, should continually mortify all our evil and corrupt affections, and daily endeavour to proceed in all virtue and godliness of living[4].

7. **Faith.** Secondly, there must be on the part of the recipient *Faith*, that is, not a mere intellectual[5] belief in Christ, but an assured confidence in the promises of God made to us in this Sacrament. These promises, as we have already seen, are (1) *the forgiveness of our sins*[6], (2) *the assistance of the Holy Spirit*, and (3), if not forfeited, *everlasting life*. These promises we must lay hold on by faith, and in all our falls and backslidings lean upon them as signed and sealed to us, and humbly expect all good from God's free mercies in Christ, although our performances fall

---

[1] See above, p. 10, and the note.
[2] See the Baptismal Service.
[3] Ὁ δὲ μετανοῶν οὐκέτι τῶν αὐτῶν ἅπτεται πραγμάτων, ἐφ' οἷς μετενόησε· διὰ τοῦτο καὶ κελευόμεθα λέγειν, Ἀποτάσσομαί σοι, Σατανᾶ, ἵνα μηκέτι πρὸς αὐτὸν ἐπανέλθωμεν. St Chrysos. *ad Illum. Catech.* II.; Opp. II. 238, n.
[4] Compare Noell's *Catechism:* "We must continually, with all our power and endeavour, travail in mortifying our flesh, and obeying the righteousness of God, and must by godly life declare to all men that we have in baptism as it were put on Christ, and have His Spirit given us."
[5] See above. p. 20, n.
[6] Compare Noell's *Catechism.* "First, we must with assured confidence hold it determined in our hearts, that we are cleansed by the blood of Christ from all filthiness of sin, and so be acceptable to God, and that His Spirit dwelleth within us." See also Archbp. Secker's *Lectures*, II. 232.

very short, and although we are at the best but *unprofitable servants*[1] (Lk. xvii. 10).

CHAPTER IV.

THE BAPTISM OF INFANTS.

1. **Adult Baptism.** Those to whom John the Baptist preached by the banks of Jordan, and whom he baptized with the Baptism of repentance; those whom St Peter admitted into the Church on the day of Pentecost, and the other Apostles after him, were chiefly adults[2], who had come to years of discretion, who could not only promise repentance and faith, but also perform and keep that promise.

2. **Baptism of Infants.** But it is obvious that infants cannot "by reason of their tender age" either repent or possess a personal faith[3]. The question, therefore, naturally arises why and on what grounds are they admitted to the Sacrament of Baptism by our Church. The reply to this enquiry as given in the Catechism is, *because they promise them both* (*i.e.* both repentance and faith) *by their sureties, which promise, when they come to age, themselves are bound to perform.*

3. **Justified by the analogy of the Old Covenant.** The propriety, however, of their admission, it may be well to consider on still broader grounds. Under the Old Covenant we find God distinctly commanding that *every man child* should be circumcised (Gen. xvii.

---

[1] See Nicholson *On the Catechism*, p. 200.
[2] See Hammond's *Works*, Vol. IV. p. 438.
[3] Still it is to be remembered that "though they bring no *virtues* with them, no *positive* righteousness, yet they bring no *obstacle* or *impediment*. They *stipulate*, they enter into contract by their *sureties*, upon a presumptive and interpretative consent, and become consecrated in solemn form to *Father, Son, and Holy Ghost.*" Waterland's *Works*, IV. 440.

10—12), and accordingly Jewish children were circumcised on the eighth day after birth (Levit. xii. 3). Under the same Dispensation also we find Moses engaging not only the captains of Israel's tribes, their elders, officers, and men, but also their *little ones, to enter into covenant with the Lord* (Deut. xxix. 11, 12), and enjoining that at the Feast of Tabernacles, not only the men and women, but *the children* should be gathered together that they might *learn and fear the Lord their God, and observe to do all the words of the Law* (Deut. xxxi. 12[1]). We might naturally, therefore, expect that in Baptism, which takes the place of the Jewish rite of Circumcision[2] (Col. ii. 11, 12), God would be willing to receive children[3] into His new and better Covenant[4], unless He has expressly revealed otherwise to us.

4. **And by the Teaching of our Lord.** But so far from revealing otherwise to us, His blessed Son, who is one with Him in will and nature, when He was

---

[1] Comp. 2 Chron. xx. 13.

[2] When our Lord bade His disciples *make disciples* or *proselytes of all nations* (Mtt. xxviii. 19), He was addressing persons, who had been accustomed to enrol in the Jewish Church their own infants and proselytes of all ages, and who, unless *expressly forbidden*, would naturally interpret His words as implying that the practice was according to His will. See Archbp. Whately *On the Sacraments*, p. 34.

[3] "Otherwise the blessings of the Old Covenant, instead of being more limited, must have been more extended than those of the New; and the Law, which was given by Moses, must have been more merciful than the grace and truth, which came by Jesus Christ." Bp. Browne on Article XXVII.

[4] See above, pp. 7, 8. "Since it is certain that the grace of God is both more plentifully found and more clearly declared in the Gospel by Christ, than at that time it was in the Old Testament by Moses, it were a greater indignity if the same grace should now be thought to be either obscurer or in any part abated." Noell's *Catechism;* and comp. Hooker's *Eccl. Pol.* v. lxiv. 3.

upon earth showed in a peculiar and very special manner that children were the objects of His care and love. For on one occasion, when His disciples would have kept back certain children whom their mothers had brought to Him (Mtt. xix. 13), He blamed them for their interference; He took the children *into His arms; He laid His hands upon them, and blessed them* (Mk. x. 16). And if the outward gesture and deed of Him, "whose slightest act was full of hidden meaning," be not enough, His words are decisive, seeing that on this occasion He proceeded to say, *Suffer the little children to come unto Me, and forbid them not, for of such is the kingdom of heaven* (Mtt. xix. 14).

5. **Apostolic Practice.** Moreover, though there is not *express* mention in the New Testament of the Baptism of children, yet we find St Peter declaring to his hearers on the day of Pentecost, that the promises of the Gospel were *for them and for their children* (Acts ii. 39); we find St Paul speaking of *the children* of his Corinthian converts as *holy* (1 Cor. vii. 14); we find him baptizing Lydia *and her household* at Philippi (Acts xvi. 15), the gaoler at the same place and *all his family* (Acts xvi. 33), as also Stephanas and *his household* at Corinth (1 Cor. i. 16), and it is difficult to believe but that these families and households included children[1].

6. **Custom of the Primitive Church.** Though, however, there is no express mention of Infant Baptism in the New Testament, we have every reason to believe that it has prevailed from the very first. Justin Martyr, writing his second Apology about A.D. 148, declares that Baptism stood in the stead of Circumcision, and mentions persons who had been made disciples to

---

[1] See Bishop Browne on Article XXVII.

Christ, that is, baptized, whilst children[1]. Irenæus says that "Christ came to save all by Himself, all, that is, who by Him are regenerated to God, infants and little ones, and boys and youths and old men[2]." Tertullian[3] also and Origen[4] testify that Infant Baptism was the custom of the Church in their day.

7. **Propriety of Infant Baptism.** Thus reason, analogy, and primitive antiquity, alike tend not only to remove all doubt about the propriety[5] of admitting Infants to Baptism, but to make us earnestly believe that our heavenly Father will "embrace them with the arms of His mercy, will give unto them the blessing of eternal life, and make them partakers of His everlasting kingdom[6]." But those, who have thus been brought in infancy to their Saviour, who thus promise repentance and faith by their sureties[7], must, when they come to age, consciously take upon themselves the promises then made. And this they are specially bound to do at

---

[1] Πολλοί τινες καὶ πολλαὶ ἐξηκοντοῦται καὶ ἐβδομηκοντοῦται, οἱ ἐκ παίδων ἐμαθητεύθησαν τῷ Χριστῷ, ἄφθοροι διαμένουσι. Just. *Apol.* II. 62. See Bingham's *Antiquities*, IV. 57.

[2] "Omnes venit per semetipsum salvare; omnes, inquam, qui per Eum renascuntur in Deum; infantes et parvulos, et pueros, et juvenes, et seniores." Iren. *adv. Hær.* II. 22, 4.

[3] See Tertullian *de Baptismo*, Cap. XVIII.

[4] "Quia per baptismi Sacramentum nativitatis sordes deponuntur, propterea baptizantur et parvuli." Origen, *Homil.* XIV. *in Lucam.* "Ecclesia ab Apostolis traditionem suscepit etiam parvulis baptismum dare." *Homil. in Rom.* v. 9, quoted in Guericke's *Antiquities*, p. 238, n.

[5] The Latin of the XXVIIth Article is more explicit than the English. "Baptismus parvulorum *omnino in ecclesia retinendus est*, ut qui cum Christi institutione optimè congruat."

[6] See the Office for Public Baptism of Infants.

[7] On sureties and sponsors, see above, p. 6, and note. In the Jewish Baptism of proselytes two or three sponsors or witnesses were required to be present. See Lightfoot on Mtt. iii. 6.

the time of their Confirmation, when they are called upon, having heard what their Godfathers and Godmothers promised for them in Baptism, "themselves with their own mouth and consent, to ratify and confirm the same, and also promise, that by the grace of God they will evermore endeavour[1] themselves faithfully to observe such things, as they, by their own confession, have assented unto[2]."

SECTION III.

The Sacrament of the Lord's Supper.

CHAPTER I.

THE OBJECT OF THE INSTITUTION OF THE LORD'S SUPPER.

1. **Connection.** The Catechism now proceeds to speak of the second of the two Sacraments ordained by Christ, and begins by enquiring the object for which the Sacrament of the Lord's Supper[3] was instituted.

---

[1] Endeavour (old E. *Endevor;* from Fr. *en devoir*) here, as in the Collect for the Second Sunday after Easter, and in the office of Ordering of Priests, is used as a reflexive verb. Compare

"I have *endeuoryred me* to make and ende."
Caxton, *Golden Legend.*

"This is called in Scripture 'a just man' that *endeavoureth himself* to leave all wickedness."
Latimer, *Serm.* p. 340.

"*Endeavour thyself* to sleep."
Shakespeare, *Twelfth Night,* IV. 2.

See the *Bible Word-Book*, p. 174.

[2] See the Order of Confirmation.

[3] Dr Waterland groups together the following successive appellations of the Sacrament. (1) *The Breaking of the Bread,* ἡ κλάσις τοῦ ἄρτου (Acts ii. 42), A.D. 33; (2) *Communion* (1 Cor. x. 16), A.D. 57; (3) *The Lord's Supper* (1 Cor. xi.

2. **The Object** of the Institution is defined to have been *for the continual remembrance of the sacrifice of the death of Christ, and of the benefits which we receive thereby.* In this definition it is assumed (1) that the death of Christ was of the nature of a sacrifice, (2) that the Supper of the Lord was ordained for a continual remembrance of (*a*) the death of Christ, and (*b*) of the benefits which we receive thereby[1].

3. **The Death of Christ a Sacrifice.** That the death of Christ was more than a mere corroboration of His teaching, more than a mere martyrdom, we have already seen[2]. The very Name[3] given Him before His Birth declared the object of His coming into the world to be *the delivery of His people from their sins*[4]. In harmony with this declaration, John the Baptist twice pointed Him out to his disciples as *the Lamb*[5] *of God*

---

20), A.D. 57; (4) *Oblation,* προσφορά (Clem. Rom. 1 *Ep. ad Cor.* c. 44), A.D. 95; (5) *Sacrament* (Plin. *Epist.* X. 97), A.D. 104; (6) *Eucharist* (Ignat. *Ep. ad Smyr.* VII. VIII. XX.), A.D. 107; (7) *Sacrifice* (Just. Mart. *Dial. cum Tryph.* 137), A.D. 150; (8) *Commemoration* or *Memorial* (Ibid. p. 345), A.D. 150; (9) *Passover* (Origen *contr. Cels.* VIII. 759), A.D. 249; (10) *Mass, Missa* (Ambros. *Epist.* I. 20), A.D. 385. Waterland's *Works,* Vol. IV. pp. 472—490; Guericke's *Antiquities,* p. 253.

[1] Compare Noell's *Catechism:* "M. For what use [was the Supper of the Lord ordained]? S. To celebrate and retain continually a thankful remembrance of the Lord's death, and of that most singular benefit, which we have received thereby."

[2] See above, pp. 29, 38, 42, and especially pp. 63, 64. Compare also Waterland on the *Doctrine of the Eucharist, Works,* IV. 512—516.

[3] See above, p. 23, and the note.

[4] Ἐνταῦθα τὸ παράδοξον ἐνδείκνυται. Οὐ γὰρ πολέμων αἰσθητῶν, οὐδὲ βαρβάρων, ἀλλ' ὃ πολλῷ τούτων μεῖζον ἦν, ἁμαρτημάτων ἀπαλλαγὴν εὐαγγελίζεται· ὃ μηδενί ποτε ἔμπροσθεν ἐγένετο δυνατόν. S. Chrysost. *in Mtt.* i. 21.

[5] Comp. Jn. i. 29, 36. It has been much debated what

who should take away the sin of the world (Jn. i. 29), and the public ministry of the Holy One had hardly begun before He intimated to Nicodemus that *as Moses lifted up the serpent in the wilderness, so should the Son of Man be lifted up, that whosoever believeth in Him should not perish, but have everlasting life*[1] (Jn. iii. 12—16). Again, in the synagogue of Capernaum, at the season of the second Passover of His public ministry, He declared that He was *the Bread of Life* (Jn. vi. 35), that the Bread He would give was *His flesh, which He would give for the life of the world*[2] (Jn. vi. 51). As the hour of His decease drew near He spake yet more plainly of His going up to Jerusalem to die; He declared that as *the good*[3], the true, the genuine *Shepherd*, He was about *to lay down His life for the sheep* (Jn. x. 15); that the *Son of Man came not to be ministered unto, but to minister, and to give His life a ransom for many* (Mtt. xx. 28).

train of thought suggested this image. (1) Some have thought that a flock of lambs may have been passing on their way to the coming Passover (Jn. ii. 13) at Jerusalem; (2) Others see in it an allusion to the lamb of the morning and evening sacrifice at the temple; (3) others have referred it to that wonderful chapter in the prophet Isaiah (liii. 7), which afterwards (Acts viii. 30—34) so powerfully arrested the attention of the Ethiopian eunuch. See St Chrysost. *Hom. in Joan.* XVII.

[1] "Est hæc prima quæ a Domino facta legitur, *Mosis* mentio." Bengel *in loc.*

[2] Comp. also Jn. vi. 53—58. "Ista hæc de carne et sanguine J. C. oratio *passionem* spectat, et *cum ea* S. Cœnam." Bengel *in loc.* See Bp. Browne on Art. XXVIII. pp. 717—721. Comp. Mk. ix. 12; Mtt. xvii. 10. "Evangelium in duas partes potest dividi, ex quibus divina Jesu methodus elucet. Prior propositi est, *Jesus est Christus;* altera *Christum oportet pati, et resurgere.* Homines sæpe omnia simul docent: non item Sapientia Divina." Bengel.

[3] Ὁ Ποιμὴν ὁ καλός. Comp. the use of καλός in 1 Tim. iv. 6; 1 Pet. iv. 10; 2 Tim. ii. 3.

4. **The Lord's Supper a Memorial of this Sacrifice.** Thus gradually and progressively[1] did the Holy One prepare the minds of His disciples to realise the idea of His death as a Sacrifice. But all previous announcements culminated in the institution of this Sacrament. For when He took Bread, and blessed, and brake it, when He took the Cup, and gave thanks, and gave it to His disciples, He bade them *do this*, not only in remembrance of Himself, but of Himself in a particular character[2], as about *to give His Body for them*, as about *to shed His Blood for them, and for many, for the remission of sins* (Mtt. xxvi. 26—28). Hence, in the words of St Paul to the Corinthians, *as often as we eat this Bread and drink this Cup*, we proclaim[3] the Lord's *death till He come* (1 Cor. xi. 26), we make continual remembrance of the full, perfect, and sufficient sacrifice, oblation, and satisfaction[4] which He made by His death for the sins of the whole world.

5. **And of the Benefits which we receive thereby.** Moreover the Lord's Supper was ordained not only for the continual remembrance of the death of Christ, but also of "the innumerable benefits which by His precious

---

[1] On the gradual and progressive training of the Apostles to associate the idea of their Lord's death with the idea of a sacrifice, see the Author's *Witness of the Eucharist*, Chaps. V. VI.

[2] "About to be crucified as a felon and a slave, He commanded that it should be remembered to the end of time—did so in the full confidence that He should at last triumph. And *the fact has been* remembered. This is the mystery—if He was not all that He claimed to be—this is truly more miraculous than anything ever so called." Young's *Christ of History*, p. 238.

[3] $Καταγγέλλειν = to\ proclaim$, announce, and this we do (1) before God, (2) before one another, (3) before the world.

[4] See above, p. 64. On the word *satisfaction*, which occurs not only in the Communion Service, but also in the Collect for the fourth Sunday in Advent, and dates from the time of Anselm, see Swainson's *Hulsean Lectures*, p. 283, and the notes.

blood-shedding He hath obtained to us[1]." For it was instituted at a Paschal Feast. Now the Passover, as often as it was celebrated by the Jews, recalled, as in a living drama, the great story[2] of the deliverance of their nation from cruel and oppressive bondage (Deut. xvi. 2, 3); a deliverance effected not *by* them, but *for* them[3]; a deliverance wrought solely by the outstretched arm of Jehovah; a deliverance which elevated them from the condition of slaves to that of a ransomed people, which placed them in a state of exalted privilege, and gave them the hope of entrance into a Promised Land. So also the Lord's Supper is a continual Memorial of the deliverance not only of a single nation, but of the whole world from the bondage of sin and Satan; a deliverance effected not *by* us, but *for* us; a deliverance planned in the counsels of eternity, and due solely to the loving mercy of God, who *spared not His own Son* (Rom. viii. 32) but gave Him to be the very[4] Paschal Lamb (1 Cor. v. 7), which was offered for us, and hath taken away the sin of the world; who "by His death hath destroyed death, and by His rising again hath restored to us everlasting life," and afforded us a hope of entry hereafter into *a better country, that is, a heavenly* (Heb. x. 19, 20; xi. 16).

---

[1] See the Exhortation in the Communion Service.

[2] Of the various festivals of the Jews, if we except those of later institution which commemorated the deliverance of the people from Haman and Antiochus Epiphanes, the Passover was the only one which rested on a distinctly historical basis. See Stanley's *Lectures on the Jewish Church*, I. 121.

[3] In which they had been not *actors* but *passive spectators*, had stood still and seen the salvation of God (Ex. xiv. 13).

[4] See the Proper Preface for Easter Day in the Communion Service. On *very* see above, p. 25, n.

CHAPTER II.

THE OUTWARD PART OR SIGN OF THE LORD'S SUPPER.

1. **Connection.** Having considered the object for which the Sacrament of the Lord's Supper was ordained, the Catechism proceeds to treat of "the outward part or sign of the Lord's Supper." This it defines to be *Bread and Wine, which the Lord hath commanded to be received.*

2. **The Command** that these elements should be received is recorded in three of the Gospels[1], and in St Paul's first Epistle to the Corinthians, where the Apostle reminds those to whom he wrote of that account of the Institution of this Sacrament, which he had already delivered to them, and which he had received by express revelation[2] from the Lord.

3. **The Paschal Feast.** The Lord's Supper, as we have already seen, was instituted at a Paschal Feast[3]. With the Passover by Divine ordinance there had always been eaten flat cakes of unleavened bread (Ex. xii. 8); and the rites of the feast by immemorial usage had been regulated according to the succession of four[4] cups of wine. These were placed before the

---

[1] Mtt. xxvi. 26—29; Mk. xiv. 22—25; Lk. xxii. 19, 20.

[2] 1 Cor. xi. 23—25: Ἐγὼ γὰρ παρέλαβον ἀπὸ τοῦ Κυρίου ὃ καὶ παρέδωκα ὑμῖν. Compare Gal. i. 12. The similarity between St Paul's account of the Institution and that given in St Luke's Gospel has often been noticed.

[3] Comp. (*a*) Mtt. xxvi. 1, 2; (*b*) Mtt. xxvi. 17, 18; Mk. xiv. 13, 14; (*c*) Lk. xxii. 10, 11; (*d*) Lk. xxii. 15.

[4] Buxtorf *de Cœna Domini*, pp. 299, 300. "Omnes in cœna Paschali oportet quatuor pocula bibere." "Four cups of wine were to be drunk by every one." Lightfoot, *Hor. Heb.* on Mtt. xxvi. 27; and compare Ps. cxvi. 12.

master of the house where the Paschal company[1] was assembled, or the most eminent guest, who was called the Celebrant, the President, or *Proclaimer of the Feast.*

4. **Rites of the Feast.** After those assembled had reclined, He took one of the four cups, known as the "Cup of Consecration," and pronounced the benediction over the wine and the feast, saying, *Blessed be Thou, O Lord our God, the King of the Universe, who hast created the fruit of the vine*[2]. Then followed ablutions, the setting out of the table with the unleavened bread, the Paschal Lamb, and the feast-offerings, the drinking of a second cup, and the *Haggadah,* or *Shewing forth*[3] of the circumstances of the Exodus. After this the President took two of the unleavened cakes, broke one of them with the words *Blessed be thou, O Lord, King of the Universe, who bringest forth fruit out of the earth,* and distributed a portion to each person around him. Then after the eating of the flesh of the Paschal Lamb, he lifted up his hands, and blessed the third cup of wine, specially known as the *Cup of Blessing,* and handed it round to each guest at the table. Thereupon followed a renewal of thanksgiving, and the drinking of a fourth cup, known as the "Cup of Song," after which a Hymn, called the Hallel[4], was sung, and the rite was concluded.

---

[1] Which might include not less than ten persons, but usually from ten to twenty, according to the family, or the number of strangers that might be present.

[2] For similar use of these words in the synagogue service for Friday evening, see Pedahzur's *Jewish Ceremonies,* p. 137.

[3] "Hence the Apostle borroweth his phrase, *As often as ye eat this Bread, and drink this Cup, ye do declare or shew forth* (καταγγέλλετε) *the Lord's death till he come,* 1 Cor. xi. 26)." Godwyn's *Moses and Aaron,* Book III.

[4] Psalms cxiii — cxviii. This explains Mtt. xxvi. 30; Mk. xiv. 26, respecting the Hymn, or rather Psalm, sung before our Lord and His disciples left the Upper-Room.

5. **Institution of the Lord's Supper.** Such, or nearly such, were the ceremonies observed at the celebration of the Passover in the time of our Lord. On the night, then, that He was betrayed, when all things had been duly prepared in the upper-room at Jerusalem, He sat down with His Apostles, and assumed the place amongst them of Master, or President of the company. Then as the feast proceeded[1], taking one of the unleavened cakes that had been placed before Him, when He had given thanks, He brake it, and gave it to His disciples, saying,

> *Take, eat; This is My Body[2] which is given for you: Do this in remembrance of Me.*

Afterwards He took a cup of wine, probably the third cup, and known as the "Cup of Blessing[3]," and when He had given thanks, He gave it to them, saying,

> *Drink ye all of this; for this is My Blood[4] of the New Testament[5], which is shed for you*

---

[1] Even if δείπνου γενομένου be the right reading in Jn. xiii. 2, the meaning is *when supper had begun*. Tischendorf and Tregelles read γινομένου.

[2] Τοῦτό ἐστι τὸ Σῶμά μου. So Mtt., Mk., Lk., and 1 Cor. xi. 24. St Luke, however, adds τὸ ὑπὲρ ὑμῶν διδόμενον = *which is being* (or *on the point of being*) *given for you*. St Paul adds τὸ ὑπὲρ ὑμῶν κλώμενον, *which is being* (or *on the point of being*) *broken for you*. Both St Luke and St Paul add, *Do this in remembrance of me*, εἰς τὴν ἐμὴν ἀνάμνησιν, on the force of which see Waterland's *Works*, Vol. IV. pp. 499—512.

[3] See above, p. 170.

[4] Τοῦτο γάρ ἐστι τὸ αἷμά μου, τῆς καινῆς διαθήκης (Mtt. xxvi. 28, but some chief MSS. omit καινῆς), τὸ περὶ πολλῶν ἐκχυνόμενον εἰς ἄφεσιν ἁμαρτιῶν = *For This My Blood of the New Testament* (or rather *the New Covenant*, or *the New Dispensation*), *which is being* (or *on the point of being*) *poured out for many unto remission of sins*.

[5] St Luke and St Paul read Τοῦτο τὸ ποτήριον ἡ καινὴ διαθήκη ἐστὶν ἐν τῷ ἐμῷ αἵματι = *This Cup is the New Covenant* (or *Dispensation*) *in my Blood*.

and for many, for the remission of sins: Do this, as oft as ye shall drink it, in remembrance of Me[1].

6. **The Elements of Bread and Wine.** Thus did our Lord ordain Bread[2] and Wine to be the outward part or sign of the Sacrament of our Redemption by His Death. In the Feast of the Passover these elements had been subordinate. He now gives to them the first importance. In the Feast of the Passover, the Paschal Lamb had occupied the chief place, it had been selected with scrupulous care (Exod. xii. 5), it had been slain with solemn ceremony, its blood had been sprinkled on the Brazen Altar in the Temple[3], and it was then not burnt, or eaten by the priests only, but by all the people[4], in memory of the delivery of the Israelites from Egypt. But now the type was succeeded by the Antitype, now the "very

---

[1] This is added in St Paul's record, 1 Cor. xi. 24.

[2] Foreshadowings of the use of Bread and Wine in this Sacrament have been traced in:
- (a) The history of Melchizedek, *King of Salem, and priest of the Most High God*, who brought forth *Bread and Wine* after Abraham's delivery of Lot (Gen. xiv. 18—20; and see Heb. vii. 1—24).
- (b) The *Manna* with which the Israelites were fed in the wilderness (Comp. Exod. xvi. 15 with Jn. vi. 31, 51, and 1 Cor. x. 4).
- (c) The Miracles of the *Feeding of the Five* (Jn. vi. 5—14), and *the Four Thousand* (Mtt. xv. 32—39; Mk. viii. 1—9; Mtt. xiv. 15—21).

[3] Comp. Deut. xvi. 5, 6; 2 Chron. xxx. 16; 2 Chron. xxxv. 10, 11.

[4] See Cudworth's *True Notion of the Lord's Supper, Works,* II. 831. In the Passover, (a) the principle of *mediation* found its highest expression; (b) the *victim* slain was in the strictest sense a *sacrifice*, and combined some of the chief features of (1) the *sin-offering*, and (2) the *peace-offering;* (c) the idea of a *sacrificial feast* was most deeply realised. See *Class-Book of O.T. History,* p. 139, and 151, n.

Paschal Lamb[1]" was come, and was about to offer Himself upon the altar of His Cross for the sins of the whole world. Of the Jewish Paschal lamb, therefore, no word is said, but in place of it our Blessed Lord puts the Bread and Wine. The lamb had been eaten as a type of Him, Bread and Wine were to be taken and received *in remembrance of Him.*

CHAPTER III.

THE INWARD PART OF THE LORD'S SUPPER.

1. **Connection.** From treating of "the outward part or sign in the Lord's Supper," the Catechism passes on to speak of "the inward part or thing signified," and this it defines to be *The Body and Blood of Christ, which are verily and indeed taken and received by the faithful in the Lord's Supper.*

2. **The words of our Lord.** The truth of this statement is sufficiently confirmed by the words of our Lord Himself. For, as we have already seen, on the occasion of the second Passover[2] of His public ministry, He declared to the Jews in the synagogue of Capernaum, that He was *the Bread of Life, the Living Bread, which came down from heaven;* that *His Flesh was meat indeed*[3], *and His Blood drink indeed*

---

[1] Compare Tyndall's Version of 1 Cor. v. 7, 8: "*Christ oure Easter-lambe is offered up for us; therefore let us kepe holy daye.*"

[2] If the Miracle of the "Feeding of the Five Thousand" was, as some hold (see Tischendorf's *Synop. Evang.* XXXIV.), wrought on a Passover-Eve, the significance of its connection with the Discourse on the following day in the synagogue of Capernaum, and with the following Passover, when the Eucharist was instituted, is very striking.

[3] The better reading is ἡ γὰρ σάρξ μου ἀληθής ἐστι βρῶσις, καὶ τὸ αἷμά μου ἀληθής ἐστι πόσις = *For My Flesh is true meat, and My Blood is true drink.* "Fateor," says Calvin,

(Jn. vi. 35, 51, 58). Again, at the following Passover, gathering up in action all that He had then expressed in words, when He gave the bread to His disciples, He said, *Take, eat; this*[1] *is*[2] *My Body;* and when He took the Cup, He said, *Drink ye all of this; for this is My Blood of the New Covenant.*

3. **The words of St Paul.** Thus also in his first Epistle to the Corinthians, reprehending the practice of some of joining in the idol-feasts, St Paul says, *I speak unto wise men; judge ye what I say. The Cup of Blessing which we bless, is it not the Communion*[3] (an actual *partaking*) *of the Blood of Christ? The Bread which we break, is it not the Communion* (an actual *partaking*) *of the Body of Christ? For we being many are one bread and one body: for we are all partakers of that one Bread* (1 Cor. x. 15—17). And, again, when rebuking the disorder and confusion[4] which had de-

"nihil hic dici quod non in Cœna figuretur ac vere præstetur fidelibus; adeoque S. Cœnam Christus quasi hujus concionis sigillum esse voluit."

[1] Τοῦτό ἐστι τὸ Σῶμά μου; Τοῦτό ἐστι τὸ αἷμά μου. Our Lord says this of the Bread in His hand, of the Cup in His hand. *This* (Bread) *is My Body*, *This* (Cup) *is My Blood*. It is not οὗτος ὁ ἄρτος, or οὗτος ὁ οἶνος, but τοῦτο in both cases. Bread being a thing without life is referred to by a neuter pronoun.

[2] For the force of ἐστι, *is*, here, compare the places where Christ says of Himself, *I am the Door* (Jn. x. 9); *I am the true Vine* (Jn. xv. 1); *I am the bright and morning Star* (Rev. xxii. 16); also St Paul's words, *that Rock was Christ* (1 Cor. x. 4).

[3] Here alone the word κοινωνία is used of the Lord's Supper, and is the origin of the name as applied to it.

[4] In early times the reception of the Communion formed part of an *Agape* or love-feast, to which the rich contributed of their wealth, and the poor of their poverty. But at Corinth the richer Christians made this feast minister to their own self-indulgence, and utterly overlooked the wants of their poorer brethren, *so that while one was hungry another was drunken* (1 Cor. xi. 21).

graded their celebration of the Holy Feast almost to the level of a heathen orgy, he declares that he who ate this Bread and drank this Cup in the unworthy and irreverent way they did, *was guilty*[1] *of the Body and Blood of the Lord;* that he ate and drank *judgment*[2] *unto himself, not discerning the Lord's Body* (1 Cor. xi. 27, 29).

4. **The solemnity of the Lord's Supper.** These words of our blessed Lord and of St Paul are sufficient to show the surpassing dignity and solemnity of this "holy mystery[3];" that it is far more than "only a sign of the love that Christians ought to have among themselves one to another[4];" that while the outward part or sign is but Bread and Wine, the inward part or thing signified is the Body and Blood of Christ, which are verily and indeed taken and received by the faithful in the Lord's Supper[5].

5. **The Passover a Feast upon a Sacrifice.** In reference to this reception it may be well to revert to the Jewish Passover, at a celebration of which, as we have seen, the Lord's Supper was instituted. The Passover, then, was a Festival of Redemption. The victim was offered up in behalf of each Paschal company[6]. Having

---

[1] Ἔνοχος ἔσται—*i. e.* crimini et poenae corporis et sanguinis Christi violati obnoxius erit. Meyer.

[2] See the margin of our Version here. The word κρίσιν, rendered *damnation*, denotes rather *judgment* or *punishment*, and refers to the *temporal chastisements* spoken of in 1 Cor. xi. 30.

[3] See the Exhortation in the Communion Service.

[4] See the XXVIIIth Article.

[5] Compare the words of the XXVIIIth Article: "The Supper of the Lord is...a Sacrament of our Redemption by Christ's death, insomuch that to such as rightly, worthily, and with faith receive the same, the Bread which we break is a partaking of the Body of Christ; and likewise the Cup of blessing is a partaking of the Blood of Christ."

[6] See *Class-Book of Old Testament History*, pp. 150, 151.

been presented before the altar in the Temple, and its blood having been sprinkled there, it was then not burnt, or eaten by the priests only, but by the entire Paschal company, for whom it had been offered, at a Sacrificial Feast. Now feasts on sacrifices were means of ratifying covenants[1] between man and God[2]; they were also peculiar to the Peace-offerings of the Jews, and indicated that what had separated the offerer from Jehovah was covered and cancelled, that He now welcomed him to His Table, and in this feast gave him a pledge of reconciliation and favour[3].

6. **The Eucharist a Feast upon a Sacrifice.** Now as the Passover was a Feast of redemption and deliverance, so is the Lord's Supper a Feast of a still greater Redemption and Deliverance[4]. He who accomplished it is none other than our Master and only Saviour Jesus Christ. By His one oblation of Himself once offered, He has "made a full, perfect, and sufficient sacrifice, oblation, and satisfaction for the sins of the whole world[5]." Having *through the Blood of His Cross become our Peace* (Col. i. 20; Eph. ii. 14), He has

---

[1] Hence our Lord said when He took the cup, *This is My Blood of*, i. e. ratifying *the New Covenant*.

[2] See Cudworth's *True Notion*, Chap. VI. Compare the scene on Sinai, when Moses, Aaron, Nadab, Abihu, and the seventy elders, after the covenant between Jehovah and His people had been solemnly ratified by sacrifices and sprinkling of blood, ate and drank of a portion of the sacrifice in His presence at a Covenant-feast, and therein received the pledge of His mercy and favour (Ex. xxiv. 9—11; Heb. ix. 19—21).

[3] As the *total consumption by fire* on the altar was the culminating point in the *burnt-offering*, so was *the sacrificial feast* of the peace-offering. See Kurtz's *Sacrificial Worship*, p. 163.

[4] See above, p. 167.

[5] See the Prayer of Consecration in the Communion Service.

instituted and ordained this Feast upon His one Great Sacrifice[1], once offered. By this sacred Banquet the peace He has made for us is accepted, the covenant He has ratified is sealed, and we are assured of God's "favour and goodness towards us[2]." At this Holy Table we are God's guests, and He "vouchsafes to feed us, who duly receive these holy mysteries, with the spiritual food of the most precious Body and Blood of His Son our Saviour Jesus Christ;" we "spiritually eat the flesh of Christ and drink His Blood; we dwell in Christ, and Christ in us; we are one with Christ, and Christ with us;" and thus verily and indeed, though after a heavenly and spiritual manner[3], under the form of Bread and Wine, are given, taken, and received by the faithful the Body and Blood of Him, who *gave His flesh for the life of the world* (Jn. vi. 51).

[1] "The Passover was a feast on a sacrifice; the Eucharist is a feast on a sacrifice. The one on the lamb; the other on the Lamb of God. The one true; the other true. But the one carnally true; *the other spiritually, and therefore even more true.*" Bp. Browne on Art. XXVIII. Sect. 2.

[2] See the Second Prayer in the Post-Communion Service.

[3] See the XXVIIIth Article, and compare the address to each communicant at the moment of receiving, "Take and eat this in remembrance that Christ died for thee, and *feed on Him in thine heart by faith with thanksgiving.*" "What these elements are in themselves it skilleth not. It is enough that unto me that take them they are the Body and Blood of Christ. His promise in witness hereof sufficeth. His word He knoweth which way to accomplish. Why should any cogitation possess the mind of a faithful communicant; but, O my God, Thou art true; O my soul, thou art happy!" Hooker's *Eccl. Pol.* Bk. v. lxvii. 12.

CHAPTER IV.

THE BENEFITS OF THE LORD'S SUPPER.

1. **Connection.** Having thus treated both of the outward part or sign and the inward part or thing signified in the Lord's Supper, the Catechism proceeds to ask, "What are the benefits whereof we are thereby partakers?" To this question it teaches us to reply, *The strengthening and refreshing of our souls by the Body and Blood of Christ, as our bodies are by the Bread and Wine.*

2. **The Benefits** which we receive are thus declared to be two, (1) *Strengthening*, and (2) *Refreshing*, and these effects are compared to those wrought on our natural bodies by the reception of bread and wine. Bread, the staff of life, *strengtheneth man's heart*[1] (Ps. civ. 15), and without it "the body fails, and falls, decays, pines away, and winders to nothing[2]." Wine *maketh glad the heart of man* (Ps. civ. 15), cheers and refreshes the body, and imparts vigour and sustenance, so that it faints not. Even so in the inner man and our spiritual nature are wrought by these holy mysteries, effects analogous to those in the outward man by "the creatures[3] of bread and wine."

---

[1] "The testimony of Geology confirms unequivocally the testimony of Revelation, and shews us that corn was not only specially created for man's use, but was also got ready specially for the appointed hour of his appearance on earth. Not the slightest trace or vestige of corn-plants occurs in any of the strata of the earth, until we come to the most recent formations, contemporaneous with man." Macmillan's *Bible Teachings in Nature.*

[2] Nicholson *On the Catechism*, p. 225; Hammond's *Practical Catechism*, p. 397.

[3] Creatures, from the Latin *creatura*, in its original sense is used of "anything created," and is not limited to "living

3. **Spiritual Strength needed.** And first by the reception of this Holy Sacrament our souls receive *strength*. Situated as we are in this world, inheriting a sin-infected nature, and exposed to the assaults of our spiritual Foe[1], we " have no power of ourselves to help ourselves," we " cannot always stand upright," " we are sore let and hindered in running the race that is set before us[2]," and are liable to continual falls[3]. We need, therefore, constantly to be strengthened for our spiritual warfare; we require that the weakness of our mortal nature should from time to time be fortified for our daily contest, that the wounds we continually inflict upon ourselves in our encounter with the world, the flesh, and the devil should be healed.

4. **Spiritual Strength supplied.** And what thus, " as long as the days of our warfare last[4]," we sorely need, He, who is *the Bread of Life* (Jn. vi. 35), and without whom we *can do nothing* (Jn. xv. 5), of His mercy and goodness vouchsafes to supply. For as often as with a true penitent heart and lively faith we receive this holy Sacrament, our communion with Him, who is "the Strength of all them that put their trust in Him[5]," is renewed, we dwell in Him, and He in us, and He im-

---

things." Compare (1) Rom. i. 25, *Who exchanged the truth of God for a lie, and worshipped and served the creature* (τῇ κτίσει) = created objects, *rather than the Creator;* (2) 1 Tim. iv. 4, *For every creature* (πᾶν κτίσμα) *of God is good.*

[1] See above, p. 131, and the notes.
[2] Collect for the Fourth Sunday in Advent.
[3] See Hammond's *Practical Catechism*, p. 397.
[4] " As long as the days of our warfare last, during the time that we are both subject to diminution and capable of augmentation in grace, the words of our Lord and Saviour Christ will remain forcible, *Except ye eat the Flesh of the Son of Man, and drink His Blood, ye have no life in you,* Jn. vi. 53." Hooker's *Eccl. Pol.* Bk. v. Chap. lxvii. 1.
[5] Collect for the First Sunday after Trinity.

parts to us grace and strength[1] according to our day and our needs (2 Cor. xii. 9). As often, again, as we fall into sin through ignorance, or frailty, or the violence of any temptation, He who is *our Advocate with the Father*[2] (1 Jn. ii. 1), in the symbols of His Body broken and His Blood *shed for the remission of sins* (Mtt. xxvi. 28) gives us the seal and pledge of His willingness to "forgive us all that is past[3]," and thus "our sinful bodies are made clean by His Body, and our souls washed through His most precious Blood" (1 Jn. i. 7, 9), and we are once more strengthened for our daily warfare (Phil. iv. 13).

5. **Need of refreshment.** Again in the valley of this mortal life, being in ourselves full of infirmity and weakness, and our consciences grieved and wearied with the burden of our sins, we are apt to be often *disquieted and cast down* (Ps. xlii. 5), to fear that God has shut up His tender mercies in displeasure, or that He has *forgotten to be gracious* (Ps. lxxvii. 9). Often also we are afflicted and distressed in mind, or body, or estate; we are tossed about with many perplexities and troubles; the path set before us is toilsome; the burden laid upon us seems more than we can bear; and we long to be refreshed and cheered, to be quickened and revived (Ps. xlii. 1).

6. **Spiritual Refreshment vouchsafed.** And the refreshment we thus need is in this holy Sacrament vouchsafed. He, who *knoweth our frame*, who *remem-*

---

[1] "By the communion of the holy supper of the Lorde, we are preserued and strengthened, that we maye be able stedfastly to stand and fyght, against the violent inuasions of sin and the power of the Deuel." Cranmer's *Catechism*, p. 206; see also Hammond's *Practical Catechism*, pp. 396, 397.

[2] Hence the need of special confession of sins before the reception of the Communion. See the Communion Service.

[3] See the Confession in the Communion Service.

bereth that we are dust (Ps. ciii. 14), speaks to us His comfortable words, saying, *Come unto Me all ye that travail and are heavy laden, and I will refresh you* (Mtt. xi. 28). He cheers[1] us with the assurance of His favour and goodness towards us. He refreshes[2] us with the Glad Tidings of the abundance of His Mercy, and of the continuance of His Intercession at the right hand of His Father (1 Jn. ii. 1). In the Holy Mysteries which He hath instituted, He gives us pledges that *neither death, nor life, nor angels, nor principalities, nor powers, nor things present, nor things to come, nor height, nor depth, nor any other creature will be able to separate us from His love* (Rom. viii. 38, 39), which endured the bitter pains of the Cross for us. Thus He encourages us to *endure unto the end* (Mtt. xxiv. 13), so to *run that we may obtain* (1 Cor. ix. 24), so to *contend that we may overcome* (Rev. ii. 7), so to *labour* that we *faint not*[3] (Rev. ii. 3; Heb. iii. 6).

CHAPTER V.

REQUISITES FOR APPROACH TO THE LORD'S SUPPER.

1. **Connection.** Such being the dignity of this Holy Mystery, and such the benefits whereof we are therein made partakers, the Catechism proceeds to treat lastly of the attitude of heart and feeling with which we should approach it. It therefore asks, "What

---

[1] Ps. xlii. 1; Isai. liv. 11.
[2] See Nicholson *On the Catechism*, p. 228.
[3] "Seying oure Savioure Christe doth gyue vs Hys Bodye to be our meat, and His Bloude to be oure drynke, and thereby doth declare that He will effectually dwel in vs, strengthen and preserue vs to euer lasting lyfe we may stedfastly belieue that Christ doth work in us, and that He will give us ghostly strength, and stedfastness, that we lyke grene braunches maye continue in the Vine and so be ful of sappe, and bryng forth good fruit." Cranmer's *Catechism*.

is required of them who come to the Lord's Supper?" To this the answer we are taught to give is, *To examine themselves*, whether

   (i) *They repent them truly of their former sins, stedfastly purposing to lead a new life;* whether

   (ii) *They have a lively faith in God's mercy through Christ, with a thankful remembrance of His death;* whether

   (iii) *They be in charity with all men*[1]?

2. **The duty of self-examination** before the reception of this Sacrament is directly taught us by St Paul. For after severely rebuking the Corinthians for the irreverent way in which they profaned this holy Banquet, making no distinction between it and an ordinary meal, and not *discerning the Lord's Body* (1 Cor. xi. 29), he continues, *But let a man examine*[2] *himself, and so let him eat of that Bread and drink of that Cup* (1 Cor. xi. 28), and adds in reference to the temporal chastisements[3] with which they had been

---

[1] Compare the Exhortation in the Communion Service. "Judge therefore yourselves, brethren, that ye be not judged of the Lord; (1) *repent* you truly for your sins past; (2) have a lively and stedfast *faith* in Christ our Saviour; (3) *amend* your lives; and (4) be in perfect *charity* with all men; so shall ye be meet partakers of these holy mysteries." See also the Exhortation before Confession.

[2] Δοκιμαζέτω ἑαυτόν = *let him put himself to the test*, which "notes a diligent and exact enquiry, such as lapidaries and goldsmiths use, to find out true metal from counterfeit, good from bad." Nicholson *On the Catechism*, p. 232. Compare for (1) the etymological sense of the word, 1 Pet. i. 7, χρυσίου διὰ πυρὸς δοκιμαζομένου, for (2) its secondary sense, 1 Thess. ii. 4; Gal. vi. 4; 1 Cor. iii. 13; 2 Cor. xiii. 5; Eph. v. 10.

[3] See 1 Cor. xi. 30, and above, p. 174, n., and compare the Exhortation in the Communion Service, "We provoke Him to plague us with divers diseases, and sundry kinds of death." Κρίμα, "non dicit τὸ κατάκριμα *condemnationem*, sed judicium aliquod, morbum, mortemve corporis." Bengel *in loc.*

visited, *If we had judged ourselves*[1] *we should not have been judged; but now that we are judged, it is by the Lord that we are chastened*[2], *that we may not be condemned with the world* (1 Cor. xi. 31, 32).

3. **Repentance.** The first point, then, respecting which we are to examine ourselves, is whether we repent us truly and sincerely of our former sins, and at the same time, since, as we have seen[3], all genuine repentance includes resolutions of amendment for the future, whether we stedfastly purpose to lead a new life, "following the commandments of God, and walking from henceforth in His holy ways[4]."

4. **Faith.** The second point for self-examination is whether we have a lively faith in God's mercy through Christ. *Without faith*, indeed, *it is impossible to please God* (Heb. xi. 6), and the possession of faith is the condition of the answering of any petition (Mk. xi. 24). But a settled persuasion[5] that for the sake of the meritorious cross and passion of His dear Son *God is faithful and just to forgive us our sins, and to cleanse us from all unrighteousness* (1 Jn. i. 9) is essential to a due participation of this Sacrament of our Redemption.

---

[1] Εἰ ἑαυτοὺς διεκρίνομεν, οὐκ ἂν ἐκρινόμεθα. Διεκρίνομεν, *dijudicaremus* ante factum, ἐκρινόμεθα, *judicaremur* post factum. Bengel.

[2] Παιδευόμεθα, *per molestias* eruditio, August. *Enarr. in Ps.* cxix. 67. Trench's *Synonyms*, p. 108. Compare Lk. xxiii. 16; Heb. xii. 5, 7, 8.

[3] On μετάνοια and the nature of genuine repentance (Jer. xxiv. 7; Joel ii. 12, 13), including (*a*) *godly sorrow* (2 Cor. vii. 8, 9), (*b*) *confession of sin* (Ps. xxxii. 5; Lk. xv. 18; 1 Jn. i. 9), (*c*) *full purpose of amendment* (Prov. xxviii. 13; and 2 Pet. ii. 20—22) see above, p. 158, n.

[4] See the Exhortation in the Communion Service.

[5] "Thus we see, beloved, that resorting to this Table, we must pluck up all the roots of infidelity, all distrust in God's promises, that we make ourselves living members of Christ's Body." First Part of the "Homily concerning the Sacrament."

And not only must we have a lively[1], a living, vigorous faith in God's mercy, and stay ourselves and rest upon it as a sure hope, but with it also a thankful[2] "remembrance of Christ's death, and of the innumerable benefits which by His precious bloodshedding He hath obtained to us."

5. **Charity.** Moreover, since *faith, if it hath not works, is dead in itself*, and if it have any living root[3] *worketh by love* (Gal. v. 6), the third point for self-examination is, whether we are living in *charity*[4] or

---

[1] Lively = *living, full of life, vigorous*, and a vital faith shows itself by good works. For this use of lively compare (1) Ps. xxxviii. 19, "Mine enemies are *lively*" (where see the margin); (2) Acts vii. 38, "Who received the *lively oracles* to give unto us;" (3) 1 Pet. i. 3, "a *lively* hope;" (4) 2 Pet. ii. 5, "*lively* stones" = "a *living* Stone," 1 Pet. ii. 4. When our Version was made, there was scarcely any distinction between "lively" and "living." Compare

"Lysistratus of Sicyone was the first that represented the shape of a man's visage in a mould from the *lively* face indeed."—Holland, *Pliny*, xxxv. 12.

"Was it well done to suffer him, imprisoned in chains, lying in a dark dungeon, to draw his *lively* breath at the pleasure of the hangman?"—Holland, *Livy*, p. 228.

"That his dear father might interment have,
The young man entered a *lively* grave."
                  Massinger's *Fatal Dowry*, Act II. Sc. 1.

See Trench's *Select Glossary*, pp. 120, 121; and the *Bible Word-Book*, p. 299.

[2] On the duty of thankfulness compare the Parable of the *Ten Lepers*, Lk. xvii. 17, 18; Col. i. 12—14, and see the Exhortation in the Communion Service, "*Above all things ye must give most humble and hearty thanks* to God the Father, the Son, and the Holy Ghost, for the redemption of the world by the death and passion of our Saviour Christ."

[3] Νεκρά ἐστιν καθ' ἑαυτήν = *is dead in itself*, not "being *alone*" as in our English Version.

[4] Charity, from the Latin *caritas*, through the Fr. *charité*, is now almost confined to *almsgiving*, but is used in our Authorized Version to translate ἀγάπη, "a word born within the bosom of revealed religion," which denotes Christian love flowing from a sense of God's love for us. See 1 Cor. xiii. 1,

love with all men. For the Lord's Supper is not only the seal and pledge of God's great love towards us, but an assurance of our union with one another (1 Cor. x. 17), of our being very members incorporate in the mystical Body of His Son, which is the blessed company of *all faithful people*[1]. But if we *love not our brother, whom we have seen, how can we love God, whom we have not seen?* (1 Jn. iv. 20), and how can we partake of that holy Feast, which declares "not only our communion with Christ, but that unity also, wherein they that eat at this table should be knit together[2]"?

6. **Proofs of Charity.** This Charity or Christian love will display itself (1) in a readiness to make restitution and satisfaction for all injuries and wrongs done by us to any other[3] (Mtt. v. 24); (2) in a willingness to forgive others that have offended us, even as we would have forgiveness for our offences from our heavenly Father (Mtt. vi. 14, 15); (3) in a forwardness to give alms of our substance to supply the wants of our poorer brethren[4], and to offer up hearty prayer for "all sorts and conditions of men," who are fellowmembers with us of the same Body and joint-heirs of the same glorious Kingdom[5].

and compare Wiclif's Version of Rom. viii. 39, "Neither death, neither lyf...neither noon othir creature mai departe us from the *charite* of God that is in Jesu Christ our Lord." See Trench's *Synonyms*, p. 43; *The Bible Word-Book*, p. 97.

[1] See the Second Prayer in the Post Communion Service; Noell's *Catechism*.

[2] See the Second Part of the Homily *Concerning the Sacrament*.

[3] See above, on the petition in the Lord's Prayer, *Forgive us our trespasses*, p. 126.

[4] Hence the occurrence of the Offertory in the Communion Service, in accordance with the usage of all the ancient Liturgies. Comp. Acts ii. 45, 46; 1 Cor. xvi. 2; Heb. xiii. 16.

[5] See above, p. 117.

I.

GENERAL INDEX.

A.

Abram, meaning of, 5
Absolution of the Church, 65
Adult baptism, 159
Adultery forbidden, 93
Almighty, meaning of, 21, 22
Amen, meaning of, 139; use in Scripture, 136, n.
Angels, services of, 120
Apostles' Creed, 13
Apostles, receive the gift of the Holy Ghost, 50; found the Christian Church, 55; inculcate the duty of prayer, 104; are taught to pray by our Lord, 105; are commanded to baptize all nations, 146; their teaching concerning baptism, 158; their practice, 162
Articles of the Creed, 18
Ascension of our Lord, 44
Athanasian Creed, 14

B.

Baptism, name given in, 5, 6; a covenant, 7, 8; vows of, 10; remission in, 61, n.; a sacrament, 139; the outward sign in, 143; of proselytes, 148; of John, 148; of our Lord, 149; mode of administration of, 150; formula of, 151; the grace of, 154; the requirements for, 156; of Infants, 160; of Adults, 160
Benefits of the Lord's Supper, 178
Birth of our Lord, 28; the new, 151
Blood of Christ shed for us, 167, 171; of the New Testament, 171; verily received by the faithful in the Lord's Supper, 177; our souls strengthened by, 179; shed for the remission of our sins, 180
Body, burial of our Lord's, 33; resurrection of our Lord's, 37; resurrection of ours, 60; duty of keeping in temperance, 93; life of the, 121; Christ's body given for us, 166, 170; verily received by the faithful in the Lord's Supper, 177; our souls strengthened by, 179; Christ's mystical body, 185
Bread, our daily, 122; Christ the bread of life, 166; unleavened, eaten at the Passover, 169; an outward sign in the Lord's Supper, 172
Burial of our Lord, 33

C.

Calvary, derivation of, 32
Catechism, meaning of, 1; derivation of, 1; of the Church of England, 1; its divisions, 2; history of, 2
Catechist, meaning of, 1
Catechumen, 1
Catholic, meaning of, 57; Church, 57
Charity, necessity of, 184; proofs of, 185
Chastity, duty of, 93
Child of God, 9
Children, duty of, 87; love of Christ towards little, 161
Christ, members of, 8; our Prophet, Priest and King, 24; meaning of the name, 24; Death of, 32; Resurrection of, 36; Ascension of, 40; our Judge, 46
Christian name, the, 5
Church, meaning of the word, 53; derivation of, 53; foundation of the, 54; spread of the, 55; Holy, 56; Catholic, 56; Militant, 57; Triumphant, 59
Comforter, the, 53
Commandments, the Ten, 74; their division, 76; the First, 77; the Second, 80; the Third, 82; the Fourth, 84; the Fifth, 87; the Sixth, 90; the Seventh, 92; the Eighth, 94; the Ninth, 96; the Tenth, 98

INDEX.   187

Communion of saints, the, 59
Confidence in God, 109
Confirmation, 163
Congregation of believers, 55
Contentment, duty of, 100
Covenant, the Mosaic, 7; the Christian, 7; baptism admits into, 7; conditions of, 9
Covetousness forbidden, 99
Creation, Sabbath a commemoration of the, 85
Creeds, origin of, 13; the Apostles' Creed, 13; the Nicene Creed, 14; the Athanasian Creed, 14
Crucifixion of our Lord, 31

D.

Death of our Lord, 32; a sacrifice, 165; the Lord's Supper a remembrance of, 167
Devil, works of the, 11; names of, 11, n.; snares of, 128
Doxology, the, 133—137; wanting in St Luke, 133; not explained in the Catechism, 133
Duty of keeping our baptismal vows, 16; towards God, 79; towards our neighbour, 87; towards parents, 89; of purity, 93; of truth and justice, 95; of keeping the tongue from lying and slandering, 97; of contentment, 100; of forgiveness, 126; of prayer, 129; of self-examination, 181

E.

Eucharist, the, 176
Ever, for, in doxology, 135
Everlasting life, 70; death, 132
Evil in the world, 130; in ourselves, 131; One, the, 131; deliver us from, 132
Examination, self, duty of, 182

F.

Faith, a vow of, 12; natural, 12; religious, 13; contained in creeds, 13, 14; required in Baptism, 159; in the Lord's Supper, 183
Fatherhood of God, the, 21, 108
Father, our, use of in Lord's Prayer, 107

Feast, the Paschal, 169; rites of the, 170; the Eucharistic, 176
Flesh, lusts of, 12
Forgiveness of others, a duty, 126; a proof of charity, 185
Forgiveness of sins: an article of the Creed, 61—65; prayed for in the Lord's Prayer, 124—129; promised in baptism, 153

G.

Glory, kingdom of, 117; in Doxology, 135
God-fathers and mothers, 6
God, our being in, 20; the Father, 21; the Son, 25; the right hand, 41; the Holy Ghost, 50; commandments of, 75; our duty towards, 79; a jealous, 81; Fatherhood of, 108; the name of, 111; names of, 112; kingdom of, 114, 116; secret will of, 118; revealed will of, 119; forgiveness of, 126
Grace, need of divine, 16; kingdom of, 115

H.

Heaven, Maker of, 22, n.; He ascended into, 40; Father in, 110; Kingdom of, 114
Hell, meaning of, 34, n.; our Lord's descent into, 35
Holy Ghost, a Person, 48; proceedeth from the Father and Son, 49; is God, 50; the giver of life, 50, 51; why called Holy, 51; the Comforter, 52

I.

Ichabod, meaning of, 5
Idolatry forbidden, 71; Egyptian, 80; warnings against, 81
Incarnation of our Lord, 27
Infant Baptism, 160; justified by the analogy of the old covenant, 160; by the teaching of our Lord, 161; by Apostolic practice, 162; by custom of the primitive church, 162; propriety of, 163
Isaac, meaning of, 5
Israelites, typical condition of the, 76; commandments addressed to the, 80

J.

Jealous, how God is, 81
Jehovah, name of, 102
Jesus, name of, 23; meaning of, 23
John, message of, 114; baptism of, 145
Joshua, name of, 23
Judge, Christ as the, 46
Judgment, by Christ, 44; of the quick and the dead, 45
Justice, duty of, 95

K.

King, Christ our, 42
Kingdom of Heaven, the, 114; of God, 114, 134; of grace, 115; of Satan, 115, n.; of glory, 117

L.

Lamb, the Paschal, 172
Life, everlasting, 70; present, 70; future, 70, 71; negative, 71; positive, 71; of the body, 121; of the soul, 123
Lord's Day, 85
Lord's Prayer, 101, 105; its form, 105; its structure, 106
Lord's Supper, 164—185
Lord, title of, 26
Lustrations, in heathen nations, 146; among the Jews, 147
Lusts of the flesh, 12
Lying forbidden, 97

M.

Maker of heaven and earth, 22
Malice forbidden, 91
Man, Christ the perfect, 28
Marriage, sanctity of, 92
Mary, the Virgin, 27
Member of Christ, a, 8; of the kingdom of heaven, 9
Militant, Church, 57
Murder forbidden, 90

N.

Name, the Christian, 5; when and by whom given, 6; of Jesus, 23; of Christ, 24; not to be taken in vain, 83; of God, 111; to be hallowed, 113
Neighbour, duty towards our, 87

O.

Obedience, duty of, 89
Olivet, the walk to, 39

P.

Paradise, 35
Parents, authority of, 88; to be honoured, 89
Paschal Feast, the, 169; Lamb, the, 172, 173
Passover, an historical memorial, 168; its rites, 170; a feast upon a sacrifice, 175
Paul, St, his teaching respecting the Lord's Supper, 168, 174; self-examination, 182; repentance, 158; prayer, 104; the union between Christ and His Church, 93; obedience to parents, 89; the joys of heaven, 71; the future judgment, 44, 45
Person, of the Father, 21; of the Son, 23; of the Holy Ghost, 48
Pilate, Pontius, governor of Judea, 30; our Lord's sufferings under, 31
Pomps of the world to be renounced, 11
Praise, ascription of, 134
Prayer, necessity of, 103; taught by our Lord, 103; by the Apostles, 105
Pride, a work of the devil, 11
Priest, Christ our, 42
Promises of God in Baptism, 153
Proselytes, baptism of, 148; new life begun by, 154; examination of Jewish, 156
Purity, duty of, 93

Q.

Quick, the, judgment of, 45

R.

Rainbow, the, a sign, 144
Redemption, the promise of, 27; the Lord's Supper, a Sacrament of, 176, 183
Refreshment, spiritual, need of, 180; vouchsafed, 180
Regeneration, 155, and notes
Renunciation, 10, 16
Repentance, nature of, 158; re-

quired in baptism, 158; in the Lord's Supper, 183
Resurrection of the Flesh, 65, n.; Old Testament hopes of, 66; New Testament reveals what is anticipated in the Old, 66; pledges of, 67; of Christ, 67; of the Body, 68
Rights of property, 94

S.

Sabbath, institution of, 84; observed amongst the Jews, 85; the Lord's day, 85; its obligation, 86
Sacrament, meaning of, 141; classical use, 140; ecclesiastical use, 140, 141
Sacraments, number of, 138; ordained by Christ, 138; generally necessary to salvation, 139
Sacrifice, the death of Christ a, 165; the Lord's Supper a memorial of, 167; the Passover a feast upon a, 175; the Eucharist a feast upon a, 176
Saints, meaning of, 58; communion of, 59; departed, 60
Salvation, two sacraments necessary to, 139
Samuel, meaning of, 5
Satan, meaning of, 11
Scriptures, our Lord's descent into Hades proved from, 35; His resurrection according to the, 37; revelations concerning future judgment, 46; speak of Holy Ghost as a Person, 49; images of applied to sin, 61
Seth, meaning of, 5
Signs, in Baptism and in the Lord's Supper, 143; use of material things as, 143
Sin, various names for, 61, 62; guilt of, 62; forgiveness of, 63; means and conditions, 64, 65; forgiven in Baptism, 65; prayer for forgiveness of, 125; a death unto, 154
Slandering forbidden, 97
Soldier of Christ, 10
Son of God, 25; of Man, 47
Soul, life of the, 123; needs of the, 123; preparation of, 156; strengthened by the Eucharist, 179

Spirit, the Holy, 49; the Giver of life, 50; of holiness, 51
Spiritual strength, 179; refreshment, 180
Sponsors, 6, 163
Stealing forbidden, 95
Strength, spiritual, needed, 179; supplied, 179
Sufferings of our Lord, 29; their prediction, 29; their fulfilment, 30
Supper, the Lord's, the object of its institution, 164; a memorial of Christ's sacrifice, 167; instituted at a Paschal Feast, 169; the outward sign of, 172; the inward part of, 173; the solemnity of, 175; a feast upon a sacrifice, 176; the benefits thereof, 178; requisites for approach to, 181; a seal and pledge of God's love towards us, 185; an assurance of our union with each other, 185
Sureties, 6, 163
Surname, 5

T.

Temptation, meaning of, 127; prayer against, 128
Thankfulness, duty of, 183
Trespasses, meaning of, 124; our own, 124; forgiveness of, 125; those of others, 126
Truth, duty of, 95

V.

Vanity of the world, 11
Vow, the Baptismal, 10

W.

Watchfulness, duty of, 129
Water, the outward sign in Baptism, 146; used for ceremonial purification, 146
Whitsunday, derivation of, 51
Wickedness of the world, 11; of our own hearts, 131
Will of God, the secret, 118; revealed, 119
Wine, used at the Passover, 169; an element of the Lord's Supper, 172
World, pomps and vanity of, 11
Wrath, children of, 151

II.
INDEX OF GREEK AND LATIN WORDS.

Ἄβυσσος, 34
Ἅιδης, 34
Ἁγιάζειν, 113
Ἀγνόημα, 62
Αἰχμαλωτίζειν, 103
Ἀλλάσσειν ἐν, 78
Ἁμαρτία, 61
Ἀμήν, 136
Ἀνάδοχοι, 6
Ἀνακαίνωσις, 156
Ἀνομία, 62
Ἄνωθεν, 151
Ἀπολύτρωσις, 64

Βασιλεία τῶν οὐρανῶν, 114
Bulla, 6

Γέεννα, 36

Caritas, 184
Concupiscentia, 99
Credo Deum, 20
—— Deo, 20
—— in Deum, 20

Delictum, 62
Διαθήκη, 171
Dies Dominica, 86
Dies lustricus, 6
Δοκιμάζειν, 182
Δουλαγωγῶ, 93

Ἐγκράτεια, 94
Ἐκκλησία, 54
Ἐπιθυμία, 99
Ἐπιούσιος, 123

Fide-jussores, 6

Ἥττημα, 62

ΙΗΣΟΥΣ, 23
Ἱλασμός, 64

Καταγγέλλειν, 167

Καταλλαγή, 64
Κατηχέω, 1
Κλάσις τοῦ ἄρτου, 164
Κοινωνία, 174
Κρανίον, 32
Κυριακή, 53
—— ἡμέρα, ἡ, 86
Κύριος, 26

Λόγχη, 33

Μετάνοια, 158
Μυστήριον, 142
Μωρέ, 91

Ὀπτανόμενος, 37
Ὀργή, 151
Ὅρος, 103
Ὀφείλημα, 62

Παλιγγενεσία, 155
Παντοκράτωρ, 22
Παράβασις, 61
Παράδεισος, 35
Παράκλητος, 49
Παρακοή, 62
Πατήρ, 108
Πειρασμός, 148
Perseverantia, 132
Προσκαρτερεῖν, 104

Renuntiare, 10
Ῥύεσθαι, 130

Σύμβολον, 13
Συναγωγή, 54
Σωζομένους, τούς, 17

Τάγμα, 68
Ταπείνωσις, 72
Tessera militaris, 13

Ὑπομονή, 132

Φυλακή, 35

III.

INDEX OF OTHER WORDS.

Abaddon, 11
Agape, 174
Allfadir, 108
Amen, 136
Apollyon, 11
Atonement, 64

Calvary, 32
Catechism, 1
Catholic, 57
Charity, 184
Comforter, 49
Creature, 178

Daily bread, 122

Endeavour, 164
Eschew, 117
Eucharist, 165

Generally, 140

Instant, 104

Jealous, 81
JEHOVAH, 112

Ghost, 48
Ghostly, 131

Grace, 102

Lively, 184

Mystery, 142

Paraclete, 49
Paradise, 35
Pharaoh, 80
Picking, 95
Potipherah, 80

Quick, 45

Rehearse, 18
Renounce, 10

Sabaoth, 22
Succour, 89
Surname, 5

Temperance, 93
Testament, 171

Very, 25

Which, 107
Whitsunday, 51

THE END.

CAMBRIDGE: PRINTED AT THE UNIVERSITY PRESS.

JANUARY, 1868.

16, BEDFORD STREET, COVENT GARDEN,

London.

MACMILLAN AND CO.'S

CLASSICAL BOOKS.

ÆSCHYLUS.—ÆSCHYLI EUMENIDES. The Greek Text, with English Notes, and English Verse Translation and an Introduction. By BERNARD DRAKE, M.A., late Fellow of King's College, Cambridge. 8vo. 7s. 6d.

> The Greek Text adopted in this Edition is based upon that of Wellauer, which may be said in general terms to represent that of the best manuscripts. But in correcting the Text, and in the Notes, advantage has been taken of the suggestions of Hermann, Paley, Linwood, and other commentators.

ARISTOTLE.—ARISTOTLE ON FALLACIES; OR, THE SOPHISTICI ELENCHI. With a Translation and Notes by EDWARD POSTE, M.A., Fellow of Oriel College, Oxford. 8vo. 8s. 6d.

> Besides the doctrine of Fallacies, Aristotle offers either in this treatise, or in other passages quoted in the commentary, various glances over the world of science and opinion, various suggestions on problems which are still agitated, and a vivid picture of the ancient system of dialectics, which it is hoped may be found both interesting and instructive.
>
> "It is not only scholarlike and careful; it is also perspicuous."—*Guardian.*

ARISTOTLE.—AN INTRODUCTION TO ARISTOTLE'S RHETORIC. With Analysis, Notes, and Appendices. By E. M. COPE, Senior Fellow and Tutor of Trinity College, Cambridge. 8vo. 14s.

> This work is introductory to an edition of the Greek Text of Aristotle's Rhetoric, which is in course of preparation.
>
> "Mr. Cope has given a very useful appendage to the promised Greek Text; but also a work of so much independent use that he is quite justified in his separate publication. All who have the Greek Text will find themselves supplied with a comment; and those who have not will find an analysis of the work."—*Athenæum.*

CATULLUS.—CATULLI VERONENSIS LIBER, edited by R. ELLIS, Fellow of Trinity College, Oxford. 18mo. 3*s.* 6*d.*

> "It is little to say that no edition of Catullus at once so scholarlike has ever appeared in England."—*Athenæum.*

> "Rarely have we read a classic author with so reliable, acute, and safe a guide."—*Saturday Review.*

CICERO.—THE SECOND PHILIPPIC ORATION. With an Introduction and Notes, translated from the German of KARL HALM. Edited, with Corrections and Additions, by JOHN E. B. MAYOR, M.A., Fellow and Classical Lecturer of St. John's College, Cambridge. Third Edition, revised. Fcap. 8vo. 5*s.*

> "A very valuable edition, from which the student may gather much both in the way of information directly communicated, and directions to other sources of knowledge."—*Athenæum.*

DEMOSTHENES.—DEMOSTHENES on the CROWN. The Greek Text with English Notes. By B. DRAKE, M.A., late Fellow of King's College, Cambridge. Third Edition, to which is prefixed ÆSCHINES AGAINST CTESIPHON, with English Notes. Fcap. 8vo. 5*s.*

> The terseness and felicity of Mr. Drake's translations constitute perhaps the chief value of his edition, and the historical and archæological details necessary to understanding the *De Coronâ* have in some measure been anticipated in the notes on the Oration of Æschines. In both, the text adopted in the Zurich edition of 1851, and taken from the Parisian MS., has been adhered to without any variation. Where the readings of Bekker, Dissen, and others appear preferable, they are subjoined in the notes.

HODGSON.—MYTHOLOGY FOR LATIN VERSIFICATION. A Brief Sketch of the Fables of the Ancients, prepared to be rendered into Latin Verse for Schools. By F. HODGSON, B.D., late Provost of Eton. New Edition, revised by F. C. HODGSON, M.A. 18mo. 3*s.*

> Intending the little book to be entirely elementary, the Author has made it as easy as he could, without too largely superseding the use of the Dictionary and Gradus. By the facilities here afforded, it will be possible, in many cases, for a boy to get rapidly through these preparatory exercises; and thus, having mastered the first difficulties, he may advance with better hopes of improvement to subjects of higher character, and verses of more difficult composition.

JESSOPP.—A MANUAL OF THE GREEK ACCIDENCE FOR THE USE OF BEGINNERS. By AUGUSTUS JESSOPP, M.A., Head Master of King Edward the Sixth School, Norwich. Fcap. 8vo. 3*s.* 6*d.*

JUVENAL.—JUVENAL, FOR SCHOOLS. With English Notes. By J. E. B. MAYOR, M.A. New and Cheaper Edition. Crown 8vo. [*In the Press.*

"A School edition of Juvenal, which, for really ripe scholarship, extensive acquaintance with Latin literature, and familiar knowledge of Continental criticism, ancient and modern, is unsurpassed, we do not say among English School-books, but among English editions generally."—*Edinburgh Review.*

LYTTELTON.—THE COMUS of MILTON rendered into Greek Verse. By LORD LYTTELTON. Extra fcap. 8vo. Second Edition. 5*s.*

— THE SAMSON AGONISTES of MILTON rendered into Greek Verse. By LORD LYTTELTON. Extra fcap. 8vo. 6*s.* 6*d.*

MARSHALL.—A TABLE OF IRREGULAR GREEK VERBS, Classified according to the Arrangement of Curtius's Greek Grammar. By I. M. MARSHALL, M.A., Fellow and late Lecturer of Brasenose College, Oxford; one of the Masters in Clifton College. 8vo. cloth. 1*s.*

MERIVALE.—KEATS' HYPERION rendered into Latin Verse. By C. MERIVALE, B.D. Second Edition. Extra fcap. 8vo. 3*s.* 6*d.*

PHILOLOGY.—THE JOURNAL of SACRED and CLASSICAL PHILOLOGY. Four Vols. 8vo. 12*s.* 6*d.* each.

PLATO.—THE REPUBLIC OF PLATO. Translated into English, with an Analysis and Notes, by J. Ll. DAVIES, M.A., and D. J. VAUGHAN, M.A. Third Edition, with Vignette Portraits of Plato and Socrates, engraved by JEENS from an Antique Gem. 18mo. 4*s.* 6*d.*

ROBY.—AN ELEMENTARY LATIN GRAMMAR. By H. J. ROBY, M.A. New Edition. 18mo. [*In the Press.*

"It contains an amount of accurate and well-digested knowledge such as is often found wanting in works of much greater pretensions. We know no book which in so small a compass, and with so little parade, contains more sound knowledge of Latin."—*Spectator.*

SALLUST.—CAII SALLUSTII CRISPI Catilina et Jugurtha. For use in Schools (with copious Notes). By C. MERIVALE, B.D. (In the present Edition the Notes have been carefully revised, and a few remarks and explanations added.) Second Edition. Fcap. 8vo. 4s. 6d.

> The Jugurtha and the Catilina may be had separately, price 2s. 6d. each.

TACITUS.—THE HISTORY OF TACITUS translated into ENGLISH. By A. J. CHURCH, M.A., and W. J. BRODRIBB, M.A. With Notes and a Map. 8vo. 10s. 6d.

> The translators have endeavoured to adhere as closely to the original as was thought consistent with a proper observance of English idiom. At the same time it has been their aim to reproduce the precise expressions of the author. The campaign of Civilis is elucidated in a note of some length which is illustrated by a map, containing only the names of places and of tribes occurring in the work.

THRING.—Works by **Edward Thring, M.A.,** Head Master of Uppingham School:—

— A CONSTRUING BOOK. Fcap. 8vo. 2s. 6d.

> This Construing Book is drawn up on the same sort of graduated scale as the Author's *English Grammar.* Passages out of the best Latin Poets are gradually built up into their perfect shape. The few words altered, or inserted as the passages go on, are printed in Italics. It is hoped by this plan that the learner, whilst acquiring the rudiments of language, may store his mind with good poetry and a good vocabulary.

— A LATIN GRADUAL. A First Latin Construing Book for Beginners. Fcap. 8vo. 2s. 6d.

> The main plan of this little work has been well tested.
> The intention is to supply by easy steps a knowledge of Grammar, combined with a good vocabulary; in a word, a book which will not require to be forgotten again as the learner advances.
> A short practical manual of common Mood constructions, with their English equivalents, form the second part.

— A MANUAL of MOOD CONSTRUCTIONS. Extra fcap. 8vo. 1s. 6d.

THUCYDIDES.—THE SICILIAN EXPEDITION. Being Books VI. and VII. of Thucydides, with Notes. A New Edition, revised and enlarged, with a Map. By the Rev. PERCIVAL FROST, M.A., late Fellow of St. John's College, Cambridge. Fcap. 8vo. 5s.

> This edition is mainly a grammatical one. Attention is called to the force of compound verbs, and the exact meaning of the various tenses employed.

WRIGHT.—Works by **J. Wright, M.A.**, late Head Master of Sutton Coldfield School :—

— HELLENICA ; Or, a HISTORY of GREECE in GREEK, as related by Diodorus and Thucydides, being a First Greek Reading Book, with Explanatory Notes Critical and Historical. Second Edition, with a Vocabulary. 12mo. 3s. 6d.

> In the last twenty chapters of this volume, Thucydides sketches the rise and progress of the Athenian Empire in so clear a style and in such simple language, that the author doubts whether any easier or more instructive passages can be selected for the use of the pupil who is commencing Greek.

— A HELP TO LATIN GRAMMAR ; Or, the Form and Use of Words in Latin, with Progressive Exercises. Crown 8vo. 4s. 6d.

> "Never was there a better aid offered alike to teacher and scholar in that arduous pass. The style is at once familiar and strikingly simple and lucid ; and the explanations precisely hit the difficulties, and thoroughly explain them."—*English Journal of Education.*

— THE SEVEN KINGS OF ROME. An Easy Narrative, abridged from the First Book of Livy by the omission of difficult passages, being a First Latin Reading Book, with Grammatical Notes. Fcap. 8vo. 3s.

> This work is intended to supply the pupil with an easy Construing-book, which may at the same time be made the vehicle for instructing him in the rules of grammar and principles of composition. Here Livy tells his own pleasant stories in his own pleasant words. Let Livy be the master to teach a boy Latin, not some English collector of sentences, and he will not be found a dull one.

— A VOCABULARY AND EXERCISES on the "SEVEN KINGS OF ROME." Fcap. 8vo. 2s. 6d.

The Vocabulary and Exercises may also be had bound up with "The Seven Kings of Rome."

MATHEMATICAL BOOKS.

AIRY.—Works by **G. B. Airy**, Astronomer Royal :—

— ELEMENTARY TREATISE ON PARTIAL DIFFERENTIAL EQUATIONS. Designed for the use of Students in the University. With Diagrams. Crown 8vo. cloth, 5s. 6d.

> It is hoped that the methods of solution here explained, and the instances exhibited, will be found sufficient for application to nearly all the important problems of Physical Science, which require for their complete investigation the aid of partial differential equations.

AIRY.—Works by **G. B. Airy**—*Continued.*

— ON THE ALGEBRAICAL AND NUMERICAL THEORY of ERRORS of OBSERVATIONS, and the COMBINATION of OBSERVATIONS. Crown 8vo. cloth, 6s. 6d.

— UNDULATORY THEORY OF OPTICS. Designed for the use of Students in the University. New Edition. Crown 8vo. cloth, 6s. 6d.

— POPULAR ASTRONOMY. With Illustrations. New and Cheaper Edition. 18mo. cloth, 4s. 6d.

> "Popular Astronomy in general has many manuals; but none of them supersede the Six Lectures of the Astronomer Royal under that title. Its speciality is the direct way in which every step is referred to the observatory, and in which the methods and instruments by which every observation is made are fully described. This gives a sense of solidity and substance to astronomical statements which is obtainable in no other way."—*Guardian.*

BAYMA.—THE ELEMENTS of MOLECULAR MECHANICS. By JOSEPH BAYMA, S.J., Professor of Philosophy, Stonyhurst College. Demy 8vo. cloth, 10s. 6d.

BEASLEY.—AN ELEMENTARY TREATISE ON PLANE TRIGONOMETRY. With Examples. By R. D. BEASLEY, M.A., Head Master of Grantham Grammar School. Second Edition, revised and enlarged. Crown 8vo. cloth, 3s. 6d.

> This Treatise is specially intended for use in Schools. The choice of matter has been chiefly guided by the requirements of the three days' Examination at Cambridge, with the exception of proportional parts in Logarithms, which have been omitted. About *Four hundred* Examples have been added, mainly collected from the Examination Papers of the last ten years, and great pains have been taken to exclude from the body of the work any which might dishearten a beginner by their difficulty.

BOOLE.—Works by **G. Boole, D.C.L., F.R.S.**, Professor of Mathematics in the Queen's University, Ireland:—

— A TREATISE ON DIFFERENTIAL EQUATIONS. New and Revised Edition. Edited by I. TODHUNTER. Crown 8vo. cloth, 14s.

> The author has endeavoured in this Treatise to convey as complete an account of the present state of knowledge on the subject of Differential Equations, as was consistent with the idea of a work intended primarily for elementary instruction. The earlier sections of each chapter contain that kind of matter which has usually been thought suitable to the beginner, while the later ones are devoted either to an account of recent discovery, or the discussion of such deeper questions of principle as are likely to present themselves to the reflective student in connexion with the methods and processes of his previous course.

BOOLE.—Works by **G. Boole, D.C.L., F.R.S.**—*Continued.*

— A TREATISE ON DIFFERENTIAL EQUATIONS. Supplementary Volume. Edited by I. TODHUNTER. Crown 8vo. cloth, 8s. 6d.

— THE CALCULUS OF FINITE DIFFERENCES. Crown 8vo. cloth, 10s. 6d.

> This work is in some measure designed as a sequel to the *Treatise on Differential Equations*, and is composed on the same plan.

CAMBRIDGE SENATE-HOUSE PROBLEMS and RIDERS, WITH SOLUTIONS:—

1848—1851.—PROBLEMS. By FERRERS and JACKSON. 8vo. cloth. 15s. 6d.

1848—1851.—RIDERS. By JAMESON. 8vo. cloth. 7s. 6d.

1854.—PROBLEMS and RIDERS. By WALTON and MACKENZIE, 8vo. cloth. 10s. 6d.

1857.—PROBLEMS and RIDERS. By CAMPION and WALTON. 8vo. cloth. 8s. 6d.

1860.—PROBLEMS and RIDERS. By WATSON and ROUTH. Crown 8vo. cloth. 7s. 6d.

1864.—PROBLEMS and RIDERS. By WALTON and WILKINSON. 8vo. cloth. 10s. 6d.

CAMBRIDGE COURSE OF ELEMENTARY NATURAL PHILOSOPHY, for the Degree of B.A. Originally compiled by J. C. SNOWBALL, M.A., late Fellow of St. John's College. Fifth Edition, revised and enlarged, and adapted for the Middle-Class Examinations by THOMAS LUND, B.D., Late Fellow and Lecturer of St. John's College; Editor of Wood's Algebra, &c. Crown 8vo. cloth. 5s.

> This work will be found suited to the wants, not only of University Students, but also of many others who require a short course of Mechanics and Hydrostatics, and especially of the Candidates at our Middle-Class Examinations.

CAMBRIDGE AND DUBLIN MATHEMATICAL JOURNAL. THE COMPLETE WORK, in Nine Vols. 8vo. cloth. £7 4s. (Only a few copies remain on hand.)

CHEYNE.—AN ELEMENTARY TREATISE on the PLANETARY THEORY. With a Collection of Problems. By C. H. H. CHEYNE, B.A. Crown 8vo. cloth. 6s. 6d.

— THE EARTH'S MOTION of ROTATION. By C. H. H. CHEYNE, M.A. Crown 8vo. 3s. 6d.

CHILDE.—THE SINGULAR PROPERTIES of the ELLIPSOID and ASSOCIATED SURFACES of the Nth DEGREE. By the Rev. G. F. CHILDE, M.A., Author of "Ray Surfaces," "Related Caustics," &c. 8vo. 10s. 6d.

CHRISTIE.—A COLLECTION OF ELEMENTARY TEST-QUESTIONS in PURE and MIXED MATHEMATICS; with Answers and Appendices on Synthetic Division, and on the Solution of Numerical Equations by Horner's Method. By JAMES R. CHRISTIE, F.R.S., late First Mathematical Master at the Royal Military Academy, Woolwich. Crown 8vo. cloth, 8s. 6d.

> The Series of Mathematical Exercises here offered to the public is collected from those which the author has from time to time proposed for solution by his pupils during a long career at the Royal Military Academy; they are in the main original: and having well fulfilled the purpose for which they were first framed, it is hoped they may be made still more widely useful.

DALTON.—ARITHMETICAL EXAMPLES. Progressively arranged, with Exercises and Examination Papers. By the Rev. T. DALTON, M.A., Assistant Master of Eton College. 18mo. cloth. 2s. 6d.

DREW.—GEOMETRICAL TREATISE on CONIC SECTIONS. By W. H. DREW, M.A., St. John's College, Cambridge. Third Edition. Crown 8vo. cloth, 4s. 6d.

> In this work the subject of Conic Sections has been placed before the student in such a form that, it is hoped, after mastering the elements of Euclid, he may find it an easy and interesting continuation of his geometrical studies. With a view also of rendering the work a complete Manual of what is required at the Universities, there have been either embodied into the text, or inserted among the examples, every book-work question, problem, and rider, which has been proposed in the Cambridge examinations up to the present time.

DREW.—SOLUTIONS to the PROBLEMS in DREW'S CONIC SECTIONS. Crown 8vo. cloth, 4s. 6d.

FERRERS.—AN ELEMENTARY TREATISE on TRILINEAR CO-ORDINATES, the Method of Reciprocal Polars, and the Theory of Projections. By the Rev. N. M. FERRERS, M.A., Fellow and Tutor of Gonville and Caius College, Cambridge. Second Edition. Crown 8vo. 6s. 6d.

> The object of the author in writing on this subject has mainly been to place it on a basis altogether independent of the ordinary Cartesian system, instead of regarding it as only a special form of Abridged Notation. A short chapter on Determinants has been introduced.

FROST.—THE FIRST THREE SECTIONS of NEWTON'S PRINCIPIA. With Notes and Illustrations. Also a Collection of Problems, principally intended as Examples of Newton's Methods. By PERCIVAL FROST, M.A., late Fellow of St. John's College, Mathematical Lecturer of King's College, Cambridge. Second Edition. 8vo. cloth, 10s. 6d.

> The author's principal intention is to explain difficulties which may be encountered by the student on first reading the Principia, and to illustrate the advantages of a careful study of the methods employed by Newton, by showing the extent to which they may be applied in the solution of problems; he has also endeavoured to give assistance to the student who is engaged in the study of the higher branches of Mathematics, by representing in a geometrical form several of the processes employed in the Differential and Integral Calculus, and in the analytical investigations of Dynamics.

FROST and WOLSTENHOLME.—A TREATISE ON SOLID GEOMETRY. By PERCIVAL FROST, M.A., and the Rev. J. WOLSTENHOLME, M.A., Fellow and Assistant Tutor of Christ's College. 8vo. cloth, 18s.

> The authors have endeavoured to present before students as comprehensive a view of the subject as possible. Intending as they have done to make the subject accessible, at least in the earlier portion, to all classes of students, they have endeavoured to explain fully all the processes which are most useful in dealing with ordinary theorems and problems, thus directing the student to the selection of methods which are best adapted to the exigencies of each problem. In the more difficult portions of the subject, they have considered themselves to be addressing a higher class of students; there they have tried to lay a good foundation on which to build, if any reader should wish to pursue the science beyond the limits to which the work extends.

GODFRAY.—A TREATISE on ASTRONOMY, for the use of Colleges and Schools. By HUGH GODFRAY, M.A., Mathematical Lecturer at Pembroke College, Cambridge. 8vo. cloth. 12s. 6d.

> "We can recommend for its purpose a very good *Treatise on Astronomy* by Mr. Godfray. It is a working book, taking astronomy in its proper place in mathematical science. But it begins with the elementary definitions, and connects the mathematical formulæ very clearly with the visible aspect of the heavens and the instruments which are used for observing it."—*Guardian.*

GODFRAY.—AN ELEMENTARY TREATISE on the LUNAR THEORY. With a brief Sketch of the Problem up to the time of Newton. By HUGH GODFRAY, M.A. Second Edition, revised. Crown 8vo. cloth. 5s. 6d.

HEMMING.—AN ELEMENTARY TREATISE on the DIFFERENTIAL AND INTEGRAL CALCULUS, for the use of Colleges and Schools. By G. W. HEMMING, M.A., Fellow of St. John's College, Cambridge. Second Edition, with Corrections and Additions. 8vo. cloth. 9s.

JONES and CHEYNE.—ALGEBRAICAL EXERCISES. Progressively arranged. By the Rev. C. A. JONES, M.A., and C. H. CHEYNE, M.A., Mathematical Masters of Westminster School. New Edition. 18mo. cloth, 2s. 6d.

> This little book is intended to meet a difficulty which is probably felt more or less by all engaged in teaching Algebra to beginners. It is that while new ideas are being acquired, old ones are forgotten. In the belief that constant practice is the only remedy for this, the present series of miscellaneous exercises has been prepared. Their peculiarity consists in this, that though miscellaneous they are yet progressive, and may be used by the pupil almost from the commencement of his studies. They are not intended to supersede the systematically arranged examples to be found in ordinary treatises on Algebra, but rather to supplement them.
>
> The book being intended chiefly for Schools and Junior Students, the higher parts of Algebra have not been included.

MORGAN.—A COLLECTION of PROBLEMS and EXAMPLES in Mathematics. With Answers. By H. A. MORGAN, M.A., Sadlerian and Mathematical Lecturer of Jesus College, Cambridge. Crown 8vo. cloth. 6s. 6d.

> This book contains a number of problems, chiefly elementary, in the Mathematical subjects usually read at Cambridge. They have been selected from the papers set during late years at Jesus college. Very few of them are to be met with in other collections, and by far the larger number are due to some of the most distinguished Mathematicians in the University.

PARKINSON.—Works by **S. Parkinson, B.D.,** Fellow and Prælector of St. John's College, Cambridge:—

— AN ELEMENTARY TREATISE ON MECHANICS. For the use of the Junior Classes at the University and the Higher Classes in Schools. With a Collection of Examples. Third Edition, revised. Crown 8vo. cloth, 9s. 6d.

> The author has endeavoured to render the present volume suitable as a Manual for the junior classes in Universities and the higher classes in Schools. In the Third Edition several additional propositions have been incorporated in the work for the purpose of rendering it more complete, and the Collection of Examples and Problems has been largely increased.

— A TREATISE on OPTICS. Second Edition, revised. Crown 8vo. cloth, 10s. 6d.

> A collection of Examples and Problems has been appended to this work which are sufficiently numerous and varied in character to afford useful exercise for the student: for the greater part of them recourse has been had to the Examination Papers set in the University and the several Colleges during the last twenty years.
>
> Subjoined to the copious Table of Contents the author has ventured to indicate an elementary course of reading not unsuitable for the requirements of the First Three Days in the Cambridge Senate-House Examinations.

PHEAR.—ELEMENTARY HYDROSTATICS. With numerous Examples. By J. B. PHEAR, M.A., Fellow and late Assistant Tutor of Clare College, Cambridge. Fourth Edition. Crown 8vo. cloth, 5s. 6d.

> "An excellent Introductory Book. The definitions are very clear; the descriptions and explanations are sufficiently full and intelligible; the investigations are simple and scientific. The examples greatly enhance its value."—*English Journal of Education.*

PRATT.—A TREATISE on ATTRACTIONS, LAPLACE'S FUNCTIONS, and the FIGURE of the EARTH. By JOHN H. PRATT, M.A., Archdeacon of Calcutta, Author of "The Mathematical Principles of Mechanical Philosophy." Third Edition. Crown 8vo. cloth, 6s. 6d.

PUCKLE.—AN ELEMENTARY TREATISE on CONIC SECTIONS and ALGEBRAIC GEOMETRY. With Easy Examples, progressively arranged; especially designed for the use of Schools and Beginners. By G. H. PUCKLE, M.A., St. John's College, Cambridge, Head Master of Windermere College. Third Edition, enlarged and improved. Crown 8vo. cloth, 7s. 6d. [*In the Press.*

> This work will, it is hoped, be found to contain all that is required by the upper classes of Schools and by the generality of students at the Universities.

RAWLINSON.—ELEMENTARY STATICS. By G. RAWLINSON, M.A. Edited by EDWARD STURGES, M.A., of Emmanuel College, Cambridge, and late Professor of the Applied Sciences, Elphinstone College, Bombay. Crown 8vo. cloth. 4s. 6d.

> Published under the authority of H. M. Secretary of State for use in the Government Schools and Colleges in India.
>
> "This Manual may take its place among the most exhaustive, yet clear and simple, we have met with, upon the composition and resolution of forces, equilibrium, and the mechanical powers."—*Oriental Budget.*

ROUTH.—AN ELEMENTARY TREATISE on the DYNAMICS of a SYSTEM of RIGID BODIES. With Examples. By EDWARD JOHN ROUTH, M.A., Fellow and Assistant Tutor of St. Peter's College, Cambridge; Examiner in the University of London. Crown 8vo. cloth, 10s. 6d.

SNOWBALL.—PLANE and SPHERICAL TRIGONOMETRY. With the Construction and Use of Tables of Logarithms. By J. C. SNOWBALL. Tenth Edition. Crown 8vo. cloth, 7s. 6d.

> In preparing a new edition, the proofs of some of the more important propositions have been rendered more strict and general; and a considerable addition of more than *Two hundred Examples*, taken principally from the questions in the Examinations of Colleges and the University, has been made to the collection of Examples and Problems for practice.

SMITH.—Works by **Barnard Smith, M.A.**, Rector of Glaston, Rutlandshire, late Fellow and Senior Bursar of St. Peter's College, Cambridge :—

— ARITHMETIC and ALGEBRA, in their Principles and Application, with numerous Systematically arranged Examples, taken from the Cambridge Examination Papers, with especial reference to the Ordinary Examination for B.A. Degree. Tenth Edition. Crown 8vo. cloth, 10*s.* 6*d.*

> This work is now extensively used in *Schools* and *Colleges* both *at home* and in the *Colonies*. It has also been found of great service for students preparing for the MIDDLE-CLASS AND CIVIL AND MILITARY SERVICE EXAMINATIONS, from the care that has been taken to elucidate the *principles* of all the Rules.

— ARITHMETIC FOR SCHOOLS. New Edition. Crown 8vo. cloth, 4*s.* 6*d.*

COMPANION to ARITHMETIC for SCHOOLS. [*Preparing.*

A KEY to the ARITHMETIC for SCHOOLS. Fifth Edition. Crown 8vo., cloth, 8*s.* 6*d.*

— EXERCISES in ARITHMETIC. With Answers. Crown 8vo. limp cloth, 2*s.* 6*d.* Or sold separately, as follows :—Part I. 1*s.*; Part II. 1*s.* ANSWERS, 6*d.*

> These Exercises have been published in order to give the pupil examples in every rule of Arithmetic. The greater number have been carefully compiled from the latest University and School Examination Papers.

— SCHOOL CLASS-BOOK of ARITHMETIC. 18mo. cloth, 3*s.* Or sold separately, Parts I. and II. 10*d.* each; Part III. 1*s.*

KEYS to SCHOOL CLASS-BOOK of ARITHMETIC. Complete in one Volume, 18mo. cloth. 6*s.* 6*d.* ; or Parts I., II., and III. 2*s.* 6*d.* each.

— SHILLING BOOK of ARITHMETIC for NATIONAL and ELEMENTARY SCHOOLS. 18mo. cloth. Or separately, Part I. 2*d.*; Part II. 3*d.*; Part III. 7*d.* ANSWERS, 6*d.*

THE SAME, with Answers complete. 18mo. cloth, 1*s.* 6*d.*

KEY to SHILLING BOOK of ARITHMETIC. 18mo. cloth, 4*s.* 6*d.*

— EXAMINATION PAPERS in ARITHMETIC. In Four Parts. 18mo. cloth, 1*s.* 6*d.* THE SAME, with Answers, 18mo. 1*s.* 9*d.*

KEY to EXAMINATION PAPERS in ARITHMETIC. 18mo. cloth, 4*s.* 6*d.*

TAIT and STEELE.—DYNAMICS of a PARTICLE. With Examples. By Professor TAIT and Mr. STEELE. New Edition. Crown 8vo. cloth, 10s. 6d.

> In this Treatise will be found all the ordinary propositions connected with the Dynamics of Particles which can be conveniently deduced without the use of D'Alembert's Principles. Throughout the book will be found a number of illustrative Examples introduced in the text, and for the most part completely worked out; others, with occasional solutions or hints to assist the student, are appended to each Chapter.

TAYLOR.—GEOMETRICAL CONICS; including Anharmonic Ratio and Projection, with numerous Examples. By C. TAYLOR, B.A., Scholar of St. John's College, Cambridge. Crown 8vo. cloth, 7s. 6d.

TODHUNTER.—Works by **I. Todhunter, M.A., F.R.S.**, Fellow and Principal Mathematical Lecturer of St. John's College, Cambridge:—

— THE ELEMENTS of EUCLID for the use of COLLEGES and SCHOOLS. New Edition. 18mo. cloth, 3s. 6d.

— ALGEBRA for BEGINNERS. With numerous Examples. New Edition. 18mo. cloth, 2s. 6d.

> Great pains have been taken to render this work intelligible to young students by the use of simple language and by copious explanations. In accordance with the recommendation of teachers, the examples for exercises are very numerous.

KEY to ALGEBRA for BEGINNERS. [*Nearly ready.*

— TRIGONOMETRY for BEGINNERS. With numerous Examples. 18mo. cloth, 2s. 6d.

> Intended to serve as an introduction to the larger treatise on *Plane Trigonometry*, published by the author. The same plan has been adopted as in the *Algebra for Beginners*: the subject is discussed in short chapters, and a collection of examples is attached to each chapter.

— MECHANICS for BEGINNERS. With numerous Examples. 18mo. cloth, 4s. 6d.

> Intended as a companion to the two preceding books. The work forms an elementary treatise on *Demonstrative* Mechanics. It may be true that this part of mixed mathematics has been sometimes made too abstract and speculative; but it can hardly be doubted that a knowledge of the elements at least of the theory of the subject is extremely valuable even for those who are mainly concerned with practical results. The author has accordingly endeavoured to provide a suitable introduction to the study of applied as well as of theoretical Mechanics.

TODHUNTER.—Works by **I. Todhunter, M.A.**—*Continued.*

— A TREATISE on the DIFFERENTIAL CALCULUS. With Examples. Fourth Edition. Crown 8vo. cloth, 10s. 6d.

— A TREATISE on the INTEGRAL CALCULUS. Second Edition, revised and enlarged. With Examples. Crown 8vo. cloth, 10s. 6d.

— A TREATISE on ANALYTICAL STATICS. With Examples. Third Edition, revised and enlarged. Crown 8vo. cloth, 10s. 6d.

— PLANE CO-ORDINATE GEOMETRY, as applied to the Straight Line and the CONIC SECTIONS. With numerous Examples. Fourth Edition. Crown 8vo. cloth, 7s. 6d.

— ALGEBRA. For the use of Colleges and Schools. Fourth Edition. Crown 8vo. strongly bound in cloth, 7s. 6d.

This work contains all the propositions which are usually included in elementary treatises on Algebra, and a large number of *Examples for Exercise.* The author has sought to render the work easily intelligible to students without impairing the accuracy of the demonstrations, or contracting the limits of the subject. The Examples have been selected with a view to illustrate every part of the subject, and as the number of them is about *Sixteen hundred and fifty*, it is hoped they will supply ample exercise for the student. Each set of Examples has been carefully arranged, commencing with very simple exercises, and proceeding gradually to those which are less obvious.

— PLANE TRIGONOMETRY. For Schools and Colleges. Third Edition. Crown 8vo. cloth, 5s.

The design of this work has been to render the subject intelligible to beginners, and at the same time to afford the student the opportunity of obtaining all the information which he will require on this branch of Mathematics. Each chapter is followed by a set of Examples; those which are entitled *Miscellaneous Examples*, together with a few in some of the other sets, may be advantageously reserved by the student for exercise after he has made some progress in the subject. In the Second Edition the hints for the solution of the Examples have been considerably increased.

— A TREATISE ON SPHERICAL TRIGONOMETRY. Second Edition, enlarged. Crown 8vo. cloth, 4s. 6d.

This work is constructed on the same plan as the *Treatise on Plane Trigonometry*, to which it is intended as a sequel. Considerable labour has been expended on the text in order to render it comprehensive and accurate, and the Examples, which have been chiefly selected from University and College Papers, have all been carefully verified.

— EXAMPLES of ANALYTICAL GEOMETRY of THREE DIMENSIONS. Second Edition, revised. Crown 8vo. cloth, 4s.

— AN ELEMENTARY TREATISE on the THEORY of EQUATIONS. Second Edition, revised. Crown 8vo. cloth, 7s. 6d.

WILSON.—A TREATISE on DYNAMICS. By W. P. WILSON, M.A., Fellow of St. John's College, Cambridge; and Professor of Mathematics in Queen's College, Belfast. 8vo. 9s. 6d.

WOLSTENHOLME.—A BOOK of MATHEMATICAL PROBLEMS on subjects included in the Cambridge Course. By JOSEPH WOLSTENHOLME, Fellow of Christ's College, sometime Fellow of St. John's College, and lately Lecturer in Mathematics at Christ's College. Crown 8vo. cloth, 8s. 6d. [*Just published.*

> In each subject the order of the Text-Books in general use in the University of Cambridge has been followed, and to some extent the questions have been arranged in order of difficulty. The collection will be found to be unusually copious in problems in the earlier subjects, by which it is designed to make the work useful to mathematical students, not only in the Universities, but in the higher classes of public schools.
>
> CONTENTS: Geometry (Euclid).—Algebra.—Plane Trigonometry.—Conic Sections, Geometrical.—Conic Sections, Analytical.—Theory of Equations.—Differential Calculus.—Integral Calculus.—Solid Geometry.—Statics.—Dynamics, Elementary.—Newton.—Dynamics of a Point.—Dynamics of a Rigid Body.—Hydrostatics.—Geometrical Optics.—Spherical Trigonometry and Plane Astronomy.

EDUCATIONAL BOOKS ON SCIENCE.

GEIKIE.—ELEMENTARY LESSONS in PHYSICAL GEOLOGY. By ARCHIBALD GEIKIE, F.R.S., Director of the Geological Survey of Scotland. [*Preparing.*

HUXLEY.—LESSONS in ELEMENTARY PHYSIOLOGY. With numerous Illustrations. By T. H. HUXLEY, F.R.S., Professor of Natural History in the Royal School of Mines. Fourth Thousand. 18mo. cloth, 4s. 6d.

> "It is a very small book, but pure gold throughout. There is not a waste sentence, or a superfluous word, and yet it is all clear as daylight. It exacts close attention from the reader, but the attention will be repaid by a real acquisition of knowledge. And though the book is so small, it manages to touch on some of the very highest problems. . . . . The whole book shows how true it is that the most elementary instruction is best given by the highest masters in any science."—*Guardian.*
>
> "The very best descriptions and explanations of the principles of human physiology which have yet been written by an Englishman."—*Saturday Review.*

LOCKYER.—ELEMENTARY LESSONS in ASTRONOMY, with numerous Illustrations. By J. NORMAN LOCKYER.
[*Preparing.*

OLIVER.—LESSONS IN ELEMENTARY BOTANY. With nearly Two Hundred Illustrations. By DANIEL OLIVER, F.R.S., F.L.S. Third Thousand. 18mo. cloth, 4s. 6d.

> "The manner is most fascinating, and if it does not succeed in making this division of science interesting to every one, we do not think anything can. .... Nearly 200 well executed woodcuts are scattered through the text, and a valuable and copious index completes a volume which we cannot praise too highly, and which we trust all our botanical readers, young and old, will possess themselves of."—*Popular Science Review.*

> "To this system we now wish to direct the attention of teachers, feeling satisfied that by some such course alone can any substantial knowledge of plants be conveyed with certainty to young men educated as the mass of our medical students have been. We know of no work so well suited to direct the botanical pupil's efforts as that of Professor Oliver's, who, with views so practical and with great knowledge too, can write so accurately and clearly."—*Natural History Review.*

> "It is very simple, but truly scientific, and written with such a clearness which shows Professor Oliver to be a master of exposition. .... No one could have thought that so much thoroughly correct botany could have been so simply and happily taught in one volume."—*American Journal of Science and Arts.*

ROSCOE.—LESSONS in ELEMENTARY CHEMISTRY, Inorganic and Organic. By HENRY ROSCOE, F.R.S., Professor of Chemistry in Owen's College, Manchester. With numerous Illustrations and Chromo-Litho. of the Solar Spectra. Fifth Thousand. 18mo. cloth, 4s. 6d.

> It has been the endeavour of the author to arrange the most important facts and principles of Modern Chemistry in a plain but concise and scientific form, suited to the present requirements of elementary instruction. For the purpose of facilitating the attainment of exactitude in the knowledge of the subject, a series of exercises and questions upon the lessons have been added. The metric system of weights and measures, and the centigrade thermometric scale, are used throughout the work.

> "A small, compact, carefully elaborated and well arranged manual."—*Spectator.*

> "It has no rival in its field, and it can scarcely fail to take its place as the text-book at all schools where chemistry is now studied."—*Chemical News.*

> "We regard Dr. Roscoe's as being by far the best book from which a student can obtain a sound and accurate knowledge of the facts and principles of rudimentary chemistry."—*The Veterinarian.*

MISCELLANEOUS EDUCATIONAL BOOKS.

ATLAS of EUROPE. GLOBE EDITION. Uniform in size with Macmillan's Globe Series, containing 48 Coloured Maps, on the same scale Plans of London and Paris, and a copious Index, strongly bound in half-morocco, with flexible back. 9*s.*

> NOTICE.—This Atlas includes all the Countries of Europe in a Series of Forty-eight Maps, drawn on the same scale, with an Alphabetical Index to the situation of more than 10,000 Places; and the relation of the various Maps and Countries to each other is defined in a general Key-Map.
>
> The identity of scale in all the Maps facilitates the comparison of extent and distance, and conveys a just impression of the magnitude of different Countries. The size suffices to show the Provincial Divisions, the Railways and Main Roads, the Principal Rivers and Mountain Ranges. As a book it can be opened without the inconvenience which attends the use of a folding map.
>
> "In the series of works which Messrs. Macmillan and Co. are publishing under this general title *(Globe Series)* they have combined portableness with scholarly accuracy and typographical beauty, to a degree that is almost unprecedented. Happily they are not alone in employing the highest available scholarship in the preparation of the most elementary educational works; but their exquisite taste and large resources secure an artistic result which puts them almost beyond competition. This little atlas will be an invaluable boon for the school, the desk, or the traveller's portmanteau."—*British Quarterly Review.*

EARLY EGYPTIAN HISTORY for the Young. With Descriptions of the Tombs and Monuments. New Edition, with Frontispiece. Fcap. 8vo. 5*s.*

> "Written with liveliness and perspicuity."—*Guardian.*
>
> "Artistic appreciation of the picturesque, lively humour, unusual aptitude for handling the childish intellect, a pleasant style, and sufficient learning, altogether free from pedantic parade, are among the good qualities of this volume, which we cordially recommend to the parents of inquiring and book-loving boys and girls."—*Athenæum.*
>
> "This is one of the most perfect books for the young that we have ever seen. We know something of Herodotus and Rawlinson, and the subject is certainly not new to us; yet we read on, not because it is our duty, but for very pleasure. The author has hit the best possible way of interesting any one, young or old."—*Literary Churchman.*

HOLE.—A GENEALOGICAL STEMMA of the KINGS of ENGLAND and FRANCE. By the Rev. C. HOLE. In One Sheet. 1*s.*

HOLE.—A BRIEF BIOGRAPHICAL DICTIONARY. Compiled and Arranged by CHARLES HOLE, M.A., Trinity College, Cambridge. Second Edition, in Pott 8vo., neatly and strongly bound in cloth, 4s. 6d.

> The most comprehensive Biographical Dictionary in English,—containing more than 18,000 names of persons of all countries, with dates of birth and death, and what they were distinguished for.
>
> "An invaluable addition to our manuals of reference, and from its moderate price, it cannot fail to become as popular as it is useful."—*Times.*
>
> "Supplies a universal want among students of all kinds. It is a neat, compact, well printed little volume, which may go into the pocket, and should be on every student's table, at hand, for reference."—*Globe.*

JEPHSON.—SHAKESPEARE'S TEMPEST. With Glossary and Explanatory Notes. By the Rev. J. M. JEPHSON. 18mo. 1s. 6d.

> "His notes display a thorough familiarity with our older English literature, and his preface is so full of intelligent critical remark, that many readers will wish that it were longer."—*Guardian.*

OPPEN.—FRENCH READER. For the use of Colleges and Schools. Containing a Graduated Selection from Modern Authors in Prose and Verse; and copious Notes, chiefly Etymological. By EDWARD A. OPPEN. Fcap. 8vo. cloth, 4s. 6d.

> "Mr. Oppen has produced a French Reader, which is at once moderate yet full, informing yet interesting, which in its selections balances the moderns fairly against the ancients..... The examples are chosen with taste and skill, and are so arranged as to form a most agreeable course of French reading. An etymological and biographical appendix constitutes a very valuable feature of the work."—*Birmingham Daily Post.*

PAULI.—PICTURES of OLD ENGLAND. By Dr. REINHOLD PAULI. Translated by E. C. OTTE. Crown 8vo. 8s. 6d.

> "A sketch at once so faithful and so picturesque of our mediæval life and manners..... For a general view of the literature and state system of our country, of the rise and history of parliaments, together with a sufficiently minute description of our old social life, we hardly know any manual that excels the present. It seems to be well suited not as a class-book, but as a preparation for the competitive examinations."—*Christian Remembrancer.*

A SHILLING BOOK of GOLDEN DEEDS. A Reading-Book for Schools and General Readers. By the Author of "The Heir of Redclyffe." 18mo. cloth.

> "To collect in a small handy volume some of the most conspicuous of these (examples) told in a graphic and spirited style, was a happy idea, and the result is a little book that we are sure will be in almost constant demand in the parochial libraries and schools for which it is avowedly intended."—*Educational Times.*

A SHILLING BOOK of WORDS from the POETS. By C. M. VAUGHAN. 18mo. cloth.

THRING.—Works by **Edward Thring, M.A.**, Head Master of Uppingham:—

— THE ELEMENTS of GRAMMAR taught in ENGLISH. With Questions. Fourth Edition. 18mo. 2s.

— THE CHILD'S GRAMMAR. Being the substance of "The Elements of Grammar taught in English," adapted for the use of Junior Classes. A New Edition. 18mo. 1s.

> The author's effort in these two books has been to point out the broad, beaten, every-day path, carefully avoiding digressions into the bye-ways and eccentricities of language. This work took its rise from questionings in National Schools, and the whole of the first part is merely the writing out in order the answers to questions which have been used already with success. Its success, not only in National Schools, from practical work in which it took its rise, but also in classical schools, is full of encouragement.

— SCHOOL SONGS. A collection of Songs for Schools. With the Music arranged for Four Voices. Edited by the Rev. E. THRING and H. RICCIUS. Music Size. 7s. 6d.

EDUCATIONAL BOOKS ON THEOLOGY.

EASTWOOD.—THE BIBLE WORD BOOK. A Glossary of Old English Bible Words. By J. EASTWOOD, M.A., of St. John's College, and W. ALDIS WRIGHT, M.A., Trinity College, Cambridge. 18mo. 5s. 6d.

(Uniform with Macmillan's School Class Books.)

HARDWICK.—A HISTORY of the CHRISTIAN CHURCH. MIDDLE AGE. From Gregory the Great to the Excommunication of Luther. By ARCHDEACON HARDWICK. Edited by FRANCIS PROCTER, M.A. With Four Maps constructed for this work by A. KEITH JOHNSTON. Second Edition. Crown 8vo. 10s. 6d.

> The History commences with the time of Gregory the Great, and is carried down to the year 1520,—the year when Luther, having been expelled from those Churches that adhered to the Communion of the Pope, established a provisional form of government and opened a fresh era in the history of Europe.

HARDWICK.—A HISTORY of the CHRISTIAN CHURCH during the REFORMATION. By ARCHDEACON HARDWICK. Revised by FRANCIS PROCTER, M.A. Second Edition. Crown 8vo. 10s. 6d.

> This work forms a Sequel to the author's book on *The Middle Ages.* The author's wish has been to give the reader a trustworthy version of those stirring incidents which mark the Reformation period.

MACLEAR.—Works by the **Rev. G. F. Maclear, B.D.**, Head Master of King's College School, and Preacher at the Temple Church:—

— A CLASS-BOOK of OLD TESTAMENT HISTORY. Third Edition, with Four Maps. 18mo. cloth, 4s. 6d.

> "A work which for fulness and accuracy of information may be confidently recommended to teachers as one of the best text-books of Scripture History which can be put into a pupil's hands."—*Educational Times.*
>
> "A careful and elaborate though brief compendium of all that modern research has done for the illustration of the Old Testament. We know of no work which contains so much important information in so small a compass."—*British Quarterly Review.*
>
> "A well-arranged summary of the scriptural story."—*Guardian.*

— A CLASS-BOOK of NEW TESTAMENT HISTORY: including the Connection of the Old and New Testament. With Four Maps. Second Edition. 18mo. cloth. 5s. 6d.

> "Mr. Maclear has produced in this handy little volume a singularly clear and orderly arrangement of the Sacred Story.... His work is solidly and completely done."—*Athenæum.*

— A SHILLING BOOK of OLD TESTAMENT HISTORY, for National and Elementary Schools. With Map. 18mo. cloth.

— A SHILLING BOOK of NEW TESTAMENT HISTORY, for National and Elementary Schools. With Map. 18mo. cloth.

— CLASS BOOK of the CATECHISM.   [*In the Press.*

PROCTER.—A HISTORY of the BOOK of COMMON PRAYER: with a Rationale of its Offices. By FRANCIS PROCTER, M.A. Sixth Edition, revised and enlarged. Crown 8vo. 10s. 6d.

> In the course of the last twenty years the whole question of Liturgical knowledge has been reopened with great learning and accurate research, and it is mainly with the view of epitomizing their extensive publications, and correcting by their help the errors and misconceptions which had obtained currency, that the present volume has been put together.

EDUCATIONAL BOOKS ON THEOLOGY. 21

PROCTER.—AN ELEMENTARY HISTORY of the BOOK of COMMON PRAYER. By Francis Procter, M.A. 18mo. 2s. 6d.

> The author having been frequently urged to give a popular abridgment of his larger work in a form which should be suited for use in schools and for general readers, has attempted in this book to trace the History of the Prayer-Book, and to supply to the English reader the general results which in the larger work are accompanied by elaborate discussions and references to authorities indispensable to the student. It is hoped that this book may form a useful manual to assist people generally to a more intelligent use of the Forms of our Common Prayer.

RAMSAY.—THE CATECHISER'S MANUAL; or, the Church Catechism illustrated and explained, for the use of Clergymen, Schoolmasters, and Teachers. By Arthur Ramsay, M.A. Second Edition. 18mo. 1s. 6d.

SIMPSON.—AN EPITOME of the HISTORY of the CHRISTIAN CHURCH. By William Simpson, M.A. Fourth Edition. Fcap. 8vo. 3s. 6d.

SWAINSON.—A HAND-BOOK to BUTLER'S ANALOGY. By C. A. Swainson, D.D., Norrisian Professor of Divinity at Cambridge. Crown 8vo. 1s. 6d.

WESTCOTT.—A GENERAL SURVEY of the HISTORY of the CANON of the NEW TESTAMENT during the First Four Centuries. By Brooke Foss Westcott, B.D., Assistant Master at Harrow. Second Edition, revised. Crown 8vo. 10s. 6d.

> The Author has endeavoured to connect the history of the New Testament Canon with the growth and consolidation of the Church, and to point out the relation existing between the amount of evidence for the authenticity of its component parts and the whole mass of Christian literature. Such a method of inquiry will convey both the truest notion of the connexion of the written Word with the living Body of Christ, and the surest conviction of its divine authority.

— INTRODUCTION to the STUDY of the FOUR GOSPELS. By Brooke Foss Westcott, B.D. Third Edition. Crown 8vo. 10s. 6d.

> This book is intended to be an Introduction to the *Study* of the Gospels. In a subject which involves so vast a literature much must have been overlooked; but the author has made it a point at least to study the researches of the great writers, and consciously to neglect none.

WESTCOTT.—THE BIBLE in the CHURCH. A Popular Account of the Collection and Reception of the Holy Scriptures in the Christian Churches. Second Edition. By BROOKE FOSS WESTCOTT, B.D. 18mo. cloth, 4s. 6d.

> "Mr. Westcott has collected and set out in a popular form the principal facts concerning the history of the Canon of Scripture. The work is executed with Mr. Westcott's characteristic ability."—*Journal of Sacred Literature.*

WILSON.—AN ENGLISH HEBREW and CHALDEE LEXICON and CONCORDANCE to the more Correct Understanding of the English translation of the Old Testament, by reference to the Original Hebrew. By WILLIAM WILSON, D.D., Canon of Winchester, late Fellow of Queen's College, Oxford. Second Edition, carefully Revised. 4to. cloth, 25s.

> The aim of this work is, that it should be useful to Clergymen and all persons engaged in the study of the Bible, even when they do not possess a knowledge of Hebrew; while able Hebrew scholars have borne testimony to the help that they themselves have found in it.

> "On the whole, we cordially recommend the work, on the ground of its correctness, size, price, and practicalness."—*British Quarterly Review.*

BOOKS ON EDUCATION.

ARNOLD.—A FRENCH ETON; or, Middle-Class Education and the State. By MATTHEW ARNOLD. Fcap. 8vo. cloth, 2s. 6d.

> "A very interesting dissertation on the system of secondary instruction in France, and on the advisability of copying the system in England."—*Saturday Review.*

BLAKE.—A VISIT to some AMERICAN SCHOOLS and COLLEGES. By SOPHIA JEX BLAKE. Crown 8vo. cloth. 6s.

> "Miss Blake gives a living picture of the schools and colleges themselves, in which that education is carried on."—*Pall-Mall Gazette.*

> "Miss Blake has written an entertaining book upon an important subject; and while we thank her for some valuable information, we venture to thank her also for the very agreeable manner in which she imparts it."—*Athenæum.*

> "We have not often met with a more interesting work on education than that before us."—*Educational Times.*

ESSAYS ON A LIBERAL EDUCATION. By CHARLES STUART PARKER, M.A., HENRY SIDGWICK, M.A., LORD HOUGHTON, JOHN SEELEY, M.A., REV. F. W. FARRAR, M.A., F.R.S., &c., E. E. BOWEN, M.A., F.R.A.S., J. W. HALES, M.A., J. M. WILSON, M.A., F.G.S., F.R.A.S., W. JOHNSON, M.A. Edited by the Rev. F. W. FARRAR, M.A., F.R.S., late Fellow of Trinity College, Cambridge; Fellow of King's College, London; Assistant-Master at Harrow; Author of "Chapters on Language," &c., &c. In One Volume, 8vo. cloth, 10s. 6d.

THRING.—EDUCATION AND SCHOOL. By the Rev. EDWARD THRING, M.A., Head Master of Uppingham. Second Edition. Crown 8vo. cloth. 6s.

YOUMANS.—MODERN CULTURE: its True Aims and Requirements. A Series of Addresses and Arguments on the Claims of Scientific Education. Edited by EDWARD L. YOUMANS, M.D. Crown 8vo. 8s. 6d.

MEDICAL BOOKS.

ANSTIE.—STIMULANTS and NARCOTICS, their Mutual Relations, with Special Researches on the Action of Alcohol, Æther, and Chloroform on the Vital Organism. By FRANCIS E. ANSTIE, M.D., M.R.C.P. 8vo. 14s.

BARWELL.—GUIDE IN THE SICK ROOM. By RICHARD BARWELL, F.R.C.S. Extra fcap. 8vo. 3s. 6d.

FOX.—On the DIAGNOSIS and TREATMENT of the VARIETIES of DYSPEPSIA, considered in Relation to the Pathological Origin of the Different Forms of Indigestion. By WILSON FOX, M.D. Lond., F.R.C.P., Professor of Pathological Anatomy at University College, London, and Physician to University College Hospital. Demy 8vo. cloth. 7s. 6d.

HUMPHRY.—THE HUMAN SKELETON (including the Joints). With Two Hundred and Sixty Illustrations drawn from Nature. By GEORGE MURRAY HUMPHRY, M.D., F.R.S. Medium 8vo. £1 8s.

HUMPHRY.—THE HUMAN HAND and the HUMAN FOOT. With numerous Illustrations. By GEORGE MURRAY HUMPHRY, M.D., F.R.S. Fcap. 8vo. 4s. 6d.

"We cordially recommend the book to the public and the profession; the former cannot but be benefited by it, and the members of the latter, even though accomplished anatomists, will be both interested and amused by the novel way in which many of its points are brought forward."—*Lancet.*

HUXLEY.—LESSONS IN ELEMENTARY PHYSIOLOGY. With numerous Illustrations. By T. H. HUXLEY, F.R.S., Professor of Natural History in the Government School of Mines. Uniform with Macmillans' School Class Books. Fourth Thousand. 18mo. 4s. 6d.

JOURNAL OF ANATOMY and PHYSIOLOGY, Conducted by Professors HUMPHRY and NEWTON, and Mr. CLARK, of Cambridge; Professor TURNER, of Edinburgh; and Dr. WRIGHT, of Dublin. Published twice a year. Parts I. and II., price 7s. 6d. each; Part III., 6s.

MAUDSLEY.—THE PHYSIOLOGY and PATHOLOGY OF THE MIND. By HENRY MAUDSLEY, M.D. Lond., Physician to the West London Hospital, &c. 8vo. cloth. 16s.

REYNOLDS.—A SYSTEM OF MEDICINE. Edited by J. RUSSELL REYNOLDS, M.D., F.R.C.P., London. The First Volume contains:—PART I. GENERAL DISEASES, or Affections of the Whole System. § I.—Those determined by agents operating from without, such as the exanthemata, malarial diseases, and their allies. § II.—Those determined by conditions existing within the body, such as Gout, Rheumatism, Rickets, &c. PART II. LOCAL DISEASES, of Affections of particular Systems. § I.—Diseases of the Skin. Vol. I. 8vo. cloth. 25s.

— A SYSTEM OF MEDICINE. Vol. II. containing Diseases of the Nervous System, the Respiratory System, and the Circulatory System. [*In the Press.*

CAMBRIDGE:—PRINTED BY JONATHAN PALMER.